POLITICS AND PROTESTANT THEOLOGY

*An Interpretation of Tillich,
Barth, Bonhoeffer and Brunner*

By René de Visme Williamson

Edited, with an introduction and notes,
By Craig M. Kibler

Afterword
By Parker T. Williamson

Revised and Expanded Edition

REFORMATION PRESS

Reformation Press
P.O. Box 2210
Lenoir, North Carolina 28645

Reformation Press books, monographs and other resources are available at special discounts in bulk purchases for educational and ministry use. For more details, contact:

Director of Publications
Reformation Press
136 Tremont Park Drive
Lenoir, North Carolina 28645

Printed in the United States of America

All Scripture references are from the King James Version of the Bible.

Table of Contents

Acknowledgments

I wish to thank the editors of the *Political Science Review* for permission to reprint the material in Books I and II, which originally appeared in that journal (II, Fall 1973, pp. 109-141; and IV, Fall 1974, pp. 105-131, respectively).

I also gratefully acknowledge permission to reprint that part of the section titled "The Meaning of Encounter" (Book V, Chapter Three), which originally appeared in *The Presbyterian Outlook* (Nov. 4, 1974, pp. 5-6).

René de Visme Williamson
Baton Rouge, La.

Introduction

By Craig M. Kibler

The unraveling of what's left of the historic unifier in Western civilization – Christianity – continues unabated as officials from the mainline denominations trample over the Great Commission to line up and condemn one governmental action after another throughout the world.

A listing of a few of the condemnations sounds like the "theme of the day" from some of today's social action movements – the war in Iraq and the Palestine/Israeli conflict; capitalism; gender, the economy and the earth; the federal budget; cabinet nominees; the presidential election; abortion; health care; water rights; the privatization of prisons; border security; marriage; the Patriot Act; election finance laws; nuclear weapons, land mines; health insurance; poverty, HIV-AIDS; child nutrition; low-income housing, the minimum wage; free trade; and education funding, among many others.

During the same timeframe (1970-2000) in which the decibel level of such condemnations was ratcheted up, and fewer resources were devoted to evangelism, staggering membership losses were suffered by the largest members of the Protestant mainline denominations – the United Church of Christ, 29.8 percent; the Episcopal Church USA, 27.3 percent; the United Methodist Church, 26.8 percent; the Presbyterian Church (USA), 23.9 percent; and the Evangelical Lutheran Church, 10.9 percent. This is a decline in total membership of more than seven million (30,768,450 to 23,475,000), according to the World Christian Database.

In pushing social issues over the proclamation of the gospel, these denominational leaders have forgotten G.K. Chesterton's warning:

> "We do not want, as the newspapers say, a Church that will move with the world. We want a Church that will move the world . . . It is by that test that history will really judge, of any Church, whether it is the real Church or no."[1]

---

1. Michael Ffinch; *G.K. Chesterton: A Biography* (San Francisco; Harper & Row; 1986); p. 277.

The upshot, in a broken world, is that these denominations are living within the shadow of the Fall with less and less of the sense of the wonder that is engendered by the hope of the Resurrection. They have become wanderers searching for the grail of cultural popularity, bereft of a safe and secure Church in which to take refuge from the continuous headlines of an outer world that seemingly has gone mad, fleeing into a bureaucracy grown more political, bloated and distorted in a failed attempt to be all things to all people.

This is not to say that such political issues are not important – they are, but is such a witness the proper role of the Church or of individual Christians?

Without question, the late René de Visme Williamson writes, it properly is the role for individual Christians. "The leadership of the mainline denominations and of the National and World Councils of Churches," he writes, "is committed to social activism. At the same time, large numbers of Christians within the mainline denominations strongly dissent from social activism and speak through some of the smaller denominations and through organizations usually described as evangelical."

Dr. Williamson, in a searching and detailed examination of their theologies against the background of political science, demonstrates that Paul Tillich, Karl Barth, Dietrich Bonhoeffer and Emil Brunner were not social activists, although they did show some concern for political and social issues.

He makes clear that the first and foremost mission of the Church is evangelism, and it must be undertaken with the utmost seriousness:

> "And Jesus came and spake unto them, saying, All power is given unto me in heaven and in earth. Go ye therefore, and teach all nations, baptizing them in the name of the Father, and of the Son, and of the Holy Ghost: Teaching them to observe all things whatsoever I have commanded you: and, lo, I am with you always, even unto the end of the world."[2]

Current trends in the thinking of mainline denominational executives and the leadership in such organizations as the National Council of Churches, the World Council of Churches and the World Alliance of Reformed Churches make it imperative that the word *evangelism* be clearly defined, Dr. Williamson writes. By evangelism, he says, such officials mean interfaith "dialogues" in which adherents of the world's many religions speak on equal terms with no interest in converting anyone, and they mean the change of all social structures that they deem unjust, oppressive and exploitive. "Salvation is interpreted as liberation in a political, social

---

2. Matthew 28:18-20.

and economic sense – which is to be achieved by revolution, if necessary. This view of evangelism is not, of course, the historic view. Neither is it the view of Barth, Bonhoeffer and Brunner."

The historic view of winning converts to the Christian faith, Dr. Williamson explains, rejects this interpretation of evangelism. "Neither liberty (liberation) nor equality is the objective of the Christian faith, and all three theologians make this point absolutely clear," he writes. "Liberty and equality are secular ideals. Even if understood in the light of the Christian faith, rather than in the light of liberal philosophy, these ideals are only by-products of the Christian faith." Moreover, he says that Barth, Bonhoeffer and Brunner are "emphatic in their denial that any ideals can be attained by structural change alone. Structural changes may be helpful in some cases, but they guarantee nothing."

However far social activists have deviated from the essentials of the Christian faith into a sociopolitical morass, no Christian should draw the conclusion that the Church should have no concern for political, social and economic issues. It should, Dr. Williamson says, but it must avoid the pitfalls of social activism and speak out only where the principle of a particular issue is very clear. There are controversial issues in which the principle is unmistakable, and the command of the hour comes through loud and clear. On these issues, the Church must make pronouncements. "Few Christians, if any, would find fault with the Declaration of Barmen in which the German Confessing Church condemned Nazism," Dr. Williamson writes. "Again, few Christians, if any, would deny that the Church pronouncement condemning compulsory racial segregation in the United States was right."

He warns, however, that there are many issues in which facts and motives are mixed, consequences contradict the principles involved, and equally dedicated and knowledgeable Christians disagree. "In these cases, the Church should remain silent, letting individual Christians and Christian groups decide for themselves what the Christian witness means. To issue pronouncements on general principles alone in the absence of a particular controversial issue is platitudinous and, therefore, ineffective."

Dr. Williamson makes a telling point regarding such pronouncements: "When a principle becomes crystallized into an issue, it gets tied up with many matters whose religious significance is nil, or practically nil, and theologically ambiguous. During the early period of the Watergate crisis, for example, there were journalists and political scientists who argued that the United States should give up the separation of powers and adopt the British parliamentary system because there would have been no delay in getting Nixon out of office. Aside from the political impracticability of this proposal, what could be the prophetic message that the Church could give on the merits of the two systems? The same observation can be made concerning proposals for fighting inflation, lowering interest rates, devaluing the dollar, raising debt ceilings, and federal financing of primary and general elections. For the Church to sponsor a political party, engage in lobbying, form coalitions with secular pressure groups, and become entangled in the decisions of private business corporations would be to take a position in precisely those issues in which the religious significance is unclear, ambiguous or nonexistent."

In spite of such clear guidelines for Church pronouncements, and clear opposition from the people in the pews, denominational officials more and more have pressed their programs of social activism. And, since they are unable to find a Scriptural basis for such social activism in the New Testament, they turn to the Old Testament. The Church, they say, should speak with a "prophetic voice," by which they mean the adoption of their stands against racism, sexism, war and other issues. But, Dr. Williamson writes, the "Old Testament basis does not fit their claims. When the Old Testament prophets spoke, they did so under divine duress, spoke reluctantly, did not enjoy their message, and paid a high price for their mission. By contrast, the would-be prophets of our day voice personal opinions, rarely run any risks, and luxuriate in denunciation. The most serious defect in the social activist demand that the Church strike a 'prophetic note' is that, in the Old Testament, a prophetic voice always is attributed to an individual. There is no instance in either the Old Testament or the New Testament in which a prophetic voice is ascribed to either the Old Israel or the New Israel."

One of the flaws in such arguments, Dr. Williamson argues, is that these social activists "downgrade the institutional church and hold the congregation in low esteem. They say that the congregation is a mutual adoration society, self-satisfied and stagnant. They contend that church members spend too much money on buildings – money that should have been spent on service – and do not go out into the world to evangelize it by ministering to human need. What these people forget is that no one can go out who is not already in. The institutional church could be compared to a pulsating heart with venous blood coming in and arterial blood going out. A stream moves into the congregation to be purified, inspired and trained. Another stream moves out to evangelize (convert and serve) those outside the church. To sustain this pulsation, you need a center, an organization, a budget, and a program. To return to Christ's analogy, salt that has dissolved into other elements, but has no saltiness, has no power – and it is the institutional church whose task it is to produce that saltiness."

An institutional church that engenders the Church in this sense is one that has kept its saltiness by being distinctively Christian. It is a community,

Dr. Williamson says, "in which one finds humility and not conceit, serenity of spirit and not existential dread, security and not inferiority complexes, reconciliation and not alienation, acceptance and not rejection, goodwill and not malice, service and not self-aggrandizement, reverence and not irreverence, freedom and not slavery, courage and not fear, kindness and not censoriousness, wisdom and not foolishness."

"The effect of such a community is to expose evil by contrast. The mask of evil is torn off and the beguiling disguises of Satan are stripped away. On the other hand, the existence of a Church that has kept its flavor is ineffably and irresistibly attractive. It proves 'what is that good, and acceptable, and perfect, will of God.'[3] Those who are spiritually weary, morally tormented, intellectually baffled, psychologically insecure and lonely turn to it as an oasis, a fortress, a refuge. In it, they find forgiveness and acceptance. They discover that the life they led is not inevitable. They discover how sweet, good, exhilarating, abundant and ennobling life can be."

What impresses such people most, Dr. Williamson finds, is the collective impact of a life that exemplifies the Christian ethic. "Secular man, like the citizens of the decadent Roman Empire, always can dismiss an outstanding Christian individual as an exception, the exception that proves the rule, someone whose stature is not attainable by ordinary mortals and does not belong to this world. But when large numbers of quite ordinary people of all races and classes and nations exemplify the Christian ethic, secular man has to take notice."

Among the many people who will take notice, he says, will be bureaucrats and politicians. Their incorporation into the Church will bring vocation, encounter, the discerning of spirits, the creativity of the Spirit into being. No one can say in advance what effect these forms of witnessing will have. As Bonhoeffer pointed out, to claim otherwise would be to walk by sight and not by faith. Furthermore, these bureaucrats and politicians will not be alone. They will be associated with similarly attracted business people, farmers, educators, lawyers, workers, ethnic groups, and age groups. The inclusiveness of the Christian community will make Christian statesmanship possible to a degree not attainable in a secular society because there can be no leadership without a following.

This achievement is the aim of evangelism in its political aspect and it is, in essence, the 20th century message that Barth, Bonhoeffer and Brunner send to the troubled 21st century.

---

3. Romans 12:2.

Preface

This book attempts to come to grips with questions that sorely divide people in our time, questions that trouble Christians and politicians. Of the issues that traditionally have divided the churches for centuries, some are especially acute in our day. Among these is the extent to which the church should involve itself in politics. The struggle, between conservatives and social activists, takes place within the mainline Protestant denominations even more than between denominations.

In the world of politics, there also are many controversies. This is nothing new, of course, as struggle is inseparable from politics. The controversies rage not so much over problems of structure and process as about values and policies. People everywhere, in the Western world at least, are disenchanted with ideologies. Liberals and socialists give lip service to philosophies that are devoid of their former power. Conservatives know quite well what they do not like, but are uncertain as to what course they should follow. For them, the problem is to bring into sharp focus a philosophy of life and politics that can be translated into a course of action.

For those who wield political power, the problem is what to do with it. What is justice and how do you attain it? How do you deal with racism and sexism? Which countries should receive foreign aid and which should not? How do you combat inflation in such a way as to be effective in lowering prices and be fair to the different categories of people who are vitally affected by it? These and many other questions confront our leaders and demand answers in terms of policies that are practical, as well as ethically and politically sound.

One might suppose that the political science profession would have some answers that political leaders could adopt and use. It is an erroneous supposition. At its best, the profession sometimes – but not often – may be in a position to tell our leaders how they might do something, but not whether they should do it. What prevents political scientists from dealing with issues of policy is a concept of objectivity that is regarded as a dogma. A political scientist must not take stands on values because they are "subjective" and, as such, are not fit for scientific inquiry. His concept of science is that of natural science. A belief in "objectivity" long has been characteristic of academic people in general. It especially is prevalent among political scientists because of the dominant school known as behaviorism, or behavioralism. The result is that the political science profession does not even raise the crucial life-and-death issues that worry people in and out of politics – issues like identity, alienation, reconciliation, guilt and forgiveness. The thinkers who raise these issues and grapple with them are the theologians, and that is why I turn to them.

In order to avoid an excessively broad survey of current theological thought that would involve unnecessary repetition and include theologians who do not have much to contribute, I have decided to concentrate on Protestant thought and limit myself to four of the greatest and most influential theologians of the 20th century – namely Paul Tillich, Karl Barth, Dietrich Bonhoeffer and Emil Brunner. I have chosen them because they are the most original, creative and comprehensive thinkers in the field of theology. Moreover, their influence on the American church has been enormous and will continue to be so for many years to come. The fact that they write in the context of the European background, German and German-Swiss, is an advantage in that perspective thereby is gained.

I cannot assume that all my readers are knowledgeable in the field of theology, especially those whose field is political science. For that reason, I had to dwell in some detail on theological positions. Because it is so easy to misrepresent or misinterpret controversial thought, I have documented my analysis very thoroughly with citations and many quotations, thus enabling the reader to judge for himself as to the accuracy, fairness and soundness of my critiques. The focus of the book, however, is not on theology as such but on the political teachings and implications of these theologians' thought. The treatment is critical, as well as expository.

The last chapter pulls together what I consider to be the strong and weak points of Tillich, Barth, Bonhoeffer and Brunner. But that chapter is no mere summary of findings. It goes beyond those findings to develop my own thinking on the contributions of the Christian faith to politics.

Perhaps I should mention that my own religious background is the Reformed tradition and my membership is in the Presbyterian Church in the United States.[1] The reader is entitled to know, in the unlikely case that it is not already obvious, that my judgments are made from the standpoint of that tradition and denomination.

---

1. The United Presbyterian Church (USA) and the Presbyterian Church US reunited in 1983 to form the Presbyterian Church (USA).

Paul Tillich

Contents

Introduction

Paul Tillich was one of the intellectual giants of the 20th century, and we can be sure that his death[1] will not diminish the range of his influence in the 21st century. Primarily a theologian and a philosopher, his interest in politics was secondary and what he said about that topic, therefore, was fragmentary. He did follow the political events that occurred during his long life, but his occasional involvement in them never was profound or significant.

It is noteworthy, too, that he showed almost no interest in any phase of political thought, with the exception of Marxism. He ignored Machiavelli, Hobbes, Locke, Rousseau, Burke, John Stuart Mill and other classic authors – not to mention his contemporaries, such as political theorists Harold D. Lasswell[2] or Robert A. Dahl.[3]

When Tillich did consider some of the great classics of political thought, he always dealt with the purely philosophical and not the political aspects. In his numerous references to Plato and Aristotle, for instance, not a word is said about the *Republic* or the *Politics*. By contrast, his knowledge of theology and pure philosophy was profound, vast and systematic. The result is that, for the most part, the political implications of Tillich's thought must be unraveled for him, since he does so little of it himself.

The son of a Lutheran clergyman, Tillich spent his early years in rural Brandenburg, Germany. Life was very traditional and authoritarian, and

---

1. Paul Tillich (1886-1965).

2. Harold D. Lasswell (1902-1978). American son of a Presbyterian minister and a schoolteacher who taught at Milikan University, University of Chicago, Columbia University and Yale University. His many books include *Politics: Who Gets What, When, How; World Politics and Personal Insecurity; Democracy through Public Opinion; Power and Society; Power and Personality; National Security and Individual Freedom* and others.

3. Robert A. Dahl (b. 1915). Sterling professor emeritus of political science at Yale University and a past president of the American Political Science Association. His many books include *Congress and Foreign Policy; Politics, Economics and Welfare* (with C. E. Lindblom); *A Preface to Democratic Theory; Who Governs? Democracy and Power in an American City; After the Revolution?; Polyarchy; Size and Democracy* (with E. R. Tufte); *Dilemmas of Pluralist Democracy; A Preface to Economic Democracy; Democracy and Its Critics; Toward Democracy: A Journey; On Democracy; How Democratic is the American Constitution?* and others.

Lutheranism permeated his whole being. "I am a Lutheran" he wrote, "by birth, education, religious experience, and theological reflection."[4] Whatever one may think of his theology, there can be no question of the depth and vitality of his Christian faith as he understood it. The intensity and warmth of his devotion is not apparent in his *Systematic Theology*[5] and other technical writings, but it shines through with an unmistakable glow in his sermons. The distinguished Roman Catholic critic, Father George Tavard, said: "One must also acknowledge the unmistakable ring of self-commitment in his sermons."[6]

When Tillich first went to Berlin, and throughout the rest of his life on two continents, he was plunged into a world that was deeply alienated from the Christian faith and even more from the Christian Church – a world so alienated that it has been described as post-Christian. Churches were empty or nearly empty, and some of them were little more than museums. In the age of the Soviet Union, this conversion of churches to museums was the result of government policy. In Western Europe, it was the result of popular ignorance, apathy and indifference. The alienation of modern secular man from Christianity was greatest among the laboring masses and the intellectuals. For these groups, the traditional language of the Christian faith was irrelevant. Concepts like faith, justification, redemption, sanctification, sin and atonement were meaningless.

Tillich saw this situation not only as a fact, but as an ever-growing fact. In his eyes, it was somewhat less characteristic of the American people because, in the United States, the churches were numerous and full, church budgets were large, and the majority of Americans subscribed – at least nominally – to the Christian faith. Nevertheless, Tillich saw Europe's present as America's future, saying: "America lives still in a happy backwardness."[7]

This situation couldn't be anything but shocking to a man of Tillich's background, and it led him to devote his entire life to a reformulation of the Christian faith in terms that, he hoped, would make Christianity meaningful to modern man and relevant to his concerns. It was his conviction that "the Church must proclaim the gospel in a language that is comprehensible to a

---

4. Tillich; *On the Boundary*, p. 74. For a full citation of Tillich's works, see the Appendix at the end of Book I.

5. Tillich; *Systematic Theology*; For a full citation of Tillich's works, see the Appendix at the end of Book I.

6. George Tavard, *Paul Tillich and the Christian Message* (Burns and Cates; London; 1962), p. 139.

7. Tillich; *The Protestant Era*, p. 249. For a full citation of Tillich's works, see the Appendix at the end of Book I.

non-ecclesiastical humanism. It would have to convince both the intellectuals and the masses that the gospel is of absolute relevance for them."

To do this, Tillich thought that the traditional language of theology and the thought forms of the Bible would have to be discarded. He also believed that previous attempts to infuse meaning and restore relevance to the gospel by creating a new terminology have been "deplorable failures. They represent a depletion of meaning, not a new creation."[8]

Tillich, therefore, decided to try his hand at it and to succeed where others had failed. In doing so, he developed a formidable array of concepts – among which one finds being, non-being, the ground of being, the New Being, abyss, alienation, estrangement, finitude, existence, dreaming innocence, essence, ontological shock, boundary situation, centered personality, the theological circle, the latent Church, the manifest Church, autonomy, heteronomy, theonomy, and ultimate concern. And even these terms do not exhaust his conceptual creativity! Some of them are original with him, some are borrowed from other contemporary theologians and philosophers. Even when he uses common terms like love, justice and power, Tillich invests them with a meaning of his own. Moreover, all these terms were fitted into a system in the German tradition of scholarship, deriving from it an impressive logical structure.

In an enterprise such as this one, there are two criteria of success: (1) the fidelity of the new concepts in translating the substance of the Christian faith and conveying it intact to modern man; and (2) the degree of success these new concepts have had in securing the understanding and acceptance of modern man. The first criterion will be discussed as we proceed with our analysis.

As to the second criterion, certain observations are in order. To a Christian steeped in Scriptural language and well-versed in the traditional concepts of Christian theology, understanding Tillich produces a reverse process from the one Tillich anticipated. The Tillichian terms are checked not merely for fidelity, but for meaning. We are like the Roman Catholic acolyte participating in a Mass that was being said for the first time in English. When he heard the priest say, "The Lord be with you," he whispered to another acolyte: "He means *Dominus vobiscum.*"

Tillich, of course, was not writing for traditional Christians. There is some question, however, as to how far he was successful in reaching alienated Christians and non-Christians. Insofar as the proletarian masses are concerned, it can be said that he failed utterly. With regard to the intellectuals, he reached only those whose training in philosophy and theology enabled them to grasp the meaning of his terminology. Others not so

8. Tillich; *On the Boundary*; pp. 64-65.

trained, like natural scientists and most social scientists, would need the frequent help of a dictionary. Their attitude would be like that of a fellow political scientist who referred to political theory as "witchcraft."

The cause of this distaste and the lack of comprehension is due to the highly abstract nature of Tillich's terminology. It is a terminology devoid of color and power. It has an abstruse and spectral quality, and cannot compare with the concrete vividness and moving power of Biblical language. To be sure, the traditional concepts of Christian theology are abstract, too, but they have the benefit of two millennia of usage that has given them definite and concrete meaning. Only time will tell whether Tillich's terminology will acquire something of the same kind of context where frequent usage, historical events, and historical figures confer upon them a similarly definite concrete meaning.

In spite of this initial handicap, Tillich's thinking has had a real impact that has grown with time. This impact has occurred through the mediation of others who use simpler terms to convey Tillich's meaning, though not always with complete accuracy. An example of this mediation is through best-selling books like Bishop Robinson's *Honest to God* (1963).[9]

The main source of this mediation, however, has come from generations of seminarians who have read Tillich's works and had Tillich's concepts drilled and drummed into them. Later, these ministers influenced the thinking of the public from their pulpits and their positions on denominational boards and agencies. In this way, Tillichian terms like "estrangement" and "finitude" have filtered into common usage and, thus, are likely to influence politics, or at least political theory, sooner or later.

---

9. John A.T. Robinson; *Honest To God* (SCM Press; London; 1963). Robinson was the bishop of Woolwich, England, and later the dean of Trinity College at the University of Cambridge.

CHAPTER ONE

Tillich's Concept of God

Whom Moses received his great commission to deliver the people of Israel from slavery at the hands of the Egyptians, he said the people would want to know the name of the one who gave him that commission. Moses asked: "What shall I say unto them?"[1] This was Tillich's problem, too.

It may be answered that everyone in Christendom knows that the name of the one is God and they use that name constantly – whether reverently, irreverently or irrelevantly. Tillich, however, finds that answer unacceptable because, he believed, that name is associated with too many false notions that cling to it like so many barnacles. That name conveys the idea that God is an object alongside other objects. What we need, Tillich believes, is a name that includes and transcends both the objective and the subjective essence and existence. Other commonly used names like "Lord" and "Father" also are objectionable to Tillich, who rejects them because they are anthropomorphic, are drawn from only a part of human experience, symbolize only a part of the divine nature, and suggest a supernaturalism that he detests.

In addition to these conceptual objections, Tillich is bothered by the emotion of embarrassment. He is embarrassed when the name "God" is used in social gatherings; he speaks of the "pain of this embarrassment" that many people feel who "have had to teach their children the divine name;" and describes himself as "stung" by the use of that name "in governmental and political speeches, in opening prayers for conferences and dinners, in secular and religious advertisements, and in international war propaganda."[2]

With typical honesty, Tillich admits that the elements behind his embar-

---

1. Exodus 3:13.

2. Tillich; *The Eternal Now*; pp. 94-95. For a full citation of Tillich's works, see the Bibliography at the end of Book I.

rassment are mixed: What one thinks of as tact may be cowardice, and awe may be a disguised form of doubt. In other words, one wonders if the embarrassment Tillich feels is caused by the name or that for which the name stands. Presumably, there is something of both in his reaction.

In a way, Tillich's problem with names is insoluble because any name that one chooses has to be symbolic and, hence, defective. What Tillich did, therefore, was to look for symbols that would have the least objectionable connotations. To do this requires that the symbols be nearly brand new, and therefore his own, for only in this way would they have a minimum of existing connotations of any kind attached to them.

This solution had its difficulties for Tillich because he laid great stress on the fact that symbols "cannot be produced intentionally" and they cannot be invented."[3] Nevertheless, he tried the impossible in pursuance of his favorite phrase "in spite of," which he says is implicit in every act of faith regardless of contradiction and error, and with the assurance supplied to him by his interpretation of the Reformation doctrine of justification by faith, which absolves not only moral guilt but also intellectual error.

This intellectual somersault is necessitated by Tillich's repeated assertion that there is no such thing as atheism. "So the paradox got hold of me," he explains, "that he who seriously denies God, affirms him. Without it, I could not have remained a theologian. There is, I soon realized, no place *beside* the divine, there is no possible atheism, there is no wall between the religious and the secular."[4]

Inconsistently, however, he has a concept of atheism: "It is as atheistic to affirm the existence of God as to deny it. God is being-itself, not *a* being."[5] But his inconsistency is only verbal. No one can live by it because everyone has an ultimate concern, whether he knows it or not. This being the case, it becomes an imperative necessity to settle on a name or names. Not to do so would be as impractical and bewildering as going into a store to buy something without knowing its name.

Tillich's favorite names for God are "the Unconditional" and "the Ground of Being." He prefers "the Unconditional" to "the Unconditioned" because the latter suggests a thing, an objective condition and, therefore, fails to transcend the subject-object dichotomy implicit in all human thinking. On the other hand, "the Unconditional" carries no such implication and merely suggests a quality. The term "Ground of Being" appeals to him because it is free of any anthropomorphic connotation. It means that not

---

3. Tillich; *The Dynamics of Faith*, p. 43. For a full citation of Tillich's works, see the Bibliography at the end of Book I.

4. Tillich; *The Protestant Era*, xiv-xv.

5. Tillich; *Systematic Theology*; Vol. I, p. 237.

only is the subject-object dichotomy transcended, but also the dichotomy between essence and existence. The German word *Grund* actually suits his purpose somewhat better than our English *ground*. In English, the word tends to emphasize the material aspect – i.e., the solid substance upon which we put our feet. The German word is more metaphysical in its emphasis, pointing to the foundation or basis of a concept. For the more material aspects, the Germans have another word (*Boden*).

In trying to create new names for God that would be as faultless as possible, Tillich, not surprisingly, ran into communication difficulties. The names did not take, and certainly did not catch the popular fancy. They are colorless, highly abstract and bloodless. Recognizing this, Tillich became less uncompromising over the years. He experimented with the phrase "the God above God" in the hope of making himself clearer. "The ultimate source of the courage to be," he wrote in 1952, "is the 'God above God;' this is the result of our demand to transcend theism." He explained what he meant in the following words that he himself italicized:

> *The courage to be is rooted in the God who appears when God has disappeared in the anxiety of doubt.*[6]

But this was not a satisfactory solution to the problem of communication. So, he experimented with the word "Spirit" with a capital "S." This was particularly true with the third volume of his *Systematic Theology*, which came out in 1963. Inasmuch as he previously had acknowledged the ambiguities of the term, the change is a concession to the average reader (if the average reader ever reads Tillich). That his reticence was not entirely overcome is apparent in his increasing use of the term "Spiritual Presence" toward the end of the volume. As applied to human beings, "spirit" (with a small "s") refers to that which underlies all human faculties (reason, emotion, will), the creative element in the "centered personality." This is Tillich's way of avoiding the word "soul," which is distasteful to him because he considers it loaded with supernaturalism and superstition. As applied to God, he explains:

> "The divine life is the dynamic unity of depth and form. In mystical language, the depth of the divine life, its inexhaustible and ineffable character, is called 'Abyss.' In philosophical language, the form, the meaning and structure of the divine life is called 'Logos.' In religious language, the dynamic unity of both elements is called 'Spirit.' Theologians must use all three terms in order to point to the ground of revelation."[7]

---

6. Tillich; *The Courage to Be*; p. 186. For a full citation of Tillich's works, see the Bibliography at the end of Book I.

7. Tillich; *Systematic Theology*; Vol. I; p. 156.

At times, especially in his sermons, Tillich uses the word "God." It seems that even he cannot help it.

And, now, we are ready to raise the question as to whether Tillich's God is the Christian God. One thing is clear: The Christian God is a person, a living person. In the Old Testament, he is presented as one who loves, hates, chastises, entreats, warns, governs and forgives. He is the one who gives Israel its name and identity, delivers the people of Israel from slavery, gives them the moral law and their mode of worship, and constantly interferes with their national life. In the New Testament, Jesus speaks of God as a father and teaches his disciples to pray to him as "our Father."

Can Tillich's "the Unconditional" be regarded as a person? Few people will think so. But does Tillich think so?

It would seem that he did: "According to every word of the Bible, God reveals himself as personal. The encounter with him and the concepts describing this encounter are thoroughly personal." He goes even further by arguing that Christianity is unique among all religions in this respect. Biblical personalism, he says, "is different from the personal relationship which is exclusive and complete."[8]

If we follow Tillich's thinking carefully, however, it becomes clear that the personal element is a necessity of the human mind and not inherent in the divine nature itself: "Man cannot be ultimately concerned about something which is less than he is, something impersonal."[9] It follows – or should follow – that God is excluded from personhood for the following reason: "A person becomes aware of his own character as a person only when he is confronted by another person. Only in community of the I and the thou can personality arise."[10] But God does not need other persons in order to be, and neither does he need a community of persons in order to have being.

The depersonalization of God is reflected in what Tillich says about prayer. There is no true person-to-person dialogue – be it petition, intercession or thanksgiving – because that would make God into another person alongside of the one who prays. What, then, is prayer?

"The essence of prayer is the act of God who is working in us and raises our whole being to Himself."[11]

A fuller explanation is offered in the third volume of his *Systematic The-*

8. Tillich; *Biblical Religion and the Search for Ultimate Reality*; pp. 22, 26. For a full citation of Tillich's works, see the Bibliography at the end of Book I.

9. Tillich; *Systematic Theology*; Vol. I; p. 223

10. Tillich; *The Protestant Era*; p. 125.

11. Tillich; *Systematic Theology*; Vol. I; p. 245.

ology: "Every serious and successful prayer – which does not talk to God as a familiar partner, as many prayers do – is a speaking to God, which means that God is made into an object for him who prays. However, God can never be an object, unless he is a subject at the same time. We can only pray to the God who prays to himself through us."

In other words, it would seem that God is merely talking to himself. But even this weird idea cannot stand because the words, being concrete, would have to be the distorted creation of the receiving side on the part of the man who prays. Any idea of "talking," with or without words, is the essence of prayer as we understand it, and this idea is explicitly rejected by Tillich. "It is the Spirit which discerns and experiences the Spirit."[12]

Still other evidence of the depersonalization of God appears in Tillich's position with regard to prophecy. God does not speak to the prophets or give them an identifiable message. "Therefore," Tillich says, "I repeat: Let us not be misled by the phrase 'word from the Lord.' It is not an oracle-word telling us what to do or to expect."[13] This position, needless to say, raises serious problems with the Old Testament. To take just one illustration of the conflict between Scripture and Tillich's position, the Bible says that King Zedekiah asked whether there was a word from the Lord, and Jeremiah answered: "There is: for, said he, thou shalt be delivered into the hand of the king of Babylon."[14] Could any answer be more specific, verbal, and better vindicated by the history that followed?

One can only imagine what Tillich would have said if he had been confronted with this passage. His doctrine of Scripture being what it was, he could have said: (1) that Jeremiah never spoke those words; (2) that these words were spoken after the event; or (3) that these words were written into the text by some well-meaning and overzealous scribe. Whichever interpretation one chooses, the effect is to deny that there was a prophecy at all. The conclusion that Tillich's God is not a person becomes inescapable when we discuss his concept of the New Being. No wonder Tillich remarks that the term "'Personal God' is a confusing symbol."[15]

Tillich's concept of God has destructive effects on classical Christian political theory. It sends Aquinas' famous classification of law[16] crashing to

12. *Ibid.*; Vol. III; pp. 119-120, 192.

13. Tillich; *The New Being*; p. 116. For a full citation of Tillich's works, see the Bibliography at the end of Book I.

14. Jeremiah 37:17.

15. Tillich; *Systematic Theology*; Vol. I; p. 245.

16. St. Thomas Aquinas (1225-1274) believed that law arises from man's participation, through his reason, in the divine wisdom of God. He classified law into four types: eternal, divine, natural and human. Law, he wrote, "is naught else but a work of reason, made and promulgated by a competent authority for the common good."

the ground. It is incompatible with Calvin's doctrine of the sovereignty of God, a doctrine that prevents Calvin's teaching on vocation from resulting in a freezing of the status quo. It is Tillich's lack of a personal God who intervenes in history that transforms Plato's ideal republic into a petrified forest of intelligible realities.

In the 20th century and through today, it plays havoc with the theory of "sphere sovereignty" propounded by the Dutch political theorists Abraham Kuyper[17] and Herman Dooyeweerd[18] that established a God-controlled pluralism whereby institutions like the family, the university and the state each are kept in their places.

And, yet, Tillich's concept of God does have political consequences. These consequences, however, are best discussed in connection with his concept of the *kairos*, with which we shall deal later in this book.

---

17. Abraham Kuyper (1837-1920). Theologian, journalist, politician, author, founder of The Free University in Amsterdam (1880) and prime minister of the Netherlands (1901-1905). "Sphere sovereignty" implies three things: (1) ultimate sovereignty belongs to God alone; (2) all earthly sovereignties are subordinate to and derivative from God's sovereignty; and (3) there is no mediating earthly sovereignty from which others are derivative.

18. Herman Dooyeweerd (1894-1977). His books include *In the Twilight of Western Thought* (1960), *The Roots of Western Culture* (1979), *A New Critique of Theoretical Thought* (1953), and *The Christian Idea of the State* (1967). He expanded on Kuyper's theory, teaching at The Free University of Amsterdam between 1926 and 1965.

CHAPTER TWO

The New Being

For Tillich, as with all Christians, it would seem that Christ is the cornerstone of the Christian faith. "Wherever the assertion that Jesus is the Christ is maintained," he says, "there is the Christian message; wherever this assertion is denied, the Christian message is not affirmed."

The coming of Jesus Christ was a historical event. Without that event, there could not have been the Christian revelation. We are not dealing here with Plato's philosopher-king, nor with the God of stoicism or deism. Jesus was an actual physical person.

"It was just this concreteness and incomparable uniqueness of the 'real' picture which gave Christianity its superiority over mystery cults and Gnostic visions. A real individual life shines through all his utterances and actions. In comparison, the divine figure of the mystery cults remains abstract, without the fresh colors of a life really lived and without historical destiny and the tensions of finite freedom."[1]

Elsewhere, Tillich reasserts this point: "Wherever the divine is manifest, it is manifest in 'flesh;' that is, in a concrete, physical, and historical reality, as in the religious receptivity of the Biblical writers. That is what Biblical religion means."[2]

In discussing revelation, Tillich makes use of the Greek concept of *kairos*, which means the fullness of time, the right time. It means that "the Unconditional" erupts into the existential, that eternity breaks through into history. Every *kairos* is a revelatory experience and has two sides – the giving side and the receiving side. The giving side is absolute and unconditional, transcending time, space and all finitude. But the receiving side, which is the *content* of the revelatory experience, always is fragmentary,

1. Tillich; *Systematic Theology*; Vol. II; pp. 97, 151.

2. Tillich; *Biblical Religion and the Search for Ultimate Reality*; p. 5. For a full citation of Tillich's works, see the Bibliography at the end of Book I.

distorted and partially idolatrous. For that reason, all secondary *kairoi* are non-permanent. Faith, which Tillich defines as ultimate concern, "is a failure in its concrete expression, although it is not a failure in the experience of the unconditional itself. A god disappears; divinity remains."[3]

The first indication that Tillich significantly deviates from orthodoxy comes in his choice of names. He always, and with impeccable consistency, refers to Jesus Christ as Jesus "the Christ." He rejects the name Jesus Christ because it generally is used synonymously with the historic Jesus of Nazareth. Jesus Christ is a proper name, whereas Jesus "the Christ" emphasizes his title. One feels that, were it not for the necessity of communication, Tillich would not even refer to Jesus "the Christ." He has another name that he prefers – the "New Being." That name, of course, has no historic connection with any person, past or present, and therefore is supposedly free of erroneous incrustations. Thus, Tillich's thinking about the name he uses for Christ closely parallels his thinking about the name of God.

The real thrust of Tillich's thinking about the historical dimension of Christianity is anti-historical. He goes so far as to assert that history never can prove or disprove that Jesus of Nazareth existed at all. He even speculates as to whether we could have Christianity without Christ, whether the "New Being" might not be independent of Jesus of Nazareth.[4] Scholars, through the "Higher Criticism," have tried to show that the New Testament record cannot be relied upon as to the authenticity of the words and deeds related in it. But, we are told, this makes no difference because history neither can prove nor disprove faith. Faith is independent of history and beyond the reach of scholars.

From this point on, Tillich proceeds to strip the Great *Kairos* free from any and every content that the Christian faith ascribes to it. We are not to rely on the words of Jesus because we cannot be sure he uttered them, Tillich says, and "the teachings of Jesus" would make him "into another person, who gives doctrinal and ethical laws." We are not to rely on the deeds of Jesus either: "Not his actions but the being out of which his actions come makes him the Christ."[5] The Virgin Birth is a legend, Tillich says, and Jesus was the son of Joseph biologically as well as legally.[6]

It makes no difference anyway: "Christianity was born, not with the birth of the man who is called 'Jesus,' but in the moment in which one of his disciples was driven to say to him, 'Thou are the Christ.' And Christian-

3. Tillich; *The Dynamics of Faith*; p. 18.

4. Tillich; *Systematic Theology*; Vol. II; p. 113.

5. *Ibid.*; pp. 122-123.

6. Tillich; *The Dynamics of Faith*; p. 52.

ity will live as long as there are people who repeat this assertion." Jesus was liable to error: "Error is evident in his ancient conception of the universe, his judgments about men, his interpretation of the historical moment, his eschatological imagination."[7]

Tillich denies the physical resurrection of Jesus, remarking that it is "absurd" and a species of "blasphemy." And, yet, something must have happened to transform a band of dispirited disciples into a victorious group of evangelists. The orthodox position is that nothing less than a physical resurrection, however unexplainable, could have brought about such a transformation, as is most evident in the case of the Apostle Thomas. But Tillich will have nothing to do with the orthodox position. In its place, he offers what he calls the restitution theory, "which is rooted in the personal unity between Jesus and God and in the impact of this unity on the minds of the apostles."[8] In other words, the resurrection of Jesus was not a physical but a spiritual event whose only basis was the subjective experience of the disciples and in that of Christians in the centuries that followed.

In Tillich's view, he was not demythologizing the life, death and resurrection of Jesus because he holds to the belief that myths are valid modes of expressing reality. What he claims to have done is to "de-literalize" them. The difference is imperceptible. He has also de-personalized them to such an extent that it is impossible for Tillich, in spite of many statements to the contrary, to see in Jesus Christ the second person of the Trinity. He gives himself away in the following passage:

> "Many Christians, many among us, cannot find a way of joining honestly with those who pray to Jesus Christ. Something in us is reluctant, something which is genuine and valid, the fear of becoming idolatrous, the fear of being split in our ultimate loyalty, the fear of looking at two faces instead of at the one divine face."[9]

One wonders how a believer in the Incarnation could be thus afflicted with double vision. Lest this judgment seem unfair, we should weigh and ponder the following:

> "Jesus is not the creator of another religion, but the victor over religion. He is not the maker of another law, but the conqueror of law. We, the ministers and teachers of Christianity, do not call you to Christianity but rather to the New Being to which Christianity should be a witness and nothing else, not confusing itself with that New Being. Forget all Christian doctrines; forget your own certainties and your doubts, when you hear the call of Jesus. For-

---

7. Tillich; *Systematic Theology*; Vol. II; pp. 97, 131.

8. *Ibid.*; pp. 156-157.

9. Tillich; *The New Being*; p. 99.

get all Christian morals, your achievements and your failures, when you come to Him. Nothing is demanded of you – no idea of God, and no goodness in yourselves, not your being religious, not your being Christian, not your being wise, and not your being moral."[10]

The radical rejection that is so eloquently expressed in the above passage was made necessary by Tillich's insistence that the receiving side of every revelatory experience is distorted and partially idolatrous. If the Great *Kairos* is to be an exception, the only way is to strip it of its content, which is exactly what Tillich has done. It reminds one of what the British have done with their maxim, "The King can do no wrong." To make it acceptable, one must see to it that the king cannot do anything (all his acts are those of his ministers, who are responsible for them and who control him). Being forced to choose between the demands of orthodoxy and those of his metaphysics, Tillich chose the latter. Why not? "Orthodoxy is intellectual pharisaism," he says.[11]

Tillich's position also is illustrated in his concept of grace. When speaking of it, he invariably uses the passive voice; e.g., one "is grasped." He follows the example of Plato who, in the allegory of the cave, also uses the passive voice: The chains of one of the dwellers "are broken" and he "is dragged" to the mouth of the cave. "This may be seen," observes Carl J. Armbruster, "if we change the proposal grammatically from the passive to the active voice: 'X accepts you.' Who or what is X? We are expressly told we cannot know."[12]

Even more pointed is George Tavard's judgment: "Of Tillich's faith in the ground of being of the philosophers above the concrete being of the Christian God, we may say with Calvin: 'But it is mockery to attribute the name of faith to pure ignorance.'"[13] We cannot even say that the New Being is ghostly because ghosts, though they have no substance, do have shape.

The political implications of Tillich's "New Being" are likely to be slight and very indirect. This would be the case even if we took the "New Being" to be the Jesus Christ of the gospels. Jesus was far less interested in political and social questions than the Old Testament prophets. Unlike the ecclesiastical bureaucrats in the World Council of Churches, the National Council of Churches and the higher echelons of the mainline denominations,

10. Tillich; *The Shaking of the Foundations*; p. 102. For a full citation of Tillich's works, see the Bibliography at the end of Book I.

11. Tillich; *On the Boundary*; p. 51.

12. Carl J. Armbruster, S.J.; *The Vision of Paul Tillich* (Yale University Press; New Haven, Conn.; 1967); p. 183.

13. George Tavard; *Paul Tillich and the Christian Message*; op. cit.; p. 81.

Jesus certainly was not a social activist. He never joined the zealots who were the radical nationalists of his day. He said not one word about the institution of slavery, which was prevalent in the Roman Empire. He denounced no Roman policies. He encouraged the Jews to pay taxes to the Roman authorities. He praised a Roman centurion for his faith. He consorted with publicans who, in a later time, were called collaborationists by the resistance leaders in Nazi-controlled Europe. Jesus passed no judgment on the economic system of his time, in spite of his compassion for the poor. He attended the synagogue regularly and held the Temple in reverence, as he showed when he drove out the moneychangers.

In short, Jesus was not a revolutionary in any sense that modern revolutionists would recognize. Not that he was soft, but he wanted to get at the moral and spiritual realities that underlie the concerns of social activists. He was like a doctor who is less interested in treating the symptoms of a disease when he has the cure for the disease itself.

If we discard the Jesus Christ of the New Testament and concentrate on Tillich's "New Being," the connection with politics is still more tenuous. As we have seen, the Great *Kairos* has been stripped of any content. It is difficult, therefore, to see at what points the "New Being" could impinge on politics. To make the "New Being" relevant to politics, it would be necessary to invest it with a specific content that included most of the questions facing our world today. This, for Tillich, would mean loading up the Great *Kairos* with distorted and idolatrous elements, and the Great *Kairos* then would become only one of many *kairoi*.

This is not to say that no relevance to politics is contained in Tillich's theological system, but that very little of it has to do with that part of his theological system that deals with the "New Being."

There is one possible connection that might appear if Tillich's theology should ever permeate through to the masses. A widespread belief in the "New Being" would encourage the idea that we can know a leader without knowing anything about him. It would introduce a curious sort of personalism whereby people would give unqualified support to political leaders without knowing their deeds, words, records and policies. It would discourage thinking about issues and, thus, promote civic laziness. If you do not need to know these things about someone as important as the "New Being," why should you be more exacting in the case of political leaders? The transposition would be easy.

We already have seen some of it in such instances as Franklin D. Roosevelt's New Deal. At the time, the Gallup organization surveyed popular opinion about New Deal policies and agencies, and found that many of the people who opposed most or all of these policies and agencies were enthusiastically ready to vote for Roosevelt for another term. The point here is not that the voters were right or wrong but, rather, that they voted for a man they really did not know or know much about, and apparently attached no importance to his policies and the agencies they created.

The same kind of Tillichian unconcern for the substance of personality, a civic laziness toward knowing *about* a person in order really to know him, was evident in much of the support received by Dwight D. Eisenhower in the 1950s, John F. Kennedy in the 1960s, Jimmy Carter in the 1970s, Ronald Reagan in the 1980s and Bill Clinton in the 1990s.

Tillich's influence, of course, was much too restricted to blame him for these undesirable political trends of unconcern, but it can be said that his concept of the "New Being" would lead in that direction were it ever to be received seriously and widely.

CHAPTER THREE

The Human Predicament

The human predicament is one of Tillich's favorite terms for what usually is called the doctrine of man, or what Voegelin[1] would call anthropology. In order to understand it, two key words are necessary: *essence* and *existence.*

Essence is true being and, as applied to man, it means man as he ought to be or, in more traditional Christian terms, man as God created him and intended him to be. With reference to human nature, essence is potentiality.

Tillich calls this state of essence "dreaming innocence." By that phrase he means to describe man before the Fall of Adam. The Fall of Adam, however, is not to be understood as an event in time: "It has no time; it precedes temporality, and it is suprahistorical." Innocence has three connotations: "It can mean lack of actual experience, lack of personal responsibility, and lack of moral guilt. In the metaphorical use suggested here, it is meant in all three senses." But innocence is not to be understood as perfection, for only God is perfect "because he transcends essence and existence. The symbol 'Adam before the Fall' must be understood as the dreaming innocence of undecided potentialities."[2]

Existence, on the other hand, is being in time and space; i.e., in history. It also can be described as the actualization of the potential. Its most characteristic feature is finitude, whereby man is the prisoner of time and space. For that reason, actualization is only partial and distorted, and that spells insecurity and anxiety.

Why and how did this transition from essence to existence take place?

Tillich's answer is that man in his state of dreaming innocence yielded to temptation by the exercise of the freedom with which God endowed him: "He stands between the preservation of his dreaming innocence without

---

1. Eric Voegelin (1901-1985). German-born American political scientist. His many books include *The New Science of Politics* and the five-volume *Order and History.*

2. *Systematic Theology;* Vol. II; pp. 33-34.

experiencing the actuality of being and the loss of his innocence through knowledge, power and guilt. The anxiety of this situation is the state of temptation. Man decides for self-actualization, thus producing the end of dreaming innocence."[3]

The transition from essence to existence, Tillich is careful to say, is not an event in time but a universal ontological occurrence. Tillich also is very insistent that the resulting immersion in finitude is not sin, but sin does occur in finitude.

It should be pointed out that the word "sin," like other traditional terms of Christian theology, is distasteful to Tillich. He wishes he could discard it, as vividly expressed in the following quotation:

> "It is a word that has fallen into disrepute. To some of us it sounds almost ridiculous and is apt to provoke laughter rather than serious consideration. To others, who take it more seriously, it implies an attack on their human dignity. And again, to others – those who have suffered from it – it means the threatening countenance of the disciplinarian, who forbids them to do what they would like and demands what they hate. Therefore, even Christian teachers, including myself, shy away from the use of the word sin. We know how many distorted images it can produce. We try to avoid it, or to substitute another word for it. But it has a strange quality. It always returns. We cannot escape it. It is as insistent as it is ugly. And so it would be more honest – and I say this to myself – to face it and ask what it really is.[4]"

Before he defines the "ugly word," we must examine another term without which sin can have no meaning for Tillich. That term is estrangement. Estrangement is the immediate effect of finitude: "Man as he exists is not what he essentially is and ought to be. He is estranged from his true being. The profundity of the term 'estrangement' lies in the implication that one belongs essentially to that from which one is estranged. Man is not a stranger to his true being, for he belongs to it." Man is estranged from God, from nature, from other human beings, and from himself.

Nevertheless, estrangement is not synonymous with sin. It is, rather, man's reaction to estrangement, "the personal act of turning away from that to which one belongs."[5] Tillich, therefore, explicitly rejects the notion of original sin because sin is neither congenital nor hereditary. It is an act of will by man in his state of existence, his refusal to accept finitude and his persistent effort to resist it.

With these terms – essence, existence, dreaming innocence, finitude,

3. *Ibid.*; p. 46.

4. Tillich; *The Eternal Now*; pp. 50-51.

5. Tillich; *Systematic Theology*; Vol. II; pp. 45-46.

estrangement, and sin (as he defines them) – we have Tillich's "deliteralization" of the story of Genesis. But that is not the whole story. The same book of Genesis teaches that man was created in the image of God, and traditional Christian theology teaches that this image was distorted but not extinguished by the Fall. Even Calvin's doctrine of total depravity does not hold that this image is completely obliterated, but only that all of man's faculties are sufficiently crippled by sin to prevent man from being able to save himself.

Tillich, of course, does not use these terms, for they, too, must be deliteralized. He says that the essence of man continues in the midst of existence and his link with the "ground of being" is not annihilated, though he is estranged from it. Man alone among all creatures has the gift of transcendence. He alone is able to transcend his environment. "Man has a world," Tillich says, "namely a structured whole of innumerable parts, a *cosmos*, as the Greeks called it, because of its structured character which makes it accessible to men through acts of creative receiving and transforming. Having a world is more than having an environment."[6]

This transcendence implies the ability to change and, sometimes, even to transform environment. Science and technology provide the most spectacular example of this ability. Man cannot only control his environment in considerable measure; he also can understand its deeper meaning. It was one of Tillich's criticisms of Americans that, while pre-eminent in control, they are deficient in understanding. He blamed it on Calvinism and Puritanism. "There is no mystical participation in nature," he complained, "no understanding that nature is the finite expression of the infinite ground of all things, no vision of the divine-demonic conflict in nature."[7]

This transcendence extends to that part of the environment that is social. Man is a product of history and an agent of history, but he can stand aside as though it were external to himself and judge it. Not only can he know history, he can understand it and incorporate it into himself. It was another of Tillich's criticisms that most Americans know historical facts, but that these facts "remained objects of their intellect and almost never became elements of their existence."[8]

Finally, man is able to transcend himself. He can look at himself as though he were another person. He can judge himself and laugh at himself. He can destroy himself psychologically so that his personality loses its cen-

---

6. Tillich; *Morality and Beyond*; p. 19. For a full citation of Tillich's works, see the Bibliography at the end of Book I.

7. Tillich; *My Search for Absolutes*; p. 19. For a full citation of Tillich's works, see the Bibliography at the end of Book I.

8. *Ibid.*; p. 27.

ter and falls to pieces, or physically by committing suicide. He also can experience "ecstasy" (standing outside oneself) when grasped by grace through faith.

It is through these several aspects of transcendence that man is aware of the infinite "ground of being," the presence of "the Unconditional." The contrast that ensues between essence and existence and the tensions that this contrast produce constitute what Tillich calls the human predicament. Man rebels against the finite. He feels the threat of non-being, what Tillich calls the ontological shock, when he realizes that both he and his world will cease to be. He is estranged from other human beings and from himself. He is sunk in the abyss of meaninglessness.

The only thing that can get man out of his predicament is grace through faith experienced in love. Every man has some ultimate concern and, if that concern really is ultimate, "the Unconditional" will shine through the paltry content of that concern and raise him to the level of the divine where subjectivity and objectivity, essence and existence, are transcended. "Suddenly," Tillich explains, "true reality appears like the brightness of lightning in a formerly dark place. Or, slowly, true reality appears like a landscape when the fog becomes thinner and thinner and finally disappears."[9]

What Tillich describes here is a mystical experience. But he does not go quite so far as that mystic who, in answer to a question about his experience, said: "If you don't know, I can't tell you; and if you knew, you would not ask." That answer would have been no help at all! In spite of the fact that such an experience is unpredictable and relatively rare, Tillich is sure that it can have lasting results.

One reason he believes this is because the glow of it continues after the experience, like the sunlight after the sun has sunk below the horizon. The other reason is that the mode in which "the Unconditional" breaks through into existence is shared by groups belonging to particular historical periods, and the experience is kept alive by symbols, liturgies and sacraments. The result of grace is to overcome estrangement and bring forth a new creation: "Therefore we can speak of the New in terms of a re-newal: The threefold 're,' namely, re-conciliation, re-union, re-surrection."[10] It vanquishes evil, which is that "structure of self-destruction which is implicit in the nature of universal estrangement."[11] It overcomes the demonic, which "is something finite and limited which has been invested with the stature of the infinite."[12]

---

9. Tillich; *The New Being*; p. 73.

10. *Ibid.*; p. 20.

11. Tillich; *Systematic Theology*, Vol. II; p. 61.

12. Tillich; *On the Boundary*; p. 40.

The process by which man is grasped by grace and shaped by the *gestalt* of grace over a period of time is called essentialization, which is Tillich's word for sanctification. In a way, it is a reversal of the process of actualization, except that its end is not a return to dreaming innocence nor a rejection of those potentialities that have been actualized. It is, rather, their union on the level of eternity where there is neither actualization nor essentialization.

At this point, Tillich again departs from orthodox Christianity. He could not, of course, expect the resurrection of the body of Christians since he denied it to Christ himself. He refuses to believe in life after death or everlasting life because they imply a continuation of time after death. His favorite term is eternity: "Eternity is neither timelessness nor the endlessness of time." Neither can it be identified with simultaneity. The only thing we know spiritually, essentially and intuitively is the present, and the present is the Eternal Now. "Past and future meet in the present and both are included in the eternal 'now.'" Further: "The eternal is not a future state of things. It is always present, not only in man (who is aware of it), but also in everything that has being within the whole of being."

Are there any penalties? Not the wrath of God, which Tillich says should be eliminated from usage. One should likewise abandon the concept of "eternal damnation" and, instead, speak of condemnation "as removal from the eternal."[13]

Tillich is very emphatic in saying that "the Unconditional" is beyond our reach. We cannot work for it. No social engineering or political manipulation can bring it about or control it when it comes. Grace is free and undeserved, accepting the unacceptable. The greatest virtue is openness or receptivity. "Listening with an open soul," he recommends "keeping an empty space in our inner life, sharpening our spiritual hearing: this is the only thing we can do. But this is much. And blessed are those whose minds and hearts are open."[14]

Is Tillich's analysis communicable?

The question has been raised as to whether modern man experiences the human predicament, the ontological shock, the existential dread, the threat of meaninglessness. Harvey Cox argues that modern man has no such worries: "The difficulty," he says, "however, is that they are obviously *not* questions which occur to everyone, or indeed to the vast majority of people. They especially do not occur to the newly emergent urban-secular man."[15]

13. Tillich; *Systematic Theology*; Vol. I, p. 274; Vol. III, pp. 395, 400; Vol. II, pp. 77-78.

14. Tillich; *The New Being*; p.124

15. Harvey Cox, *The Secular City* (Macmillan; New York; 1965); p. 79.

The same point was made more graphically by a New York taxicab driver who was asked what he thought about communism. "Don't bother me with those cosmic problems," he said. "I've got my own troubles."

And it is true that the majority of Americans feel comfortable and secure in their lives, liberty and property. Threats to these things still are very recent, like the 9-11 attacks, but they have not changed the general attitude to an appreciable extent.

Where does this leave Tillich's human predicament?

Joseph Haroutunian came to the rescue by suggesting that Tillich was wrong only in making finitude the cause of anxiety. "However, my thesis is that it is love rather than finitude that makes man anxious," Haroutunian says. "It is loss, the loss of people and things with whom we transact, as reminders of the total loss of the world in death, that suffuses life with anxiety."[16]

We do worry about our wives and children because we love them. We are anxious about our jobs because they are important to us. We fear to lose our good name and our position in society because we care for them. We worry about illness, physical and mental, because we place a high value on health.

All these things are true enough, but they are not what Tillich has in mind. These worries are present mainly during periods of crisis, which do not occur all the time. Such worries can be treated by marriage and vocational counselors, personnel directors, public relations experts, physicians and psychiatrists. These people can handle various types of maladjustments, but they cannot handle the human predicament.

Take the case of the psychiatrist: "He must, for example, be willing to distinguish between existential anxiety to be conquered by a courage created by the Spiritual Presence and a neurotic anxiety to be conquered by analysis, perhaps in combination with methods of medical healing."[17] No psychiatrist can deliver a patient from death or the fear of death. In other words, for Tillich, existential anxiety is beyond human healing. Only grace can cope with it.

The Tillichian account of the human predicament and his solution to it do not leave much room for the politician or the political theorist. Politics, of course, is very much influenced by the phenomenon of estrangement, a word that has slipped into common usage. We see it in ideological conflicts, racial tensions, the class struggle, the search for identity among new nations, the disappearance of a sense of direction and mission in the older

16. Joseph Haroutunian; "The Question Tillich Left Us;" *Religion in Life: A Christian Quarterly of Opinion and Discussion;* XXXV (Winter 1966); p. 717.

17. Tillich; *Systematic Theology;* Vol. III; p. 281.

nations. But, if Tillich's analysis means anything, it is that there is no salvation by politics.

Social activists, who are so much in the saddle today, can draw very scanty support from Tillich. In 1942, he made the following comment:

"I do not make concrete suggestions about possible political actions in the name of religion. This is impossible, and it never should be tried. Religion as such cannot suggest war aims or social reforms."[18]

Would that the leading figures in the World Council of Churches and the National Council of Churches and similar organizations had the same self-restraint and humility.

---

18. Tillich; *The Protestant Era*; p. 191.

CHAPTER FOUR

The Protestant Principle

One of the fundamental concepts in Tillich's theology is what he calls the Protestant Principle. He gives no formal definition of it, but dwells at length on its consequences. It is possible, though, to give something of a formal definition that conveys what he means.

The Protestant Principle is that all revelations of "the Unconditional" become denatured as soon as they are given a specific content. It is his interpretation of the commandment: "Thou shalt have no other gods before me."[1] In Tillichian language, "It is the guardian against the attempts of the finite and conditioned to usurp the place of the unconditional in thinking and acting."[2] It is on the theological and philosophical levels what a *kairos* is on the historical level. Nothing must be treated as absolute that is relative, and only "the Unconditional" is absolute. All principles, being creations of the human mind, are relative – except the Protestant Principle itself.

The Protestant Principle does not necessarily refer to any Protestant "era" or any of the churches that now call themselves Protestant. It certainly is not the historic Protestant principle that says that the sole authority rests with Scripture (*sola scriptura*). Tillich explicitly rejects that historic principle as Biblicistic and un-Protestant. The Protestant "era" may disintegrate and the Protestant churches may disappear, but the Protestant Principle is permanently valid and will never disappear.

How can Tillich make such an affirmation when he holds that all revelations of "the Unconditional" are distorted and ephemeral? By the same process of deliteralization he employed in dealing with God and the "New Being." Substantively (for the philosopher and the theologian), it means having no principle at all. Operationally (for the statesman), it has been

---

1. Exodus 20:3.

2. Tillich; *The Protestant Era*; p. 163.

45

called the principle of hesitancy. For he who thinks, the Protestant Principle casts doubts on every affirmation. For he who acts, the Protestant Principle casts doubts on every alternative.

Does this have a paralyzing effect on the philosopher, the theologian and the statesman? No, Tillich says, or at least not necessarily. What the first two need is the courage to think, and the third needs the courage to act. Tillich admits that there are few who possess that kind of courage.

Closely associated with the Protestant Principle is his concept of the "boundary situation." He explains this concept as follows:

> "When I was asked to give an account of the way my ideas have developed from my life, I thought that the concept of the boundary might be the fitting symbol for the whole of my personal and intellectual development. At almost every point, I have had to stand between alternative possibilities of existence, to be completely at home in neither and to take no definitive stand against either. Since thinking presupposes receptiveness to new possibilities, this position is fruitful for thought; but it is difficult and dangerous in life, which again and again demands decisions and thus the exclusion of alternatives. This disposition and its tension have determined both my destiny and my work.[3]"

Every situation to which the Protestant Principle must be applied is a boundary situation. But "boundary situation" in political terms means "on the fence." Fence-sitters sometimes may stay in office, but they do not accomplish anything. The combination of the Protestant Principle and the boundary situation is peculiarly excruciating for the statesman because he has to make decisions. He is faced with choosing among alternatives and has no way to decide which is right and which is wrong. Indeed, it would be better to say that the only assurance he has is that it will be the wrong one, and the best that he can hope for is that at least it will be partly right.

This is the inevitable consequence of being deprived of a guiding principle that is specific and concrete enough to have meaning. One might say that the more intelligent and better informed a statesman is, the greater his hesitancy will be, a hesitancy that easily can lead to total paralysis. He may be like the proverbial donkey who, standing at a point equidistant between two haystacks, died of starvation because he could not decide to which haystack to go. It also could be said, of course, that he was an ass figuratively as well as literally.

But we do not have to cite this apocryphal story to illustrate the point. We have the historic example of General Maurice Gamelin, the commander in chief of the French army at the opening of World War II.

---

3. Tillich; *On the Boundary*; p. 13.

Gamelin was highly regarded as an intellectual. Deeply versed in military history, strategy and tactics, he anticipated every move the German forces might make, including the one they did make, and had thought out a course of action for each of these moves. His trouble was that he could not make up his mind which course of action to act upon. Neither did it occur to him to take the initiative by launching an attack while the bulk of the German army was occupied in Poland, and for the same reason – he could not face the risk of choosing any one line of attack. The result was military disaster when the German army broke through his lines, and he was relieved of command in May 1940.

By contrast, we have the case of Otto von Bismarck. The Iron Chancellor followed a course of combined diplomatic and military moves that brought him brilliant success. After victories in the war of 1866 and the Franco-German War, he created an alliance of kingdoms that later led to the formation of the German Empire in 1870.

Like Gamelin, von Bismarck had analyzed every alternative but, unlike Gamelin, he was able to make a decision and take risks. Why the difference? It was not native intelligence or professional training. It was, rather, that Bismarck had a guiding principle – the unification of Germany under the Hohenzollerns. No Protestant Principle encumbered his commitment to the principle of nationalism under dynastic leadership.

The Protestant Principle has an even greater deleterious effect on the masses. The masses cannot be expected to stand committed to principles that they regard as dubious. No one understood this better than Adolf Hitler. There were no ifs, buts, perhapses, and maybes in the principle of the *voelkischer Fuehrerstaat* as he expounded it with such fervor and which the German masses accepted with unquestioning enthusiasm. Hitler was so convinced of this necessity that he decreed that the 24 planks in the Nazi platform were "unalterable."

It is all very well to say that Hitler's principle was immoral and sacrilegious, which it was. But it still is true that, if men are to make history rather than merely endure it and be tossed to and fro by every fortuitous event that comes along, there must be commitment on the part of both leaders and masses. Tillich's Protestant Principle, therefore, is destructive of politics, political science and political theory.

CHAPTER FIVE

The Sacred Void

The sacred void is Tillich's name for the situation in which our society is caught. It is the human predicament raised to the socio-political level. It is extremely painful. Among its characteristics, Tillich discusses familiar themes like the failure to treat individuals as people; the technology that enslaves mankind to machines; the reduction of the proletariat to mere objects or tools; the loss of feeling for the translucence of nature and a sense of history; the demotion of our world to a mere environment; the demonic quality of modern nationalism; the search for identity; the hopelessness of the future.

Space does not permit us to elaborate on these themes, which Tillich discusses thoroughly, at length, and often brilliantly. Perhaps a single quotation will give the reader an idea of what all this adds up to in Tillich's thinking:

> "Little is left of our present civilization which does not indicate to a sensitive mind the presence of this vacuum, this lack of ultimacy and substantial power in language and education, in politics and philosophy, in the development of personalities, in the life of communities. Who of us has never been shocked by this void when he has used traditional or untraditional, secular or religious language to make himself understandable and has not succeeded and has made a vow of silence to himself, only to break it a few hours later? This is symbolic of our whole civilization.[1]"

Though Tillich never would admit it, the sacred void is the direct result of the deliteralization of God, the "New Being" and the Protestant Principle. The question is: Can we get rid of the sacred void and, if so, how?

The Bible, for Tillich, is not the answer because it is not the written Word of God. It is only one source among others for religious thinking, a source composed of the words of fallible men who were the product of their

---

1. Tillich; *The Protestant Era*; p. 60.

times – times that were very different from ours. The Reformation doctrine of *sola scriptura* is nothing but Biblicism which, for Tillich, definitely is a pejorative term.

We must not look to the Church either, he said, because we can get no help from that quarter. As usual with traditional terms, Tillich discards the visible church and the church universal and invisible. The basic defect he finds in these terms is that they are limited to Christianity. He therefore substitutes his own terms: The Spiritual Community, the Latent Church and the Manifest Church.

The Spiritual Community includes all mankind because every living human being has an ultimate concern which, it will be recalled, is Tillich's name for faith. The professed atheist and the avowed Communist are just as much members of that church as the Christian, and the fact that they neither know it nor recognize it does not exclude them. The Spiritual Community is composed of the Latent Church and the Manifest Church. Those belonging to the Latent Church are those who have not known "the impact of the Spiritual Presence and therefore revelation," but are destined to know it. The Spiritual Community is latent so long as it has not had "an encounter with the central revelation" and becomes manifest "after such an encounter."[2] That encounter, of course, is with the "New Being" which, while final in Jesus "the Christ," is partially manifest in other instances of revelation.

The consequences of Tillich's concept of the Church, needless to say, are radical and numerous. "It is not permissible to designate as 'unchurched' those who have become alienated from organized denominations and traditional creeds. In living among these groups for half a generation I learned how much of the Latent Church there is within them."[3]

The traditional missionary role toward non-Christians must be discarded, according to Tillich: "Therefore in our dialogues with other religions we must not try to make converts; rather, we must try to drive the other religions to their own depths, to that point at which they realize that they are witness to the Absolute but not the Absolute themselves."[4] Further: "Not long ago, many people, especially members of the church, felt qualified to judge others and to tell them what to believe and how to act. Today we feel deeply the arrogance of this attitude."[5]

Conversion, in Tillich's view, has another meaning than making Christians out of non-Christians: "Conversion can have the character of a transi-

2. Tillich; *Systematic Theology*; Vol. III; pp. 152-153.

3. Tillich; *On the Boundary*; p. 67.

4. Tillich; *My Search for Absolutes*; pp. 140-141.

5. Tillich; *The Eternal Now;* p. 82.

tion from the latent stage of the Spiritual Community to its manifest stage."[6]

It must be remembered, he reminds us, "that the history of religion and culture is a history of permanent demonic distortions of revelation and idolatrous confusions of God and man."[7]

Finally, not much hope is to be placed in the Manifest Church, Christian or otherwise, because it necessarily is hierarchical and, hence, cannot be expected to do much in promoting social justice, "for every system of religious hierarchies is conducive to social injustice."[8]

Tillich finds no refuge in conscience as ordinarily understood because it is part of existence, with all the ambiguities that existence entails. "It has no special demands; it speaks to us in the 'mode of silence.' It tells us only to act and to become guilty by acting, for every action is unscrupulous." Tillich has a concept of what he calls the "transmoral conscience," but it does not help us to distinguish right from wrong either:

"The good, transmoral conscience consists in the acceptance of the bad, moral conscience, which is unavoidable wherever decisions are made and acts performed."[9]

The transmoral conscience, however, is more sensitive than the ordinary one: "Those who have a sensitive conscience cannot escape the question of the transmoral conscience. The moral conscience drives beyond the sphere in which it is valid to the sphere from which it must receive its conditional validity."[10] And, so, Tillich throws us back again to the Unconditional-impersonal, inaccessible to all of man's efforts to grasp it, and bare of any concrete substance that could guide us.

Law fares no better at the hands of Tillich. The trouble with law is that it is heteronomous; i.e., something external imposed on man and, therefore (for Tillich), tyrannical and destructive of "the centered personality." Tillich recognizes that law is necessary for the maintenance of society, but its content is ever changing and of necessity ambiguous. It can be of little use, therefore, in guiding decisions. This is as true of the moral law as it is of the civil law because both are externally imposed. "Then we can and must resist it," Tillich advises us, "because it denies our own dignity as persons."[11]

---

6. Tillich; *Systematic Theology*; Vol. III; p. 220.

7. Tillich; *The Protestant Era*; p. xxviii.

8. Tillich; *Systematic Theology;* Vol. III; p. 205.

9. Tillich; *The Protestant Era;* p. 148. The italics are Tillich's.

10. *Ibid.*; p. 149.

11. Tillich; *My Search for Absolutes*; p. 95.

Tillich's condemnation of law is harshest in the following passage:

"And certainly, the written code in its threatening majesty has the power to kill. It kills the joy of fulfilling our being by imposing upon us something we feel as hostile. It kills the freedom of answering creatively what we encounter in things and men by making us look at a table of laws. It kills our ability to listen to the calling of the moment, to the voiceless voice of others, and to the here and now. It kills our courage to act through the scruples of our anxiety-driven conscience. And among those who take it most seriously, it kills faith and hope, and throws us into self-condemnation and despair."[12]

The same applies to natural law: "The natural law cannot answer the question of the content of justice."[13] The only way in which natural law can be made acceptable is if we regard it as identical with the structure of our own being, internal and not external to ourselves.

The nearest Tillich comes to an answer on the subject of law is in his concept of love as the reunion of the estranged.[14] But, here again, love has no content other than that which an individual must decide for himself at any particular moment of time when confronting a concrete situation. Tillich's view on this matter of love has proved to be the breeding ground from which spawned Bishop Robinson's new morality, Joseph Fletcher's situational ethics,[15] Paul Lehmann's contextual ethics,[16] and the vast permissiveness that more and more is engulfing today's society.

For the Christian – and the non-Christian, too – who is looking for intelligible standards of conduct, some point of reference for his or her thinking, Tillich's concept of love is not the answer. His attitude toward law, if widely shared, would have a disastrous effect on American thinking about the U.S. Constitution. The Constitution is the supreme law of the land and, being a written code, is heteronomous; i.e., externally imposed. It assumes that the rules and principles contained in the Constitution are intelligible realities

12. Tillich; *The Eternal Now*; p. 90.

13. Tillich; *Love, Power, and Justice: Ontological Analyses and Ethical Implications*; p. 82. For a full citation of Tillich's works, see the Bibliography at the end of Book I.

14. *Ibid.*; p. 25.

15. Joseph Fletcher; *Situational Ethics* (Westminster Press; Philadelphia; 1966). Situationalism argues that every situation is different. Therefore, absolute rules are inappropriate because they are too inflexible. The only ethical "rule" is love alone because it has its own moral compass and can be trusted to know what to do in any situation.

16. Paul L. Lehmann; *Ethics in a Christian Context* (Harper & Row; New York; 1963). He argues that it is only as human motivation and judgment converge within the conscience that God and humans come in contact with one another as "the aims and the direction, the motivations and the decisions, the instruments and the structures of human interrelatedness are forged into a pattern of response – a style of life."

with an objective existence. They do stand in need of interpretation, but there has to be something to be interpreted. Without that assumption, the oath of office required by Article VI of every public official – federal, state and local – is utterly pointless. Without that assumption, the intent of the Constitution, which is to guide and circumscribe official discretion, is nullified.

Tillich, then, provides a theological base for those legal positivists who assert that law is official behavior – what officials do. We must remember his attitude toward law, especially the written law. Law kills. Were Tillich's attitude toward law to become general, it would indeed kill – every constitutional republic, including our own.

Does politics hold the answer to the problem of the sacred void?

Once again, Tillich gives us no hope. The state, unlike individual persons, has no organic center; hence, the rulers have to act as the deciding center of the group. Tillich's view is strangely elitist for someone as individualistic as he is: "It is not the group which decides," he tells us, "but those who have the power to speak for the group and force their decision upon all the members of the group." In every ruling group, there always is "tension between power by acknowledgment and power by enforcement."[17] Both acknowledgment (which he prefers to consent) and enforcement are necessary, and both are rooted in the "vocational consciousness" of the group, and that vocational consciousness (sense of mission, purpose, direction) is the manifestation of a secondary *kairos*.

Getting down to specifics, we find Tillich very favorably disposed toward socialism. He accepts the Marxist interpretation of bourgeois culture, but rejects its materialistic and anti-religious basis. He believed so strongly in what he called "religious socialism" that, at the end of World War I, he saw it as a *kairos*. By the end of World War II, he gave up that idea, but continued to believe in religious socialism. Unfortunately, his discussion of religious socialism is too vague to supply either the rulers or the ruled with meaningful guidance.

His endorsement of democracy is a qualified one. He saw democracy as "the best way discovered so far to guarantee the creative freedom of determining the historical process to everyone within a centered historical group." But democracy and democratization are not to be identified with the Kingdom of God.[18] Moreover, he thought that the period following World War II "will create tasks for which the ordinary democratic methods

---

17. Tillich; *Love, Power, and Justice: Ontological Analyses and Ethical Implications*; pp. 93-94.

18. Tillich; *Systematic Theology*; Vol. III; pp. 347, 385.

cannot be used at all."[19] So, democracy is not the answer either.

Tillich was skeptical about revolution as well. The revolutionist is in a quandary for, "if he revolts against the authorities which have shaped him, he does it with the tools he has received from them. The language of the revolutionary is formed by those against whom he revolts. The protest of the reformer uses the tradition against which he protests. Therefore, no absolute revolution is possible."[20]

And, yet, Tillich does have an answer and he gives it in terms of the *kairos* and eschatology. It should be noted that he calls the void that plagues us the "sacred void." What makes it sacred is his belief that this void is the precursor of another *kairos* for which the world is waiting. A *kairos* "describes the moment in which the eternal breaks into the temporal, *and the temporal is prepared to receive it*."[21]

All *kairoi* are secondary; i.e., partial intrusions of "the Unconditional" into existence because there was only one Great *Kairos*, which was the appearance of the "New Being." Nevertheless: "Mankind is never left alone. The Spiritual Presence acts upon it in every moment and breaks into it in some great moments, which are the historical *kairoi*."[22] These *kairoi*, however, are of variable intensity, like electric light bulbs that give a dull glow or a brilliant light depending on the amount of electric power they receive. They take three forms: Heteronomy, autonomy and theonomy. Tillich defines these forms thus:

> "Autonomy asserts that man as the bearer of universal reason is the source and measure of culture and religion – that he is his own law. Heteronomy asserts that man, being unable to act according to universal reason, must be subjected to a law, strange and superior to him. Theonomy asserts that the superior law is, at the same time, the innermost law of man himself, rooted in the divine ground which is man's own ground: the law of life transcends man, although it is, at the same time, his own."[23]

Clearly, Tillich favors theonomy as the highest form of the *kairos*, next but not equal to the Great *Kairos*.

The appearance of these secondary *kairoi* is subject to certain "regularities." It is at this point that the concept of eschatology must be brought in. All history must have some structure of meaning – otherwise, it would be what some cynics have characterized as "one damn thing after another."

19. Tillich; *The Protestant Era*; p. 244.

20. Tillich; *The New Being*; p. 84.

21. Tillich; *The Protestant Era*; p. xix. Italics supplied.

22. Tillich: *Systematic Theology*; Vol. III; p. 140.

23. Tillich; *The Protestant Era*; pp. 56-57.

There have been two answers to this problem of the structure of meaning of history. One of them is the cyclical concept, which the ancient Greeks believed in. This concept states that history consists of a series of cycles that repeat themselves over and over again like the seasons in nature. The other is the eschatological concept, usually called the doctrine of last things, whereby history is deemed to move from a beginning to an end.

Tillich professes to believe in the eschatological concept, and says so more than once. Eschatology originally was a Christian concept, often associated with St. Augustine, but it has been transposed in a number of secular ideologies like those of Hegel,[24] Marx[25] and Auguste Comte.[26] The difference between them is that the secular ideologies conceive of the end as here on Earth, in history. The Christian concept places the end as above and beyond history. The Christian and secular concepts are alike in that both are linear, and it is to the Christian concept that Tillich claims to adhere.

His concept, however, is in some ways more cyclical than eschatological. The "regularities" of the secondary *kairoi* are that they appear and reappear in a particular order. Thus, according to Tillich, the early Middle Ages were theonomous, the later Middle Ages were heteronomous, and the

---

24. Georg Wilhelm Friedrich Hegel (1770-1831); German academic. His books include *Science of Logic*, which attributes the unfolding of concepts of reality in terms of the pattern of dialectical reasoning (thesis – antithesis – synthesis); *Encyclopedia of the Philosophical Sciences*, which describes the application of this dialectic to all areas of human knowledge; and *Phenomenology of Mind*, which criticized the traditional epistemological distinction (objective from subjective) and offered his own dialectical account of the development of consciousness from individual sensation, through a social concern with ethics and politics, to the pure consciousness of the World-Spirit in art, religion and philosophy.

25. Karl Marx (1818-1883); German-born journalist, writer and historian. Although he shared Hegel's belief in dialectical structure and historical inevitability, Marx held that the foundations of reality lay in the material base of economics rather than in the abstract thought of idealistic philosophy. In *Economic and Political Manuscripts of 1844*, he argued that the conditions of modern industrial societies invariably result in the alienation of workers from their own labor. Marx later wrote a systematic explanation of his economic theories in *Das Capital* and *Theory of Surplus Value*. With his colleague Friedrich Engels, Marx issued the *Communist Manifesto* in the explicit hope of precipitating social revolution. It describes the class struggle between proletariat and bourgeoisie, distinguishes communism from other socialist movements, proposes a list of specific social reforms, and urges all workers to unite in revolution against existing regimes.

26. Auguste Comte (1798-1857). French philosopher known as the "Father of Sociology." He developed Positivism, a philosophical system of thought maintaining that the goal of knowledge is simply to describe the phenomena that is experienced, not to question whether it exists or not. He believed that the solution to persistent social problems might be found by the application of certain hierarchical rules – reconciling science, religion, the ideals of 1789 and the doctrine of counter-revolution – that would lead mankind toward a superior state of civilization.

modern period was autonomous. His diagnosis of the situation of contemporary man is that "*he is the autonomous man who has become insecure in his autonomy.*"[27] He is ready for a new theonomy. That Tillich's doctrine of the *kairos* is not truly eschatological is evident in the following statement: "There is, in the doctrine of the *Kairos*, no final stage in which dialectics, against its nature, ceases to operate."[28]

Other elements in Tillich's theology seriously contradict his assertions that his thinking is eschatological. There is no universal history. "History has no aim, either in time or in eternity." He finds that "there is no progress from one mature style to the other."[29] He says: "Mankind does not become better; good and evil are merely raised to a higher plane."[30] He also says: "The state of ultimate concern admits no more of progress than of obsolescence or regression."[31]

Though he does not realize it, in this case as in so many others, Tillich is more Greek than Christian.

Tillich's conclusion is that the problem of the sacred void can be solved only by the coming of a theonomy, that we must wait for it, and that we cannot know when it will come. In non-Tillichian language, that means we must wait for a miracle and hope it will not be too long delayed.

27. Tillich; *The Protestant Era*; p. 192. The italics are Tillich's.

28. *Ibid.*; p. 48.

29. Tillich; *Systematic Theology*; Vol. III; pp. 341, 352, 334.

30. Tillich; *On the Boundary*; p. 77.

31. Tillich; *Systematic Theology*; Vol. III; p. 336.

CHAPTER SIX

Conclusion

A review of Tillich's thought shows that Tillich was a liberal, theologically and politically. He himself admitted as much: "Since my first political decision a few years before World War I, I have stood with the political left, even to opposing very strong conservative traditions."

His liberalism was a reaction against the authoritarianism prevailing in his family and in rural Brandenburg. It was the typical self-assertion of a very young man against his background, an act of personal independence, and he did not outgrow it with adulthood as most of us do. "Once a man has broken with the taboos of the most sacred authorities," he confessed, "he cannot subject himself to another heteronomy, whether religious or political."[1]

There is only one point at which Tillich deviates significantly from the contemporary liberal position, especially as we find it among Protestant clergy – he was not a social activist. This deviation probably can be attributed to the Lutheranism in which he was brought up, a remnant of which clung to him for the rest of his life.

Tillich essentially was an individualist. His individualism is apparent in his concept of theonomy because, in it, you have all the advantages of autonomy without any of the disadvantages. In theonomy, the self is neither extinguished nor denatured, but retained and elevated to a higher level – the realm of the eternal. Tillich reminds one of Rousseau in his individualism:

> "The problem is to find a form of association which will defend and protect with the whole common force the person and goods of each associate, and in which each, while uniting himself with all, *may still obey himself alone* and remain as free as before."[2]

---

1. Tillich; *On the Boundary*; pp. 44, 38.
2. Jean Jacques Rousseau; *The Social Contract* (J.M. Dent & Co.; London and Toronto; 1927); p. 14. Italics supplied.

This is the crux of Tillich's position, too, for – in the grip of "the Unconditional" – the individual person obeys himself alone. The same parallel can be drawn between the two thinkers with regard to moral liberty. Rousseau said it "alone makes him truly master of himself" and that "obedience to a law which we prescribe to ourselves is liberty."[3] That is precisely what Tillich thinks, for any other conception of law would be heteronomous, even if decreed by "a heavenly tyrant."

Why, then, not be satisfied with autonomy pure and simple? Because autonomy is not as deeply rooted in "the Unconditional" as theonomy.

Tillich's liberalism also shows itself in his likes and dislikes. Good words, for him, are openness, receptivity, freedom, risk, democracy and socialism. Bad words are Biblicism, fundamentalism, supernaturalism and authoritarianism. For those bad words, there is no boundary situation, no relativity. It often is overlooked, especially by liberals, that liberalism is not exempt from intolerance. Some things are beyond the pale, and others are not. It just depends on which ones.

It will be recalled that we gave two criteria for success in an enterprise like Tillich's: (1) the fidelity of the new concepts in conveying intact the substance of the Christian faith to modern man; and (2) the degree of success these new concepts have had in securing the understanding and acceptance of modern man.

Our survey of Tillich's theology makes it clear that he has failed to meet the first criterion. What he actually has done is invent a new religion. But we must admit that his is a fascinating, exciting, challenging, impressive, mind-stretching, and spirit-stretching failure. As such, it deserves sincere admiration even from those who cannot accept his religion.

As to the second criterion, Tillich has achieved a considerable measure of success. His religion has many followers and has influenced many of those who are not his followers. His influence probably will continue to grow for some years in this new century, but it will not be enduring. His theology is too abstract and disembodied.

Tillich's problem will be like that of a contemporary of Voltaire, who had concocted a new religion that he thought far more rational and acceptable than Christianity. The trouble was that he could not get anybody to believe in it.

So, he turned to Voltaire and asked: "What can I do to get people to believe in my religion?"

To which Voltaire, that master of sardonic humor, replied:

"You might try to get yourself crucified, die and rise again on the third day."

---

3. *Ibid.*; p.19.

Major Works of Paul Tillich

Systematic Theology; 3 vols. (University of Chicago Press; Chicago; 1951, 1957 and 1963).

The Protestant Era (University of Chicago Press; Chicago; 1948).

The Shaking of the Foundations (Charles Scribner's Sons; New York; 1948).

The Courage to Be (Yale University Press; New Haven and London; 1952).

The New Being (Charles Scribner's Sons; New York; 1955).

The Eternal Now (Charles Scribner's Sons; New York; 1955).

Biblical Religion and the Search for Ultimate Reality (University of Chicago Press; Chicago; 1955).

The Dynamics of Faith (Harper & Row; New York; 1957).

Love, Power, and Justice: Ontological Analyses and Ethical Implications (Oxford University Press; New York; 1960).

Morality and Beyond (Harper & Row; New York and Evanston, Ill.; 1963).

On the Boundary: An Autobiographical Sketch (Charles Scribner's Sons; New York; 1966).

My Search for Absolutes (Simon & Schuster; New York; 1967).

BOOK II

Karl Barth

Contents

Introduction

The impact of Karl Barth[1] on theology was a shattering event. Nothing has been or could remain the same again after that. In spite of a number of serious reservations, Barth was a hero in the eyes of conservative evangelicals because they saw in him the giant who slew the dragon of modernism.

To liberals, he was a monumental challenge for, however much they disagreed with him, his theology simply could not be ignored. Moreover, liberals are inclined to forgive much in the man who took such a strong stand against Adolf Hitler and who was the moving spirit behind the Declaration of Barmen. To virtually all theologians and Christian churchgoers, he was the acknowledged founder of neo-orthodoxy.

The secular world also was challenged to its very core because he called into question every culture and civilization, every political and economic system, and every social institution.

What is so shattering about Barth's theology?

God is the God of Abraham, Isaac and Jacob; he was incarnate in Jesus Christ; and he lives and rules in the Church and in the world. Gone is the kindly, bewhiskered grandfather up in the sky, the vague "Supreme Being" floating around somewhere, the concept of the Deists, the "first cause" of the philosophers.

In his majesty, glory and power God is wholly Other. Gone is the overly familiar being who invites familiarity, manipulation and indifference.

Jesus Christ is the Son of God and the second person in the Trinity. Gone is the mere teacher, the amiable leader among many leaders, the good example easily followed by men of goodwill.

The Bible is the Word of God, the sword of the Spirit, the infallible rule of faith and practice. Gone is the "good book," the collection of religious wisdom among many such collections, the merely and wholly human words of time-bound and culture-bound writers.

Christianity is the true religion. Gone is the pluralism that asserts Christianity is only one religion among many in the world, each of which contains variable amounts of truth and untruth.

---

1. Karl Barth (1886-1968).

Sin is an inescapable reality restored to all its stark destructiveness. Gone is the fatuous optimism that man inherently is good and liable only to "mistakes" and feelings of "inadequacy" originating in his environment, that progress is inevitable, that science and technology can answer all the problems of life.

The impact of Karl Barth has been mediated largely through his interpreters and popularizers in seminaries, religious journals, pulpits, contemporary confessions of faith, and the reports of denominational boards and agencies. Several factors account for this fact. Barth is an impressively erudite scholar – most forbiddingly so – who assumes a vast and detailed knowledge of theology and church history and who uses uncompromisingly technical terms. The sheer quantity of his writings is in itself an obstacle demanding a great deal of patience and perseverance. His style is tempestuous, torrential and powerful – and repetitious and verbose as well. His thought forms and way of approaching problems are profoundly German so that, even in English translation, they are alien to the American reader. As a result, the impact of his theology suffers from a time lag between the publication of his thoughts and its reception by the American public.

Barth was a theologian, not a political scientist or a political theorist. He undoubtedly would have liked to confine himself exclusively to theology. The natural consequence of a theology as transcendental as Barth's is to make political events seem small and insignificant, like automobiles that look like ants when viewed from an airplane or the top of a skyscraper. What are such problems as poverty, racial discrimination, economic recessions and politics when compared to the majesty, glory and omnipotence of God? Indeed, a sense of the infinite distance between the concerns of a theology so conceived and the concerns of politics never left Barth.

Barth, however, lived to be 82 years old. During that long life, he lived through the Great Depression and two world wars and their aftermath. He saw the rise of communism in Russia, national socialism in Germany and fascism in Italy – each of which was a new phenomenon in world history. He saw the rise of the so-called Third World in Asia and Africa. He saw the rise and fall of the League of Nations and the rise and floundering of the United Nations. Like Martin Luther, Barth was compelled much against his will to face political issues. His involvement in these issues was centered on national socialism because he took sides, and on communism because he refused to take sides. In both cases, he was forced to defend his position at considerable length.

The sense of the infinite distance previously referred to between theology and politics prevented him from being a social activist or a systematic political philosopher. The political implications of his theology are clearest in his writings before and after World War II, and his refusal to take sides in the conflict between East and West represents a return to his pre-war position.

The one exception is his passionate and eloquent repudiation of Nazism. Even here, however, it could be argued that his involvement was not really an exception and could be justified on the basis of his views before and after World War II. It must be conceded that taking sides against the Nazis was an instance of social activism in a practical sense, but he did not justify it in terms of the philosophy of social activism such as we find in the pronouncements of mainline Protestant denominations, the National Council of Churches, the World Council of Churches and similar organizations.

CHAPTER ONE

Revelation

R evelation, for Barth, is absolutely fundamental. Being "wholly Other," God cannot be discovered by any human process – be it reason, intuition or experience. "God is therefore neither an axiom nor a datum of experience." A conception of him arrived at in such ways is nothing "but a hypostatized reflection of man." Natural theology is something arrived at by human means, does not extend to salvation, and is "the attempted replacement of the divine work by a human manufacture." Man is "better served if no use is made of natural theology at all."[1]

Revelation is the self-disclosure of God that imposes itself upon man. Because he is wholly Other, revelation is the only way by which we could know him or anything about him. Revelation entails a human response to a call. Without that call, there can be neither revelation nor authentic response. "Modernist thought hears man answer without anyone having called him. It hears him talk to himself."[2]

The source of revelation is the Bible: "The revealed Word of God we know only from the Scripture adopted by Church proclamation based on Scripture."[3] It follows that the Church "cannot assess and adjudge Scripture from a view of revelation gained apart from Scripture and not related to it." For Barth, the Bible is the normative witness to revelation. "A witness," he says, "is not absolutely identical with that which it witnesses."[4] The Bible is not a systematized body of propositions and it sometimes is necessary "to repudiate certain of its detailed and perhaps not unimportant statements."[5]

---

1. Barth; *Church Dogmatics*; Vol. II-2; pp. 3, 298, 302. For a full citation of the works of Barth, see the Bibliography at the end of Book II.

2. *Ibid.*; Vol. I-I; p. 68.

3. *Ibid.*; p. 136.

4. *Ibid.*; Vol. 11-2; pp. 3, 463.

5. *Ibid.*; Vol. I-I; p. 6.

Barth's view of Scripture has drawn criticism, especially from Reformed theologians like Cornelius van Til,[6] because it seems to deny the authority and infallibility of Scripture. And it is true that some contemporary church-goers have used this concept of normative witness as a means of affirming the validity of some parts of the Bible and denying it to other parts. It is very doubtful that Barth intended his concept of normative witness to be used in this way. His voluminous, meticulous, comprehensive, and exhaustive search of Scripture to establish every point in his theology proves that such was not his intention at all. Furthermore, we have his very words for this when he says that "what we hear in the witness itself is more than witness, what we hear is revelation, and therefore the very Word of God."[7]

Barth also has been criticized for making a distinction between the Word of God and "the Mighty Acts of God." This, too, is a misinterpretation. He admits that, except for some cases when speaking or writing amounts to taking a stand and therefore acting, there is a difference between word and deed. "But for the Word of God these distinctions do not hold. For it is precisely as a mere word that it is an act."[8] When Genesis relates that God said "Let there be light,"[9] for example, it was both a word and a deed since there was light.

This matter of speaking as action with reference to God sheds light on Barth's treatment of the Book of Genesis. He denies that the Genesis account of creation is either myth or legend, for myth refers to something that never happened and legend to something that only has some basis in fact. The word he uses is "saga," by which he means that the Genesis account of creation is historical in that it took place in time and space, but pre-historical in that it took place before any recorded history and, therefore, is not subject to the usual techniques of historical investigation. It should be noted that the word "saga" is the noun form of the German *sagen*, which means to speak. When God spoke, he acted. The French translators of the Bible must have had the same point in mind for, when they came to the word *Logos* in the prologue of the fourth Gospel, they translated it by *le Verbe* (which denotes action) and not by *la Parole* (which does

---

6. Cornelius Van Til (1895-1987). A Dutch-born American minister and seminary professor, his books include *The New Modernism* (Presbyterian & Reformed Publishing Company; Phillipsburg, N.J.; 1946), *The Defense of the Faith* (Presbyterian & Reformed Publishing Company; Phillipsburg, N.J.; 1955) and *Christianity and Barthianism* (Presbyterian & Reformed Publishing Company; Phillipsburg, N.J.; 1962), plus several syallabi and numerous reviews and articles. He was joint editor of *Philosophia Reformata*, a quarterly devoted to Calvinistic philosophy.

7. *Ibid.*; Vol. 1-2; p. 473.

8. *Ibid.*; p. 164.

9. Genesis 1:3.

not denote action).

In accordance with his rigorously Christocentric theology, Barth asserts, "For God is not known and is not knowable except in Jesus Christ."[10] He is himself the Word of God, the only Word of God.

Here, again, Barth has been misunderstood by those who try to draw a wedge between the Word-in-the-flesh and the Word-in-the-script. Barth intends no such distinction: "The personification of the concept of the Word of God, which we cannot avoid when we remember that Jesus Christ is the Word of God, does not signify any lessening of its verbal character."[11] And we need to remember that, for Barth, the verbal and the incarnate are one and the same when we refer to God.

It would seem that limiting revelation to Christ and the Bible has the effect of denying any revelation of God in nature and history. If so, Barth surely is parting company with Calvin, who asserted otherwise. It is well to remember, however, that Calvin was careful to say that natural revelation is enough to convict us, but not enough to save us. As a matter of fact, Barth does speak of "lesser lights," but they are emanations from the one true light in Jesus Christ who rules over all men and not just Christians. Commenting on one of the Psalms, Barth points out that man can see God's handiwork in the firmament, but this requires the eyes of faith that not all men possess, and faith is a gift of God who was incarnate in Jesus Christ.

---

10. *Ibid.*; Vol. 11-2, p. 509.

11. *Ibid.*; Vol. I-1, p. 157.

CHAPTER TWO

Barth's Doctrine of Man

Man is body and soul, and the two are inseparable. In this, Barth follows the Hebraic teaching rather than the Greek, which held that the soul can exist without the body. That which distinguishes man from animals is his ability to know God, the creature's ability to know its Creator. This ability, however, is not inherent in human nature but, instead, is the result of revelation. How else could man know someone who is wholly Other from himself? Barth's position – knowing God is what makes man distinctively human – separates him from Aristotle, who ascribed it to reason; from Reinhold Niebuhr,[1] who ascribed it to self-transcendence; and Hobbes,[2] who ascribed it to speech.

Man is not what God intended him to be because he is a sinner. The only true and fully human man was Jesus of Nazareth. By virtue of this characteristically Christocentric position, Barth departs from the popular view that speaks of "true humanity" and "mature humanity." The trouble with

---

1. Reinhold Niebuhr (1892–1971). American minister and seminary professor, writer, socialist and political activist. In books such as *Moral Man and Immoral Society* (1932), *Christianity and Power Politics* (1940) and *The Nature and Destiny of Man* (2 vol., 1941-43), he urged clergy to take an interest in social reforms as well as the beliefs that men are sinners, that society is ruled by self-interest, and that history is characterized by irony, not progress. Other books include *Faith and History* (1949), *A Nation So Conceived* (1963), *Man's Nature and his Communities* (1965) and *Faith and Politics* (ed. by R. H. Stone 1968).

2. Thomas Hobbes (1588-1679). English philosopher. He rejected Cartesian dualism and believed in the mortality of the soul; rejected free will in favor of a determinism that treats freedom as being able to do what one desires; and rejected Aristotelian and scholastic philosophy in favor of Galileo and Gassendi, who largely treated the world as matter in motion. The *Leviathan* (1651) is the most complete expression of his philosophy. It begins with a clearly materialistic account of human nature and knowledge, a rigidly deterministic account of human volition, and a pessimistic vision of the consequently natural state of human beings in perpetual struggle against each other. It is to escape this grim fate, Hobbes argued, that we form the state to keep peace and order, surrendering our individual powers to the authority of an absolute sovereign.

this view is that it is humanistic in its secular meaning by leaving Jesus Christ out and substituting a sociological criterion.

Barth also rejects introspection as a source of knowing human nature because introspection is imperfection looking into imperfection, elimination or at least downgrading of the community aspect of human life, and an unhealthy preoccupation with the self that can lead to mental illness and even suicide.

It is only when we encounter the person of Jesus Christ that we realize the heights and the depths of human existence. It is in this encounter that we perceive God's judgment upon us and God's forgiveness of us. Barth holds to the doctrine of substitutionary atonement whereby Jesus Christ, by his crucifixion and resurrection, stands in our place, justifies us, and intercedes for us.

Jesus was the elected man and the electing God. Saving all men, regardless of all human merit and demerit, is the effect of grace born of the love of God for the whole world. Grace embraces all men regardless of behavior or belief. Sin, which is born of pride and sloth, is the attempt of man to reject grace, an attempt that cannot succeed because no man successfully can resist the will of God. Man may be blind or refuse to accept it, but both are ineffectual. The point that grace is irresistible, universal, and all-embracing is repeated by Barth over and over again in all his writings.

It is clear that Barth is a universalist in his assertion that all men will be saved and none rejected. His universalism is not that of secular humanism. Neither is it an espousal of Tillich's famous, "You are accepted." Barth's universalism is strictly Christocentric for, without Christ, no one would be saved. He points to Christ's own statement that he came into the world not "to destroy men's lives, but to save them."[3]

Nevertheless, Barth's universalism is open to criticism on his own Biblical and Christocentric ground. The same fourth Gospel says: "He that believeth on him is not condemned: but he that believeth not is condemned already, because he hath not believed in the name of the only begotten Son of God."[4] Again and again, in the Synoptics and the Book of Acts, it is said that repentance and faith are necessary for salvation. The Apostle Paul's central message is that we are saved through faith. Barth's universalism, obviously, is a radical departure from the Reformed and Calvinistic teaching in which he was brought up and trained.

This universalism raises many problems. What has the Christian got that non-Christians do not have? Barth deals with this question by describing

---

3.   Luke 9:56.

4.   John 3:18.

the quality of life that is specifically Christian. Perhaps the most important point he makes in this connection is that the Christian alone knows he is not responsible for the outcome of his witnessing. It is not demanded of him that he be successful, since that is God's decision, but only that he be faithful. The works of non-Christians "are done under the pressure of the anxious question as to the consequences. The Christian community does not stand under this pressure."[5]

Barth's departure from the full and clear teaching of Scripture on the subject of salvation by espousing universalism forces him to draw on non-Biblical sources. His doctrine of evil, for instance, cannot be squared with the Biblical conception of evil as something real, alive and personalized. He therefore speaks of "impossible possibilities" and borrows from the existentialists the pale concept of nothingness. "Nothingness," he says not very helpfully, "is not nothing."[6]

Whether hell exists or not becomes irrelevant because nobody is going there: "Jesus Christ has gone into hell and locked it up for us, and sealed it off."[7]

Heaven becomes hazy and blurred, at least insofar as the individual's destination is concerned, because Barth becomes embroiled in Tillichian discussions of time, timelessness and eternity. Had he not departed from the principle of *sola scriptura*, these difficulties would have been circumvented. Such is the price Barth has to pay for his universalism, which removes him from Biblical teachings and plunges him into metaphysics.

Man, Barth says, becomes truly human only in encounter. "'I am' – the true and fulfilled 'I am' – may be thus paraphrased: 'I am in encounter.'" What he means by this is not man as a social animal in the sense that he has to have transactions with other men. It is a matter of the "I–thou" relationship so dear to the existentialists. Not mere service is what we owe to our fellow man, but our very self. We really must look at him and see him. We must hear him in the sense of really listening. We must speak to him and not merely pass him and engage in what amounts to a monologue. "Two monologues do not constitute a dialogue." Too often, even in sermons and lectures, our words are "an inhuman and barbaric affair." "Each fellow man is a whole world, and the request he makes of me is not merely that I should know this or that about him, but the man himself, and therefore his whole world." In order to give man and woman the motivation for an "I–thou"

---

5. Barth; *Church Dogmatics*, Vol. IV-3; p. 750.

6. *Ibid.*, Vol. III-3; p. 349.

7. Barth; *Against the Stream: Shorter Post-War Writings*; p. 97. For a full citation of the works of Barth, see the Bibliography at the end of Book II.

encounter and give them their first experience of it, God created sex and
sexuality and prescribed monogamy, thus dissipating what would otherwise
be an intolerable and inhuman loneliness.[8] As far back as Genesis, it is
stated that it is not good for man to be alone.

Complete humanity, however, is not fulfilled by the "I–thou" relationship alone. There also must be an "I–Thou" (capital "T") relationship. We
must have fellowship with God as well, which means with Jesus Christ.
Man's encounter with Christ comes through in encounters with his fellow
man. This is not necessarily because a fellow man is a believer in whom the
presence of Christ is evident. It comes just as much, if not more so, from
our fellow men who are not Christians in any sense: "Genuine fellowship is
grounded upon a negative: it is grounded upon what men lack. Precisely
when we recognize that we are sinners do we perceive that we are
brothers."[9]

And it is only as we experience the forgiveness of Christ that we know
we are sinners.[10] The result of the "I-Thou" relationship is to impart to an
encounter with a neighbor "a sacramental significance" so that he
"becomes a visible sign of invisible grace, a proof that I, too, am not left
alone in this world, but am borne and directed by God."[11]

8. Barth; *Church Dogmatics*, Vol.III-2; pp. 247, 259, 260, 258, 293.

9. Barth; *The Epistle to the Romans*; p. 101. For a full citation of the works of Barth, see
    the Bibliography at the end of Book II.

10. Barth; *Church Dogmatics*; Vol. II-2; p. 768.

11. *Ibid*; Vol. I-2; p. 436.

CHAPTER THREE

Some Specific Applications of Barth's Doctrine of Man

The purpose of this section is to examine what Barth thinks are the consequences of his Doctrine of Man as it applies to individual decisions on specific issues and, thus, reserve the larger political issues for a later section.

The most individual and personal decision a man can make is marriage. "There is no necessity of nature or general divine law," Barth says, "in virtue of which every man is permitted to take a wife, or every woman a husband. If this is permitted and commanded, it is a special distinction, a special divine calling, a gift and grace. A man enters and remains in the married state because he recognizes that this is the divine will for him and therefore obligatory."

Marriage, like all "I-thou" relationships, has a sacramental character and is monogamous: "Monogamy is authoritatively ordered because it is ordered by Jesus Christ."

It follows that "it is impossible to accept either a fickle eroticism or polygamy in the relationship of man and woman." Barth is aware, of course, that there are societies in which the missionary encounters polygamy as an institution. In such cases, Barth finds that "it would be sheer brutality for the Christian Church to confront men with the choice between baptism and institutional polygamy." In this matter, we must not think "legalistically," but must have "a clear recognition of matter and purpose, but not the brutality of form and method."[1]

With regard to divorce, it would appear at first that Barth takes the Roman Catholic position: "Divorce is quite impermissible." In this case, as in so many others, appearances are deceptive. True marriages are made in heaven and, as such, are subject to the rule that no man may rend asunder

---

1. Barth; *Church Dogmatics*; Vol. III-4; pp. 183, 199, 203.

those whom God has joined. But not all marriages are true marriages. Marriages for sexual satisfaction, money, prestige, family favor, and professional advantage are "a flagrant disobedience to the command of God" and are "only approached and not entered into." Marriage is not "a purely private undertaking" and, therefore, requires a public wedding regulated by law, but such a wedding "does not constitute marriage."

Divorce in such cases is no divorce in a Christian sense, though it may well be in a legal sense, because there was no true marriage in the first place. In such cases, the Church should give its benediction to second marriages.[2]

The effect of Barth's teaching on marriage is to cast a shadow on every marriage. He admits this in so many words, for a man "may live in marriage which stands deeply under the shadow of the question whether it might not lack the divine joining together and therefore genuine and essential permanence. There is no marriage which may be said to stand altogether outside this shadow."[3]

Holy as true marriage is, however, it must not result in having and rearing a family as an end in itself – precisely because it is holy. The weakening of family ties is the result of just such a shadow that "takes the form of an attack upon the family for its own sake; and the family has been in truth not a holy thing but the voracious idol of the erstwhile middle classes."[4] What Barth says about shadows is of crucial importance because by no means are they confined to marriage – they hover over every decision an individual makes.

Human life is a gift of God and, therefore, should be respected and protected. The man who takes his own life "violates the commandment and murders as well as kills." But for him, as well as for all sinners, there is forgiveness. For "the incurably infirm, the insane, imbeciles, the deformed, persons who are by nature or accident or war completely immobilized and crippled," the answer is not mercy killing – since the answer to mercy killing is "an unequivocal 'No!'"

Capital punishment is wrong in principle because "the state leaves the human level and acts with usurped divinity." Barth is critical of the Church for having been a spectator during the increase in capital punishment that accompanied the expansion of Christianity. Capital punishment is justified, however, in cases when a man's existence "threatens the state and its stabil-

---

2. *Ibid.*; pp. 205, 219, 226, 213.

3. *Ibid.*; p. 210.

4. Barth; *The Word of God and the Word of Man*; p. 292. For a full citation of the works of Barth, see the Bibliography at the end of Book II.

ity" to such an extent that no other choice is available, such as spying and desertion.

Tyrannicide[5] is justifiable if the avenger has "a clear and categorical command from God to do it." War necessitates the destruction of life, but "is no part of the normal task of the state." Most wars cannot be justified, Barth believes. Among those are the wars of territorial aggrandizement, prestige, power, the balance of power, the containment of revolution abroad, and the pursuit of some supposed national mission. War in self-defense, however, is justifiable[6] and so is a righteous war such as that against "the inherent Godlessness of National Socialism."[7]

"A soldier or a policeman is not a murderer,"[8] he says. Pacifism should not be condoned because it condemns all wars in spite of the fact that some wars are justified, and anti-militarism "leads to an illegitimate type of conscientious objection." Conscription is desirable because it eliminates the danger of mercenary or professional armies and broadens political responsibility by making the citizens personally participate in the decisions of their government.[9]

With respect to work, Barth thinks that Protestantism, especially in its Calvinistic form, has overemphasized work as a virtue. "It is obvious," he remarks, "that the Jesus of the Synoptics and the Fourth Gospel cannot be claimed in support of this high estimation of work."

Not only did Jesus not direct any of his disciples to engage in secular work, but he "seems to have summoned His disciples away from their secular work." It is true that the Apostle Paul engaged in the secular work of tent making. "But his work is done on the fringe of his apostolic instruction. It is evident that Paul has no positive interest either in work itself or in its achievement."[10]

Barth, therefore, condemns work for work's sake – just as he did the family for the family's sake. He went so far as to say that he would not be "surprised and indignant, at least not to the depths of our soul, if the Spartacists and communists make answer that they would rather perish and

---

5. Tyrannicide – the act of killing a tyrant.

6. Barth; *Church Dogmatics*, Vol. III-4; pp. 405, 423, 445, 437, 446, 448, 449, 458, 461, 462.

7. Barth; *The Church and the War*; p. 5. For a full citation of the works of Barth, see the Bibliography at the end of Book II.

8. Barth; *Karl Barth's Table Talk*; p. 80. For a full citation of the works of Barth, see the Bibliography at the end of Book II.

9. Barth; *Church Dogmatics*; Vol. III-4; pp. 468, 466.

10. *Ibid.*; p. 472.

see all perish with them than return again to the yoke of *work for its own sake*."[11] Competition as a motivating force in the workplace does not help. On the contrary, to Barth it always means "an inhuman activity" that "can never stand before the command of God."[12]

The fault that Barth finds in all of these cases is that they violate the most fundamental duty of man, which is that of witnessing to his Lord. Whether he marries, fights or works, he must do these things for the glory of God. That is his vocation. In line with Calvin, Barth says that a man must accept his station in life – whatever it is – as an assignment from the Lord. Neither for Calvin nor for Barth does the Doctrine of Vocation have the effect of freezing the status quo because God is not dead, but alive and ruling. Man, therefore, always must be in "readiness to be called elsewhere."[13]

As we review these specific applications of Barth's Doctrine of Man, the question naturally arises as to whether Barth can be classified with the advocates of situational ethics.[14] There certainly are similarities. Barth shares with them, and with modern thought generally, a distrust of legalism, philosophical systems, principles, ideologies and propositional truth. The effect of this distrust is to blur and weaken the standards upon which men must rely to make decisions.

Barth does not, however, discard these standards. He claims, instead, that his Christocentric position merely relativizes them. He does not follow Fletcher's teaching that an individual must face a concrete problem, analyze it and then do "the loving thing" whereby the individual makes his or her own decision independently. The difference lies in the notion of command that is fundamental for Barth and non-existent for Fletcher: "We obey God, not a principle or idea." Again: "We do not decide on principles, but on conclusions."[15]

For Barth, revelation always is concrete and very particular. A general command, such as we find in the Decalogue, becomes real and effective only in "the hour of command."[16] The decision, therefore, is not the individual's but God's, not independent but obedient, not rooted in some culture-bound subjective conception of "the loving thing," but in the objective will

11. Barth; *The Word of God and the Word of Man*; p. 293. The italics are Barth's. For a full citation of the works of Barth, see the Bibliography at the end of Book II.

12. Barth; *Church Dogmatics*; Vol. III-4; p. 541.

13. *Ibid.*; pp. 642, 646.

14. See Book I, Chapter Five.

15. Barth; *Karl Barth's Table Talk*; pp. 81-82.

16. Barth; *Church Dogmatics*; Vol. III-4; p. 15.

of God. The command of the hour is perceived by and through conscience and is absolutely decisive.

Barth relates that some people in the Netherlands during the Nazi occupation asked him if there were circumstances under which it would be legitimate to lie. "I answered: Do it – but not with a bad conscience. If you have a bad conscience, then do not do it."[17]

He did not approve of Count von Stauffenberg's[18] attempt to assassinate Hitler, not because tyrannicide is wrong, but because the count did not have "a clear and categorical command from God to do it." Barth believed the proof that von Stauffenberg did not have such a command lies in the fact that "no one was prepared to go through with it in absolute disregard for his own life."[19]

---

17. Barth; *Karl Barth's Table Talk*; p. 79.

18. Count Claus Schenk Graf von Stauffenberg (1907-1944). German military officer. During World War II, he grew disillusioned with the Nazis and eventually joined a plot to kill Adolf Hitler. Von Stauffenberg planted a briefcase bomb during a staff meeting with the German leader in July of 1944. Though the bomb went off as planned, Hitler was not killed. Von Stauffenberg escaped the blast, but was captured and executed the next day.

19. Barth; *Church Dogmatics*; Vol. III-4; p. 449.

CHAPTER FOUR

Barth's View of Politics

B arth's original and enduring position with regard to politics is evident in the early work – *The Epistle to the Romans* – that first made him famous. Politics deals with individuals, humanity and history. How does he view these things? "The word 'humanity' means unredeemed men and women; the word 'history' implies limitation and corruption; the pronoun 'I' spells judgment." Because of this, we can expect little from politics.

He condemns conservatism – using the word "Legitimism," which historically refers to political conservatism – as evil because it attempts to justify the status quo which, like all things human, is corrupt and stands under judgment. He also condemns revolution because it fights evil with evil instead of overcoming evil with good and strives for ideals which, like all human ideals, are a delusion. A third alternative, reform, likewise is ruled out: "All reformers are Pharisees."[1]

In a truly unique interpretation of Romans 13, Barth recommends *not doing* as his conclusion, a conclusion that means Christians must neither support nor oppose the status quo. "Our whole visible behaviour," he writes, "is either an acceptance of the present order or a denial of it; and in both cases we do wrong. We can do right only in the 'not-doing' of our relationship to God." The role of the politician, he says, is futile: "A political career, for example, becomes possible only when it is seen to be essentially a game ... in which human possibilities have been renounced."[2]

This pessimism extends to the international level, as shown by his contempt for diplomats: "Our gain is that the intelligent person no longer takes any notice when diplomats – if there are still any real diplomats – foregather, since he knows in advance that nothing of any true importance is likely to emerge."[3]

---

1. Barth; *Epistle to the Romans*; pp. 85, 509.

2. *Ibid.*; p. 489.

3. Barth; *Church Dogmatics*; Vol. III-4; p. 556.

If we move from political action – whether conservative, revolutionary or reformist – to political thought, Barth's answer is not one bit more optimistic. The reason is not that he is unacquainted with political theory and ideologies. The first two chapters of his *Protestant Thought: From Rousseau to Ritschl*[4] show a thorough knowledge of political theory, including a remarkably accurate survey of the theories of Rousseau, Locke and Hobbes. Regrettably, however, that book is pure exposition and contains no evaluation or appraisal whatsoever. Barth was opposed to all systems, whether in the form of natural theology, natural law or any political "ism." And he denied that his own theology was a system. Taking his cue from what Marx once said about not being a Marxist, Barth could well have said that he is not a Barthian. His objection to all systems is that they originate in human pride by ignoring the finite and sinful nature of man and by presuming to know what only God can know.

Barth was no admirer of the state. He speaks of it as a graceless order. "This graceless order," he says, "corresponding to the form of this world overcome and abolished in principle by Jesus Christ, is the political order, the rule of law, which is established and protected by threats and the use of physical force."[5] He elaborates his position with even more vigor and detail in the following passage:

"The civil community embraces everyone living within its area. The members share no common awareness of their relationship to God, and such awareness cannot be an element in the legal system established by the civil community. No appeal can be made to the Word or Spirit of God in the running of its affairs. The civil community as such is spiritually blind and ignorant. It has neither faith nor love nor hope. It has no creed and no life, and its members are not brothers and sisters."[6]

Barth knows, of course, that the state takes many forms, such as democracy, monarchy, aristocracy, dictatorship, etc. These forms do not make much difference because "the various political forms and systems are human inventions which as such do not bear the distinctive mark of revelation and are not witnessed to as such – and can therefore not lay claim to belief."[7] The function of government is "essentially the same" regardless of

---

4. Barth; *Protestant Thought: From Rousseau to Ritschl*; For a full citation of Barth's works, see the Bibliography at the end of Book II.

5. *Ibid.*, Vol. II-2; p. 722.

6. Barth; *Community, State and Church*; p. 151. For a full citation of Barth's works, see the Bibliography at the end of Book II.

7. Barth; *Against the Stream*; p. 25.

state forms.[8]

Were we to limit ourselves to Barth's conception of the state as exemplified in the above quotations, we would have to conclude that he radically departs from Calvin. Calvin held to a very lofty view of the state in which the state is not confined to the punishment of the wicked and the maintenance of law and order, but has a moral and religious mission to perform. As part of the Providence of God, the state is instituted for the good of man and the glory of God.

Barth, however, makes other statements that constitute a modification of his apparent pessimism. The state, he concedes, is not "the soulless, despotic and cannibalistic beast of the abyss,"[9] but "serves to protect man from the invasion of chaos"[10] and "is ordained of God, so that those who try to evade or oppose it resist the ordinance of God and the kingly rule of His Son." Forgetting what he said in the 1920s in *Epistle to the Romans* about "not-doing," the 1950s found him demanding that Christians be active in politics – even in "that provisional, graceless order of earthly things." What does Barth expect from the participation of Christians in politics? Time – time to carry out the most fundamental of all obligations of Christians; i.e., witnessing to their Lord. "That God wills to give the world and the Church time to receive grace is the secret purpose of the political order."[11]

In spite of what he said about the relative unimportance of state forms, we must be aware of differences of degree. "Thus there is clearly no cause for the Church to act as though it lived, in relation to the State, in a night in which all cats are grey."[12] Barth is willing to say that democracy comes nearer to being an ideal state than any other political system and that socialism comes nearer to being an ideal economic system than capitalism.[13] He stresses more than once that neither anarchy nor tyranny is a state at all and, therefore, is not included in the admonition of Romans 13 to obey the powers that be. In this connection, we must note that, "democracy is not the middle between anarchy and tyranny, but is above both, above this dichotomy."[14]

By democracy, Barth does not mean absolute majoritarianism, since the Church "always stands for the constitutional State," including the separa-

8. Barth; *The Church and the War*; p. 22.

9. Barth; *Church Dogmatics;* Vol. III-4; p. 465.

10. Barth; *Against the Stream*; p. 21.

11. Barth; *Church Dogmatics;* Vol. II-2; pp. 721, 722.

12. Barth; *Community, State, and Church*; p. 119.

13. Barth; "Letter to American Christians" in *The Church and the War*; p. 39.

14. Barth; *Karl Barth's Table Talk*; p. 81.

tion of powers between the legislative, executive and judicial branches. The Church should "concentrate first on the lower and lowest levels of human society,"[15] but should beware of absolute equalitarianism because "the mutual fellowship of men" and not "equality" is the objective that should be pursued.[16] Another characteristic of democracy that meets with Barth's approval is the willingness of democracy to bring things into the open, since "the Church is the sworn enemy of all secret policies and secret diplomacy."[17]

Having made all these concessions to democracy, it is important to remember that Barth always insists that the Church must never identify itself with any political system, even democracy, and that democracy, therefore, is a qualified and conditional political system.

The position against revolution that is so categorical in the *Epistle to the Romans* is seriously modified in his other writings and becomes much more conventional. In very circumspect language, he offers three criteria for legitimate revolution, namely: (1) that it have an unquestionably just cause; (2) that all legal and peaceful means of redress have been exhausted so that the overthrow of the regime is the only possible course; and (3) that there are convincing reasons for believing that revolution will result in a better situation.[18] It should be noted that the first two criteria are the classic ones spelled out in the writings of John Locke[19] and in the American Declaration of Independence, but Barth leaves out the third criterion – that only the majority of the people have the right to overthrow the government by revolution. He gives no reason for this omission and the substitution of his own third criterion.

When asked if there ever was a revolution that met his three criteria, Barth's reply was: "Perhaps, the American Revolution." He went on to comment on the American Declaration of Independence, saying that the word

---

15. Barth; *Against the Stream*; pp. 35, 38, 36.

16. Barth; *Church Dogmatics*; Vol. IV-3; p. 899.

17. Barth; *Against the Stream*; p. 39.

18. Barth; *Karl Barth's Table Talk*; p. 76.

19. John Locke (1632-1704); British philosopher, academic, medical researcher and political activist. Much of his work is characterized by opposition to authoritarianism, both for individuals and for institutions such as government and the church. For the individual, Locke wants each of us to use reason to search after truth, rather than simply accept the opinion of authorities. For institutions, he says it is important to distinguish the legitimate from the illegitimate functions of institutions, and to make the corresponding distinction for the uses of force by them. Locke's most famous work is *An Essay Concerning Human Understanding*. Others include *Two Treatises of Civil Government*, the *Letters Concerning Toleration*, *The Reasonableness of Christianity* and *Some Thoughts Concerning Education*.

"evident" would be preferable to "self-evident" as applied to the truths we hold because the latter term "smacks of natural theology." Barth says it would be better to say that all men are created "in togetherness and mutual responsibility" because the phrase created equal is "too formal," and that the liberty with which men are endowed by their Creator should read "freedom of life within the bounds of a rightfully established common order."[20]

Outlined thus far, Barth's political views are somewhat vague, inconclusive and hesitant. They might well have remained so had he not become involved, much against his will, in acrimonious controversies over the Nazi and Communist regimes. The result of his involvement was to bring his political views into a much sharper focus.

Barth's detestation of and opposition to the Nazi regime was absolute and total. Nevertheless, that animosity was slow to grow and surface, even after he had been fired from his professorship in a German university for refusing to take an oath of loyalty to Hitler. Barth has been criticized for his slowness in opposing National Socialism, but there was a reason for it that lies at the core of his theology. He does not like abstractions and philosophical systems of whatever kind, including political "isms." He regards them as unreal until they have reached fruition in action. "The Church can never defend and proclaim – or even attack – abstract norms, ideals, historical laws and socio-political ideologies as such. Its concern must never be with political principles, creeds, and catechisms but only with definite and concrete political constellations. It cannot make itself responsible either for any -ism or for rejecting it."[21]

When the Nazi regime first came into power, "the Church in Germany at that time – this is still my conviction today – had the right and the duty to confine herself to giving it, as a political experiment, first of all time and a chance, and therefore to adopting herself first of all to a strictly neutral position. In this regard neutrality was in plain terms at that time the form of Church decision enjoined."[22]

Even when he had reached the conclusion that the Nazi regime was "a definite and concrete political constellation," Barth believed that there were wrong or inadequate reasons for opposing it. In his letter to British Christians written in the midst of the war, he warned against appealing to such grounds as the values of Western civilization, the freedom of the individual, and the infinite value of human personality. He also warned against argu-

---

20. *Ibid.*; p. 77. The substitutions suggested by Barth that are in quotation marks are italicized by Barth in his original text.

21. Barth; *Against the Stream*; p. 91.

22. Barth; *The Church and the War*; p. 31.

ments based on natural law as completely ineffective in coping with the Nazi monster: "All arguments based on Natural Law are Janus-headed.[23] They do not lead to the light of clear decisions, but to the misty twilight in which all cats become grey. They lead to – Munich."[24] These grounds and arguments, aside from being tainted because they are human inventions, do not generate enough direction and power to overcome incarnate evil.

What, then, were adequate grounds for fighting the Nazis to the finish? The Hitler regime "is the enterprise of an evil spirit," the incarnation of an "overwhelming flagrant injustice," and "the inbreaking of open inhumanity."[25] Bearing in mind what Barth said about anarchy and tyranny not being included in the admonition of Romans 13 to obey the powers that be, it is a decisive conclusion that "this State is anarchy tempered by tyranny, or tyranny tempered by anarchy, but it is certainly no State."[26] The Nazi regime had its roots in the German "heritage of a paganism that is mystical" and in Luther's erroneous understanding of the relations of the temporal and spiritual that "confirmed and idealized the natural paganism of the German people, instead of limiting and restraining it."[27] In other words, Nazism was a pagan religion.

If there was one thing about the Nazi regime that most infuriated Barth, and was absolutely conclusive for him, that thing was anti-Semitism. "He who is a radical enemy of the Jews, were he in every other regard an angel of light, shows himself, as such, to be a radical enemy of Jesus Christ. Anti-Semitism is sin against the Holy Ghost."[28] So great is his emphasis on this particular aspect of Nazism that we must give our attention to what Barth has to say about the Jews.[29]

For Barth, the continued identity of the Jews as a people over the centuries is a miracle, the evidence of the reality and faithfulness of God. Many people, including Jews, have asked the question: What is a Jew? The Jews are not a race. They belong to the Semitic race, but they are not a race because there are other Semites, notably their arch-enemies, the Arabs.

23. Janus was the Roman god of gates and doors, beginnings and endings. He was portrayed with a double-faced head, each looking in opposite directions.

24. Barth; *A Letter to Great Britain from Switzerland*; pp. 16-17. For a full citation of Barth's works, see the Bibliography at the end of Book II.

25. *Ibid.*; pp. 11, 34.

26. Barth; *The Church and the War*; p. 55.

27. Barth; "First Letter to the French Protestants" in the Bibliography to *A Letter to Great Britain from Switzerland*; p. 36.

28. Barth; *The Church and the War*; p. 51.

29. Barth; The longest and most detailed account, here summarized, is to be found in *Church Dogmatics*; Vol. III-3; pp. 210-26.

They do not have a language because only a minority of Jews speak Hebrew. They have no specific culture of their own, like the French and the Germans, because their contributions have been to the cultures of the nations in which they lived. They have no state or territory, for the state of Israel is quite new and includes only a very small percentage of the Jews in the world. They have had no common, connected history since Biblical times. They do not even have a common religion because many Jews do not subscribe to Judaism.

What, then, do they have?

The simple fact that they were, are and will continue to be the Chosen People of God. Their existence can be accounted for only in the faithfulness of God, who keeps his Covenant even though the Jews do not.

Why, Barth asks, is anti-Semitism so universal and pervasive throughout all history? Is it because the Jews have unpleasant characteristics? No. All people have unpleasant characteristics. The Jews are the living witness of what it means to exist by divine election and that alone. Since all men are elected, all men ought to live by it. But only the Jews live by it, however unwillingly. Non-Jews find their identity and security in their nation, money, social prestige, political power, cultural traditions. In doing so, they reject and conceal from themselves the grace of God in divine election. The Jews are a constant reminder of our disbelief in the faithfulness of God and, in them, our mask is torn off and our cloak is stripped from us – and we do not like it! In the deepest sense, therefore, Barth's opposition to the Nazi regime was a religious one.

While Barth took a strong stand against Nazism, it is well known that he refused to do the same against communism. He did make it clear that he was not a Communist, was on record as disapproving of communism and "its system and its methods," and dismissed the classless society as a "grotesquely optimistic" belief that "can occur only to dreamers and visionaries."[30] Yet, he was slow in responding to demands that he take a stand. "I regard anti-communism as a matter of principle an evil greater than communism itself,"[31] he says.

Several things are wrong with anti-communism, according to Barth. It is a cause and, as such, one of those ideologies in which the Church has no interest. "Man has not to serve causes; causes have to serve man."[32] Writing to a pastor in East Germany, Barth said that the Christian message is "just

---

30. Barth; *Against the Stream*; pp. 116, 91.

31. Barth; *How I Changed My Mind;* p. 63. For a full citation of Barth's works, see the Bibliography at the end of Book II.

32. Barth; *Against the Stream*; p. 35.

as repugnant and embarrassing to the West as it is to the East," and perhaps more so.[33] In view of this, how can anti-communism justifiably recast "the Eastern collective man into an angel of darkness and the Western 'organization man' into an angel of light?"[34] Moreover, he says, Soviet Russia, in spite of "very bloody and very dirty hands," was engaged in the pursuit of a "constructive idea" by tackling "the social problem."

Barth, speaking again in favor of the East, says that, unlike Nazism, communism has not tried "to falsify Christianity" and "never committed the basic crime of anti-Semitism." Fundamentally, then, the conflict between East and West during the Cold War was nothing but a struggle for power between the United States and the Soviet Union.[35]

Barth admitted his pro-Western leanings, but not enough to issue a pronouncement that would cast "all kinds of fuel in the fire of anti-communism" when he believed there was no necessity for doing so.[36] It was not necessary because he saw communism as not being at all tempting to the West anyway, thereby differing greatly from Nazism, which "hypnotized" the West even in the churches "as a rabbit by a giant snake."[37] For all these reasons, the same man who refused to take an oath of loyalty to Hitler was able to tell an East German pastor: "I would not see any difficulty, were I in your shoes, in offering this loyalty to the East German Republic, and thus in truthfully pledging the oath that is required of you."[38]

It is easy to see how Barth was influenced by his anti-intellectual attitude toward political "isms" and philosophical systems, since it led him to seriously not take communism as a doctrine, however misguided such an attitude was. But it is difficult to understand why he could not recognize the Soviet Union at that time as one of those "definite and concrete political constellations" that he says fall within the purview of the Church. It is even more difficult to understand why Barth took no notice of Soviet anti-Semitism which, though not a part of Marxist doctrine, very much was a Soviet policy.

33. Barth; *How to Serve God in a Marxist Land*; p. 52. For a full citation of Barth's works, see the Bibliography at the end of Book II.

34. Barth; *How I Changed My Mind*; p. 64.

35. Barth; *Against the Stream*; pp. 139-140, 128.

36. Barth; Letter to a Pastor in the German Democratic Republic in *How to Serve God in a Marxist Land*; p. 49.

37. Barth; *Against the Stream*; p. 115.

38. Barth; Barth; Letter to a Pastor in the German Democratic Republic in *How to Serve God in a Marxist Land*; p. 68.

CHAPTER FIVE

The Institutional Church and Political Activity

We have touched upon the problem of the institutional church and political activity from time to time in connection with other topics. Now, we are ready to examine what Barth has to say about it more systematically.

When theologians and church bodies deal with this problem, they usually do so under the rubric of reconciliation as it is understood in the horizontal aspect of doing away with the alienation of men from each other, treating it under the heading of the ministry or service of the Church to humanity. It is the diaconate function of the Church.

The first observation to make is that Barth is not very much interested in this problem. His allocation of space to it is in itself indicative of his attitude. He devoted three fat tomes of his *Church Dogmatics* to the topic of reconciliation. All of the first two volumes and the major part of the third volume deal with the vertical aspect of reconciliation; i.e., the reconciliation of man to God. In the 901 pages of this third volume, only 71 pages are devoted to the horizontal aspect. In a section titled "The Ministry of the Community," most of the pages deal with theological topics like proclaiming, teaching, preaching, evangelizing, theologizing, praising, foreign missions, and prayer. The last part of this section deals with the diaconate (serving humanity). Only 12 pages are allocated to the topic and, of these 12 pages, a mere five are devoted to the so-called "prophetic" function of the Church!

If we look at Barth's conception of the diaconate, we discover that it is quite traditional, in the sense of having very little of what today is called the social gospel. The diaconate, he explains, consists of such activities as "caring for the sick, the feeble, and the mentally confused and threatened, looking after orphans, helping prisoners, finding homes for refugees, stretching out a hand to stranded fellow men of all kinds." It is true that Barth says the Church should "summon the world to reflect on social injus-

91

tice and its consequences and to alter the conditions and relationships in question." It is true that he advises the Church "to tackle at their social roots the evils by which they are confronted in detail."[1] Such statements do point to a social gospel, and would appear to be an espousal of the popular concept of "corporate responsibility" as applied to the Church.

Barth does not, however, deal with these social aspects at all systematically, and he hardly goes beyond scattered and disconnected comments – occasionally denunciatory and always critical – of such things as capitalism, militarism, nationalism and racism as these come up, mostly in his political writings. He does not go into detail on these matters or dwell on them. Most significant is the striking fact that these comments always are negative, and he never provides one scintilla of positive suggestions or programs.

The explanation for this attitude lies deep in his conception of Providence – the world is ruled by Providence. Man "cannot anticipate God's providence or its use in God's living hand;"[2] there is no "system of Christian truth;"[3] and man cannot know "the strategic plan of the divine world-governance." Barth throws out the window, therefore, the theological fad of discovering "what God is doing in the world" that fills so much of denominational literature. This rejection is a part of his conception of God as wholly Other. "He is not like a schoolmaster who gives the same lesson to the whole class, or an officer who moves his whole squadron in the same direction, or a bureaucrat who once an outlook or principle is embedded in his own little head rules his whole department in accordance with it."[4] God is free and, therefore, unpredictable.

"Have we not observed the simple fact," he asked British Christians, "that we cannot shape the future in the smallest things, not to speak of the great?"[5] In advising French Protestants, he wrote that this advice "was in no sense an attempt to assume the role of a prophet."[6] He criticized American Christians for devoting "superfluous time and energy" to formulating war aims and speculating on what the post-World War II period would or should be like. "Doesn't your Bible, too, contain the command not to take thought for the morrow because sufficient to the day are the evils thereof?"[7] What,

1. Barth; *Church Dogmatics*; Vol. IV-3; pp. 891, 892, 893.

2. *Ibid.*; Vol. III-3 p. 52.

3. *Ibid.*; Vol. I-1; p. 88.

4. *Ibid.*; Vol. III-3; pp. 260, 138.

5. Barth; *A Letter to Great Britain from Switzerland;* p. 23.

6. Barth; "Second Letter to the French Protestants" in the Bibliography to *A Letter to Great Britain from Switzerland*; p. 44.

7. Barth; "A Letter to American Christians" in *The Church and the War*; pp. 36-37.

then, is a Christian layman or a Church body or a Christian public official to do? We have already seen what Barth's answer to that question is: Wait for "the command of the hour."

How do we know what "the command of the hour" is and when it has struck?

Barth's answer is that it is disclosed to us when we are under an inner and external compulsion to take a stand, and not before or after. To the French Protestants, he said: "I wrote as I felt I must write in the circumstances of that time in the discharge of my responsibility to the Holy Scriptures."[8] In explaining to an East German pastor why he had been so long and so reluctant in saying anything about the conflict between East and West, he said, "It is because as time goes on, I like less and less to discuss a matter unless both outer necessity and inner necessity compel me to say something definite."[9] In defending Switzerland against French criticism of its neutrality, Barth contended that the Swiss never should "voluntarily" discard their policy of neutrality "without the compulsion of external pressure."[10]

As for the Church, Barth says, "It cannot and must not be a harum-scarum, demanding to be heard on every occasion and in every situation. It can and must speak only when an inner compulsion of its own impels it to speak."[11] The Church is issuing much paper, which is not necessarily a bad thing, but it should be very careful as to "what is written on this paper, and whether or how far it is genuinely Christian."[12] As it does so, "It cannot attach itself to any world-view, nor can it produce, propagate and defend any supposed Christian world-view of its own."[13]

It is this particular danger that makes Barth hostile to political parties. He asserts that "parties are one of the most questionable phenomena in political life," and that the chief interest of the Church "must be rather that Christians all not mass together in a special party, since their task is to defend and proclaim, in decisions based on it, the Christian gospel that concerns all men." A "non-political Christianity" is impossible, but its political aspect comes with the participation of Christians as individuals in political

---

8. Barth; "Second Letter to the French Protestants" in the Bibliography to *A Letter to Great Britain from Switzerland*; p. 44.

9. Barth; *How to Serve God in a Marxist Land*; p. 47.

10. Barth; "First Letter to the French Protestants" in the Bibliography to *A Letter to Great Britain from Switzerland*; p. 31.

11. Barth; *Against the Stream*; p. 92.

12. Barth; *Church Dogmatics*; Vol. III-4; p. 557.

13. *Ibid.*; Vol. IV-I; p. 837.

parties, provided they do so anonymously, because "waging a political battle for the Church ... will inevitably bring discredit and disgrace on the Christian name."[14]

What saves Barth from pessimism about politics is his conviction that God is in full control, turning evil into good. Everyone would concede, for instance, that Pilate's deed of ordering the crucifixion of Jesus[15] was a travesty of justice by a Roman official who was too cowardly to jeopardize his political career by doing what he knew was right – i.e., releasing an innocent man. Barth, however, says no because without the crucifixion there would have been no atonement and no resurrection. Pilate was carrying out God's plan without the slightest inkling that he was doing so. Therefore, Barth says, Pilate "became the involuntary agent and herald of divine justification," and a Roman governor "became the virtual founder of the Church."[16]

For Barth, then, the guiding hand that controlled a Roman politician 2,000 years ago also controls the politicians of our time. Christians have no reason to despair of the present; to be anxious for the morrow; to waste time devising ideologies, policies and programs that are stricken by finiteness and tainted by sin; and to ineffectually attempt to crystal-gaze what God is doing in the world. All they have to do, in Barth's view, is to be receptive and responsible to the will of God as it is disclosed to them in "the command of the hour."

---

14. Barth; *Against the Stream*; pp. 45, 22, 46.

15. Matthew 27:23-26.

16. Barth; *Community, State, and Church*; pp. 113, 111.

CHAPTER SIX

Conclusion

A s we review Barth's monumental theological edifice, we find it impossible to classify him as a conservative or a liberal, either theologically or politically. He simply defies classification. Barth draws too much from both camps, and some of his contributions are uniquely his own.

Officially, he was an adherent of the Reformed faith, was a member of the Reformed Church, had a profound admiration for Calvin, and felt a strong sentimental attachment to the Reformed tradition. In his reliance on the authority of Scripture, his emphasis on the centrality of Jesus Christ as the Son of God, his acceptance of the Virgin Birth and his view of the transcendence of God, he was a Calvinist and a conservative. On the other hand, his universalism, his concept of evil and his fuzzy handling of heaven and hell had more affinity with theological liberalism.

In the political realm, too, it is difficult to pin a label on him. His instinctive attitude toward conservatism and liberalism essentially was "a plague on both your houses!" And he would not have gone beyond this position had not circumstances propelled him into saying something more enlightening.

On the whole, it would be fair to say that Barth leaned more toward the liberal direction because of his distrust for propositional truth; his critique of society, and especially capitalism; his sympathy for socialism and mixed feelings about communism; and his individualism in giving to each person the sole right and duty of discovering and obeying "the command of the hour." And, yet, liberals could not be too happy about his attitude toward revolution and reform; his disbelief in secular goals and programs; and his profound skepticism about the value and Christian authenticity of most of the pronouncements by the Church.

Let us, therefore, give up any attempt to pin a label on Barth that would place him somewhere in the conservative-liberal spectrum and, instead, ask ourselves what in Barth's theology has contributed to political theory that could help potential thinkers and practical politicians.

On the plus side, one could say that Barthian theology, if adhered to, would make it impossible for anyone to treat political ideologies, party programs and state policies as idols. Every political doctrine is robbed of its divisiveness by being placed in the perspective of the majesty, glory and omnipotence of God. The contrast between the righteous God and an unrighteous world has the effect of sensitizing the individual and collective conscience to the scandal of human injustice and suffering. No one in a Barthian world, which Barth regards as God's handiwork and the theater of God's action, would be guilty of desecrating, exploiting and polluting man's physical environment.

But there is a minus side to Barth's influence, too – very much so, unfortunately. Its main source is what one is obligated to characterize as his anti-intellectualism. Principles, rules and laws have no authority for him because he regards them as abstractions and, therefore, ineffectual either as guides or as restraints. They have no authority whatever until they become "definite and concrete political constellations." He applies this limitation to public officials, whether Christian or non-Christian, quite as much as to Church bodies. This means that there can be no forethought and no preparation until "the definite and concrete political constellation" stares us in the face. It means that we can do nothing about a crisis until we are in its very midst, and then we only can hope for that "command of the hour" that does not always come.

Barth's anti-intellectual attitude is unrealistic in that it makes no room for the power of ideas. We do not have to take the Hegelian position that ideas make conditions or the Marxist position that conditions make ideas. It is enough to say that ideas and conditions interact and, because they do, we cannot afford to ignore the influence of ideas and ideologies on politics. As men believe, so they will act – whatever circumstances and conditions may have led them to believe what they do.

It was Barth's failure to appreciate the impact of ideas – ideas prior to their becoming "definite and concrete political constellations" – that is responsible for his failure to ascribe to Communist doctrine its true importance. It is quite unnecessary to argue that the doctrine of Marx and Lenin accounts entirely and solely for Soviet-era policies. It is perfectly accurate to recognize that Soviet-era policies were influenced by geography and inherited much from czarist policies, but it would be thoroughly inaccurate to imagine that the doctrine of Marx and Lenin had no part in influencing Soviet-era policies. Can anyone imagine that czarist Russia would have benefited from fifth columns and subservient political parties in Western Europe and in the Americas? To imagine such a thing would be sheer nonsense, or worse.

By his negativism with regard to social and political action, Barth does something else that has had enormous political consequences: He denies political and social goals to humanity. If the Allies in World War II had had no conception of what they were fighting for, no vision of a world better than the inferno exemplified in the Nazi regime that they could hold up to their peoples, the outcome of the war might have been very different. It was precisely the failure of the U.S. government to have or to make clear the goals behind the Vietnam War that brought upon the country the disastrous and disgraceful consequences that many of us have had to live through. Contrast that ambiguity with the clear goals,[1] whether one agrees with them or not, behind the allied worldwide war on terrorism in the aftermath of the 9-11 attacks in the United States.

In his emphasis on God as "wholly Other," Barth forgot that this very God gave us minds with which to think, and did not sentence us to be the prey of the pressures of the moment. Taking for granted that people by nature are finite and biased, we should not conclude that people cannot think of goals for the future and programs for the present. These goals and programs, if adhered to with the humility to admit that nothing human is perfect and free from error, are sufficient to make the difference between a better world and a blind and hopeless subjection to a mere trial-and-error existence. Rather ironically, the non-Barthian and the non-Christian are better off because they can set goals and make plans without being restrained by Barthian qualms about objective truth and the ability of public officials to change and improve conditions.

With this passionate fealty to the Word of God in Scripture, Barth should have remembered that the Bible tells us that, without vision, the people perish.[2]

---

1. The declared objectives, among other things, included the destruction of al-Qaeda and other transnational terrorist organizations; the transformation of Iraq into a prosperous, stable democracy; the democratization of the rest of the Middle East; the eradication of terrorism as a means of irregular warfare; and an end to the proliferation of weapons of mass destruction to real and potential enemies worldwide.

2. Proverbs 29:18

Major Works of Karl Barth

Church Dogmatics; 4 vols. (Charles Scribner's Sons and T&T Clark; New York and Edinburgh, Scotland; 1936-1962).

The Epistle to the Romans (Oxford University Press; London; 1933).

The Church and the Political Problems of Our Day (Charles Scribner's Sons; New York; 1939).

A Letter to Great Britain from Switzerland (Sheldon Press; London; 1941).

The Church and the War (Macmillan; New York; 1944).

Against the Stream: Shorter Post-War Writings, 1946-52 (SCM Press; London; 1954).

The Word of God and the Word of Man (Harper and Brothers, Publishers; New York; 1957).

Protestant Thought: From Rousseau to Ritschl (Harper and Brothers, Publishers; New York ;1959).

How to Serve God in a Marxist Land, containing Letter to a Pastor in the German Democratic Republic (Association Press; New York; 1959).

Community, State, and Church (Doubleday & Co.; New York; 1960).

Karl Barth's Table Talk (Oliver & Boyd; Edinburgh, Scotland; 1963).

How I Changed My Mind (John Knox Press; Richmond, Va.; 1966).

Dietrich Bonhoeffer

Contents

Introduction

Dietrich Bonhoeffer[1] is one of the most influential of 20th century theologians. The reason for this influence is not that he produced a monumental theological edifice, as was the case with Tillich and Barth. He was much too involved with struggles within the German Lutheran Church and with the Nazi regime for such an achievement. He was at least as much of a churchman as he was a theologian. Moreover, he was only 39 when he died. We can only imagine what he might have written in his forties, fifties and sixties. Bonhoeffer's influence is due mainly to two circumstances: (1) he was a 20th century Christian martyr; and (2) he was the author of the phrases "religion-less Christianity" and "the world come of age."

It is true that some German Lutherans denied him the title of Christian martyr because he was executed on account of his involvement in a conspiracy to assassinate Adolf Hitler, to overthrow the Nazi regime, and to obtain a negotiated peace with the Allies. These German Lutheran critics technically were right, but their view was unjustifiably narrow because it ignored the fact that Bonhoeffer's involvement was the direct result of his Christian faith. In any case, the world now universally accords him the title of Christian martyr and respects him as such. The weight of his life stands behind the thrust of his words.

The phrases "religion-less Christianity" and "the world come of age" have aroused a powerful response, even today. They appealed to a generation that was distrustful of all institutions and hostile to orthodoxies of every kind; to a culture so unconcerned with God that some "theologians" pronounced him dead; and to a world increasingly secularized and which, nevertheless, somehow wanted to be told that secularization was right and good. These phrases spread far and wide. They were applauded because they seemed to depict the sickness unto death of our age as a condition of its robust health.

Bonhoeffer would be the first to reject this outburst of ill-begotten popularity. The phrases in question occur only in the last work he wrote, *Letters and Papers from Prison*, and were not interpreted in the context of his other

---

1. Dietrich Bonhoeffer (1906-1945).

works. They had not yet been developed into clear and well-defined concepts but, instead, represented bits of tentative exploratory thinking on Bonhoeffer's part, as he was the first to admit:

> "I am only gradually working my way to the non-religious interpretation of
> biblical concepts; the job is too big for me to finish just yet."[2]

As a matter of fact, Bonhoeffer was very Lutheran and very German,
being intensely proud of his religious and national heritage. To the last, he
was loyal to both and he never ceased to be a churchman.

---

2.   Bonhoeffer; *Letters and Papers from Prison*; p. 195. For a full citation of Bonhoeffer's
     works, see the Bibliography at the end of Book III.

CHAPTER ONE

Bonhoeffer's Theology

Because he was so actively engaged in the ecclesiastical and political struggles of his time, and because his life was cut off so early, Bonhoeffer has left us nothing so comprehensive as Tillich's *Systematic Theology* or Barth's *Church Dogmatics*. His theology must be pieced together from his various works, therefore, and can be summarized without going to great lengths.

God is the Creator and Sustainer of everything that was, is and will be, according to Bonhoeffer. God is a person, not a concept or an idea. For that reason, he cannot be known by the study or contemplation of nature. "Any attempt ... to grasp the person by the work remains unsuccessful because the work is ambivalent. ... It is essential to know the person if the work is also to be known."[1] Even in purely human handiwork, the full meaning is not clear until we know whose handiwork it is. This is still truer of God's handiwork. Creation bears the imprint of its maker, but this imprint is visible only to the person to whom its maker chose to reveal himself. All this means, to Bonhoeffer as well as to Barth, is that there neither is ultimate reality nor salvation through natural theology.

History is no more helpful than nature, Bonhoeffer says, because "history has no rationally perceptible purpose"[2] and both participants and spectators are afflicted with sin and guilt. "There is no absolute ground of faith in history."[3] Hegelian attempts to find God in history are foredoomed to failure.

For Bonhoeffer, God is a person. Because God is a person, there is

---

1. Bonhoeffer; *Christ the Center*; p. 38. For a full citation of Bonhoeffer's works, see the Bibliography at the end of Book III.

2. Bonhoeffer; *The Communion of Saints: A Dogmatic Inquiry into the Sociology of the Church*; p. 61. For a full citation of Bonhoeffer's works, see the Bibliography at the end of Book III.

3. Bonhoeffer; *Christ the Center;* p. 75.

absolutely no way to know him except as he chooses to reveal himself. Even on the human level, a person is a mystery concealed from all other persons as though by a veil. Only as the person discloses himself by a glance, expression, gesture, word or deed is the veil momentarily lifted. What we see in such instances is a living being, and the experience of encountering that being always has something so new and so unique that we characterize the self-disclosure as revelation – and do not feel guilty of exaggeration in putting it that way. So it is with our knowledge of God, except that it is more fragmentary and unfathomable than the revelation of one human being to another.

As Bonhoeffer sees it, any person-to-person revelation (and there can be no other) takes place in action. Action is existence itself. "For man, to exist means to stand under God's claim, to conduct oneself, to make decisions."[4] Bonhoeffer describes God's creation as "wresting out of non-being." God does this by speaking, which means "the concrete thing itself."[5] Clearly, wresting and speaking thus understood are forms of action. "From that it seems an inescapable conclusion that God can be known only in the act, i.e., existentially."[6]

The one and only revelatory act of God is his incarnation in Jesus Christ. Outside of Jesus Christ, there is no revelation, no knowledge of God, and only one way from God to man. In this respect, Bonhoeffer is as radically Christocentric as Barth. For Tillich's theonomy, Bonhoeffer substitutes Christonomy: "The antinomy of heteronomy and autonomy is here resolved in a higher unity which we may call Christonomy."[7] Bonhoeffer recognizes, of course, that there is such a thing as the orders of creation, but they have meaning only in the light of Jesus Christ. As such and of themselves, these orders are dumb; i.e., voiceless. Any argument that proposes we should attempt to discover God and his will in the orders of creation is futile: "The danger of the argument lies in the fact that just about everything can be defended by it."[8]

If we know God only through Jesus Christ, the next question for Bonhoeffer is: How do we know Jesus Christ? The answer is twofold: We know

---

4. Bonhoeffer; *Act and Being*; p. 99. For a full citation of Bonhoeffer's works, see the Bibliography at the end of Book III.

5. Bonhoeffer; *Creation and Fall*; pp. 23, 20. For a full citation of Bonhoeffer's works, see the Bibliography at the end of Book III.

6. Bonhoeffer; *Act and Being;* p. 96.

7. Bonhoeffer; *Ethics*; p. 264. For a full citation of Bonhoeffer's works, see the Bibliography at the end of Book III.

8. Bonhoeffer; *No Rusty Swords: Letters, Lectures and Notes*; p. 165. For a full citation of Bonhoeffer's works, see the Bibliography at the end of Book III.

him through the Bible and through the Church.

Bonhoeffer asserts that "the self-attestation of Jesus Christ is none other than that which is handed down to us by Scripture, and it comes to us in no other way than by the word of Scripture."[9] The key concept here is witness. "It is not a book which contains eternal truths, doctrines, norms or myths, but it is a unique witness of the God-man Jesus Christ."[10] In interpreting Scripture in this way, "we may never stick at one point, but must move over the whole of the Bible, from one place to another, just as a man can only cross a river covered in ice floes if he does not remain standing on one particular floe but jumps from one to another." We are not confronted here with fundamentalist literalism, since the Bible has flaws. "But the Risen One encounters us right through the Bible with all its flaws."[11]

The second answer is that we know Jesus Christ through the Church: "The church is the presence of Christ on earth, the church is the *Christus praesens*" (present Christ).[12] Again: "Christ is present in the church as a person." Or: "That in turn means that Christ can only be conceived of existentially, viz. in the community." For Bonhoeffer, as has been pointed out, the truth is not an abstraction to be grasped by the mind or an object to be apprehended by the senses. The truth of revelation in Jesus Christ is a reality that is personal and, therefore, communal. "Truth is not something which rests in itself and for itself, but something which takes place between two persons. Truth happens only in community."[13] From this personal and communal nature of the knowledge of God, it follows that the Church is the indispensable link between man and God: "The question of church membership is the question of salvation. The boundaries of the church are the boundaries of salvation."[14]

There is astonishingly little in Bonhoeffer's theology that deals with sin and guilt. He probably takes the Lutheran position on sin and guilt for granted, interpreting sin as disobedience and therefore rebellion against God, and guilt as the consequence of sin that can be wiped out only by the death and resurrection of Jesus Christ accepted in faith.

Bonhoeffer says almost nothing about personal salvation because he is suspicious of it as an "individualistic question" that should not get in the

---

9. Bonhoeffer; *Christ the Center*; p. 75.

10. Bonhoeffer; *No Rusty Swords*; p. 317.

11. Bonhoeffer; *Christ the Center*; p.76.

12. Bonhoeffer; *No Rusty Swords*; p. 161.

13. Bonhoeffer; *Christ the Center*; pp. 43, 47, 51.

14. Bonhoeffer; *The Way to Freedom: Letters, Lectures and Notes*; p. 93. For a full citation of Bonhoeffer's works, see the Bibliography at the end of Book III.

way when "there are more important things" to consider. It is apparent that this view troubles him a little, for he remarks: "I know it sounds pretty monstrous to say that."[15] But he says it nonetheless!

---

15. Bonhoeffer; *Letters and Papers from Prison*; p. 156.

CHAPTER TWO

Bonhoeffer's
Concept of Command

So far, Bonhoeffer's theology has been quite traditional except, perhaps, for its radically Christocentric character. It is when we reach the concept of command that we find something much more original and distinctive in Bonhoeffer. It is not that he is the only theologian to make use of it, but that no one else pushed it quite so far. In Bonhoeffer's theology, God sounds more like an army officer than a lawgiver. Everything is "thou shalt," "thou shalt not," "this is permitted," "this is not permitted," "ours is not to question why, but to do or die."

If this seems like an exaggeration not quite fair to Bonhoeffer, let us consider what he says about discipleship. He makes the comment that Jesus had "not the slightest interest in the psychological reasons for a man's religious decisions." When Jesus called someone, he expected the man to drop forthwith whatever he was doing and follow him. This compliance was "a testimony to the absolute, direct, and unaccountable authority of Jesus." Even more precisely: "To follow in his steps is something which is void of all content. It gives us no intelligible programme for a way of life, no goal or ideal to strive after. It is not a cause which human calculation might deem worthy of our devotion, even the devotion of ourselves."[1]

"God's commandment is the speech of God to man. Both in its concrete contents and in its form it is concrete speech to the concrete from time and place; it can only be heard in a local and temporal context. If God's commandment is not clear, definite and concrete to the last, then it is not God's commandment."[2] Obviously, God's commandment is unconditional and total, but what prevents it from being law in the generally accepted sense is

---

1. Bonhoeffer; *The Cost of Discipleship*; p. 48-49. For a full citation of Bonhoeffer's works, see the Bibliography at the end of Book III.

2. Bonhoeffer; *Ethics*; p. 245.

its specificity in time and place. It is a matter of the moment and, therefore, strictly individual. The orders of creation are at best the vehicle through which the command reaches us. "Thus the concept of orders of creation must be rejected as a basis for the knowledge of the commandment of God. Hence, neither the Biblical law as such nor the so-called orders of creation as such are for us the divine commandment which we perceive today."[3]

How do we know that God has commanded us to do something and how do we know what that something is? Many Christians probably would answer conscience. But not Bonhoeffer. He says quite definitely that conscience "is not the voice of God,"[4] though it "pretends to be the voice of God and the standard for the relation to other men." It should be seen "to be the most ungodly self-justification"[5] and regarded "as man's attempt at self-salvation."[6] One of its effects is "to put man to flight from God."[7] Another effect is to interfere with the discharge of one's responsibility to his fellow man. It is in command that man finds his liberation from the pangs of conscience, by Jesus Christ "who is the Lord of conscience."[8] But this merely confirms what Bonhoeffer already has said – namely, that conscience does not tell us what God's command is.

Another answer often given, especially by conservative Protestants, is the Bible. One might think that Bonhoeffer, as a good Lutheran who subscribes to *sola scriptura*, would accept this answer. But he does not. Bonhoeffer is willing to say that the Bible is the test for the truth of Christian doctrine, but he is unwilling to say that a man's course of action can be determined on this basis. "Only the truth of a doctrine can be proved by Scripture, never the rightness of a particular course." Proving the rightness of a course of action by Scripture, Bonhoeffer says, "absolves us from acting in faith. We want to see the way before we go along it." Such an attempt would turn the Bible into "an insurance policy" and would mean that man "looks for justification by his works before God."[9]

In determining the what and the when of a command, it is important to be patient. It is not merely that impatience leads to mistakes on the part of he who yields to it, but that it makes it harder for others to detect what the

3.   Bonhoeffer; *No Rusty Swords*; p. 166.

4.   Bonhoeffer; *Creation and Fall*; p. 83.

5.   Bonhoeffer; *Ethics*; pp. 149, 212.

6.   Bonhoeffer; *Act and Being*; p. 162.

7.   Bonhoeffer; *Creation and Fall*; p. 82.

8.   Bonhoeffer; *Ethics*; pp. 204, 216.

9.   Bonhoeffer; *The Way to Freedom*; pp. 175-177.

command is. "Impatience disrupts fellowship."[10] Here, we must remember that, according to Bonhoeffer's view of the communal aspect of the person-to-person nature of revelation, command usually is heard in fellowship.

The issue of patience in recognizing what, if any, is God's commandment in a particular crisis was faced more than once in Nazi Germany. One such crisis was the issue of legalization. The question was whether the pastors of the Confessional Church should register with the state church. Without such registration, they could not be assigned a living and the practice of their calling would be illegal. On the other hand, to register might be interpreted as accepting various Nazi decrees, such as the one applying the infamous Aryan paragraph[11] to ecclesiastical positions.

What is the command of God in such a predicament?

In this particular situation, Bonhoeffer set forth certain criteria that are important enough to be quoted in full:

"I want to try to clarify some things in principle. 1. In times of uncertainty the following rules hold for us: a) I should never make a decision in uncertainty; the status quo has precedence over change, unless I recognize the need for change with certainty. b) I should never act alone, firstly because I need the advice of the brothers, secondly because the brothers need me, and thirdly because there is a church discipline which I must not treat lightly. c) I should never make a hasty decision or allow it to be forced on me. If one door closes for me today, God will open another one when he wills."[12]

In the final analysis, Bonhoeffer's contention is that God's commandment is self-authenticating. "If God's commandment is not clear, definite and concrete to the last, then it is not God's commandment,"[13] and "the nature of this will of God can only be clear in the moment of action."[14] In the contention that God's commandment is self-authenticating, there undoubtedly is a mystical element which, for Bonhoeffer and people like him, must be regarded as a fact of experience.

Curious as it may seem to Americans who are inclined to think that whatever is compulsory, *ipso facto*, is a denial of freedom, Bonhoeffer

---

10. *Ibid.*; p. 200.

11. Aryan paragraph. Legislation in Nazi Germany that stated: "Anyone who is not of Aryan descent or who is married to a person of non-Aryan descent may not be appointed as a pastor or official. Pastors or officials of Aryan descent who marry non-Aryans are to be dismissed. The only exceptions are those laid down in the state law."

12. Bonhoeffer; *True Patriotism: Letters, Lectures and Notes*, 1939-1945; p.187. For a full citation of Bonhoeffer's works, see the Bibliography at the end of Book III.

13. Bonhoeffer; *Ethics*; p. 245.

14. Bonhoeffer; *No Rusty Swords*; p. 43.

argues the exact opposite – namely, that the commandment of God is the foundation of all freedom and the taproot of personal responsibility. We have seen his argument that God's commandment liberates man from enslavement to his conscience. Man also is liberated from the restrictions and uncertainties of ethical rules: "The Christian message stands beyond good and evil,"[15] he says. Moreover, there is another side to God's commandment that must not be overlooked: "It does not only forbid and command; it also permits. It does not only bind; it also sets free; and it does this by binding."[16]

Bonhoeffer illustrates this permissive and empowering aspect of commandment by commenting on the commandment that forbids adultery. There can be no true marriage when adultery is practiced. In that sense, the commandment is the "pre-condition" of marriage, but it becomes "the permission to live in marriage in freedom and certainty." It would surely be in line with Bonhoeffer's thought to remind ourselves that happily married couples do not worry about adultery, as well as pointing out that literally millions of men and women live their whole lives through without ever knowing the legal provisions governing marriage and divorce, the rights and duties of parents and children, the rights of husbands and wives. These legal provisions have a direct bearing on personal and property relationships in the family. Yes, these legal provisions do exist and they are, indeed, obligatory. They are commands. Nevertheless, most people go through life without knowing them. It is only in the case of trouble, perhaps some violation of a command, that people have to go to a lawyer and become aware of these legal provisions.

The point of Bonhoeffer's argument is that command makes responsible freedom possible, and that the existence of the community depends upon it. To the lawbreaker, command does appear as the denial of freedom – quite the contrary is true: It is the affirmation of responsible freedom.

In view of this, it would be a mistake to suppose that the commandment of God is heard and heeded only in "intensely conscious moments of crisis," only "at the crossroads" of life, and "always before him."[17] Most of the time, the commandment lies quietly behind us because we have obeyed it as a matter of course. As such, the commandment lies buried in our subconscious because no struggle against it brought it to the surface. The commandment, then, is the tacit foundation stone of communal life because it would occur to no one to question it.

---

15. *Ibid.*; p. 41.

16. Bonhoeffer; *Ethics*; p. 244.

17. *Ibid.*; p. 250

CHAPTER THREE

The Concept of Mandate

One of the points at which Bonhoeffer's theology most clearly impinges on politics is the concept of mandate. He defines it thus:

"By the term 'mandate' we understand the concrete divine commission which has its foundation in the revelation of Christ and which is evidenced by Scripture; it is the legitimation and warrant for the execution of a definite divine commandment, the conferment of divine authority on an earthly agent."

In choosing this word "mandate," Bonhoeffer rejected several others – specifically institution, order and office – because he felt they were too secularized and that usage had robbed them of their spiritual significance. For example, he says, "the term 'office' is now so completely secularized, and has come to be so closely associated with institutional bureaucratic thinking, that it cannot possibly render the sublime quality of the divine decree."[1] We already have seen why he rejected the concept of orders of creation. It is true that in one place he halfheartedly substituted the concept of orders of preservation, but it would seem that, without actually saying so, he replaced that one with the concept of mandate.

This concept of mandate is so important to Bonhoeffer that it is best to quote him at some length:

"The world is relative to Christ, no matter whether it knows it or not. This relativeness of the world to Christ assumes concrete form in certain mandates of God in the world. The Scriptures name four such mandates: labour, marriage, government and the Church. We speak of divine mandates rather than of divine orders because the word mandate more clearly refers to a divinely imposed task rather than to a determination of being. It is God's will that there shall be labour, marriage, government, and church in the

---

1. Bonhoeffer; *Ethics*; p. 254.

world; and it is His will that all these, each in its own way, shall be through Christ, directed towards Christ, and in Christ. God has imposed all these mandates on all men. He has not merely imposed one of these mandates on each individual, but He has imposed all four on all men."[2]

The reason for selecting these four mandates is that, for Bonhoeffer, they are provided for and established by Scripture. They are not the result of some rational analysis of social conditions, though they are not contrary to reason. Besides the test of Scripture, there also is that of the direction from which the mandate comes. A mandate, as a kind of cluster of divine commandments and a series of assignments to particular human beings, is always from above, never from below. Each mandate has its own allotted functions.[3]

Though all of Bonhoeffer's mandates receive some degree of spelling out, only one seems unduly vague and in need of special clarification. Marriage, church and government are reasonably clear, but labor is not. In one place, Bonhoeffer defines it thus: "Labour embraces here the whole range of work which extends from agriculture by way of industry and commerce to science and art."[4] In several places, he uses "culture" and "labour" synonymously. It is the broadest of his categories, which, though the economic aspects form a large part of it, touches every aspect of occupational or professional life.

It is under this mandate that Bonhoeffer discusses vocation or calling (preferring the term "deputyship") and personal responsibility. It is clearly a very important mandate which, like all mandates, comes directly from God and is not mediated through the state or the Church. For that reason, the government "must never itself try to become the subject, the driving force, in this domain of labour and its own divine mandate."[5] Institutions like the corporation, the labor union, the professional association and the university have a special status and sanctity, "their own origin in God, an origin which is not established by government. ... This means that for these fields the significance of government is *regulative* and not *constitutive.*"[6]

Lest this discussion give rise to the idea that Bonhoeffer's mandates, especially that of labor, are all-inclusive, it is worth noting that much is excluded – namely, whatever does not "possess a concrete divine commission and promise which has its foundation and evidence in revelation."

2.   *Ibid.*; p. 73.

3.   *Ibid.*; p. 264.

4.   *Ibid.*; p. 309.

5.   Bonhoeffer; *Christ the Center*; p. 76.

6.   Bonhoeffer; *Ethics*; p. 309. Emphasis supplied.

Among the things that are specifically excluded are listed people, race, class, the masses, society, nation, country, and empire. The trouble with these sociological items is that they have no basis in Scripture and derive whatever authority they have *from below.*

On that basis, government can be legitimized as a mandate, but the state cannot. "The concept of the state is foreign to the New Testament. It has its origin in pagan antiquity,"[7] he says. Government itself is a mandate; but the form of government is not because it comes from below. This does not mean that non-mandate forms are illegitimate, but only that they are permissive and, therefore, do not enjoy what we would call indispensable constitutional status and protection.

The importance of the direction from which authority emanates becomes clear in Bonhoeffer's discussion – which was very courageous at the time he made it – of the leadership principle (*Fuehrersprinzip*) so dear to the Nazis. He distinguished the authority of the office and the authority of the person. The leader, he said, "has authority from below" and that from below "is borrowed authority," while the "authority of an office is original authority." It is the leader's job, therefore, "to lead his following away from the authority of his person to the recognition of the real authority of orders and of offices."[8] But even the authority of office is itself only a stepping stone to God, who *is* (and not just "has") authority. "Here our being is invaded by a new being."[9]

The concept of mandate is important in two other respects, according to Bonhoeffer. One of these is that God's commandments, though personal, always are issued through one of the mandates. "God's commandment, which is manifested in Jesus Christ, comes to us in the Church, in the family, in labour and in government."[10] There is only one source, but there are four channels. This helps to determine whether God has spoken and, if he has, what he has said. The reception of the commandment, however, continues to be a fact of personal experience that cannot be demonstrated to someone else, though it can (and, indeed, must) be obeyed.

The other important aspect is that no human authority can claim sovereignty – especially not popular sovereignty, which comes from below and, therefore, is invalid. There is no sovereign but God.

> "Because the commandment of God is the commandment which is revealed in Jesus Christ, no single authority, among those which are

---

7. *Ibid.*; pp. 295, 297.

8. Bonhoeffer; *No Rusty Swords*; pp. 200, 202.

9. Bonhoeffer; *Christ the Center*; p. 37.

10. Bonhoeffer; *Ethics*; p. 245.

authorized to proclaim the commandment, can claim to be absolute. The authorization to speak is conferred from above on the Church, the family, labour and government, only so long as they give effect to God's commandment in conjunction and collaboration with one another and each in its own way. No single one of these authorities can exclusively identify itself with the commandment of God."[11]

It is clear that Bonhoeffer is taking sides with those who advocate decentralization, whether it be called federalism, pluralism or sphere sovereignty. In doing so, he is not only rejecting the dictatorship of Hitler and the empire of the Hohenzollerns, but reaching back to an ancient and romanticized German past.

It is in connection with his discussion of mandates that Bonhoeffer introduces the idea of vocation, or calling. Once again, he uses his own favorite word – namely, deputyship. A deputy is someone who is appointed to act for and on behalf of other people. Bonhoeffer cites the father, the teacher and the statesman as examples of what he means. God himself has appointed him to be responsible for his children, his students or his people, as the case may be. "Thus in a real sense he is their deputy. He is not an isolated individual, but he combines in himself the selves of a number of human beings. Any attempt to live as though he were alone is a denial of the actual fact of his responsibility." Every human being has his own appointed place, he says. "No man can altogether escape responsibility, and this means that no man can avoid deputyship."[12]

At this point, we must be careful not to read into Bonhoeffer's concept of deputyship the pseudo-democratic notion that a deputy is a bellhop for his constituents. That is not his idea at all. He adheres to the Burkean[13] idea whereby the deputy acts in accordance with his own conscience and judgment as to what the true welfare of the community – which includes his constituents – requires.

This is not an easy position to be in. A complicating factor is that almost every man simultaneously is involved in all four mandates as a father, a teacher, a worker, a churchman and a statesman. The extent of his involvement in these mandates varies, in that his statesmanship might extend no

11. *Ibid.*; p. 246.

12. *Ibid.*; p. 206.

13. Edmund Burke (1729-1797); British statesman, parliamentary orator, writer and political thinker. His works, which may be described as a defense of sound constitutional statesmanship against prevailing abuse and misgovernment, include *A Vindication of Natural Society* (1756), *A Philosophical Inquiry into the Origin of Our Ideas of the Sublime and Beautiful* (1757), *Observations on the Present State of the Nation* (1769), *On the Causes of the Present Discontents* (1770), *American Taxation* (1774), *Conciliation with America* (1775), and *Letter to the Sheriffs of Bristol* (1777).

further than being a voter. But there always is the possibility of confusion as to the commandment or commandments he hears, or thinks he hears, as a participant in each mandate. This necessitates choice, which means decision – and decision is an indispensable part of being a person.

There also is the fact that, for most people, the exercise of personal responsibility – i.e., acting as a deputy – is severely limited. Bonhoeffer repeatedly refers to the "limitedness of responsible life and action" and reminds us that "there is inherent in every thing its own law of being, no matter whether this thing is a natural object or a product of the human mind, and no matter whether it is a material or an ideal entity." For people – like factory workers, apprentices, clerks, etc. – who are engaged in "monotonous daily work," the area of responsibility is small because most activities are pre-decided. Some of these cramping limitations are inevitable but, whether inevitable or not, they result in the individual person's being "ethically emasculated" and deprived of "creative moral power." But even those few people, like statesmen and business executives, who enjoy a large measure of discretion and, therefore, of responsibility must work under limitations, too. There is a technical side to every position, however lofty, that must be learned, mastered and adhered to. Technique limits even the most powerful.

Finally, it is well to bear in mind that there are problems that "are simply insoluble." Some of these problems are important indeed: "The problem of the poor and the rich can certainly never be solved otherwise than by remaining unsolved."[14]

Bonhoeffer does not regard these limitations – which, in varying degrees, bind everybody – as grounds for pessimism. There is a liberation that comes through Christ: "It is not in the loyal discharge of the earthly obligations of his calling as a citizen, a worker and a father that a man fulfils the responsibility which is imposed on him, but it is in hearing the call of Jesus Christ. This call does indeed summon him to earthly duties, but that is never the whole of the call, for it lies always beyond these duties, before them and behind them." Man no longer is fenced in by any boundary: "Its boundary is broken through not only from above, that is to say by Christ, but also in an outward direction."[15]

To illustrate his point, Bonhoeffer cites the example of a physician who, if he works under the concept of deputyship, sees his responsibility as involving much more than the cure of the patient under his care. Beyond the health of his patient lie other ranges of responsibility – from contribu-

14. Bonhoeffer; *Ethics*; pp. 204, 206, 218, 219, 206, 319-320.

15. *Ibid.*; pp. 223, 225.

tions to medical science or to political activity for or against some bills affecting the medical profession.

Whoever knows that God has made him the deputy of other people and takes that deputyship seriously becomes inventive and resourceful. There is no job so menial, monotonous and humble that can't be turned into something significant – certainly for the one who performs it, and usually for the one for whose benefit the job is done.

CHAPTER FOUR

Bonhoeffer's
Concept of Government

The first thing to note about government is that it is divinely instituted, one of God's four mandates. Its authority comes from above.
Bonhoeffer spells out these points quite clearly:

> "Government is divinely ordained authority to exercise worldly dominion
> by divine right. Government is deputyship for God on earth. It can be
> understood only from above. Government does not proceed from society,
> but it orders society from above."[1]

In spite of this high conception, Bonhoeffer by no means deifies government. For him, government "cannot engender life" and "it is not creative."
There is no "Christian state," the government's mandate "is certainly not to
confess Christ," and "the state possesses its character as government independently of the Christian character of the person who governs. There is
government also among the heathen." The task of government is that of
"preserving the world, with its institutions which are given by God, for the
purpose of Christ." The legislative and coercive power of government "pre-
serves the world for the reality of Jesus Christ."[2]

The elimination of a religious function from the task of the state is not
replaced by any secular idealism. "God hates visionary dreaming; it makes
the dreamer proud and pretentious."[3] Furthermore, he says: "Whenever the
state becomes the executor of all the vital and cultural activities of man, it
forfeits its own proper dignity, its specific authority as government."[4]

---

1. Bonhoeffer; *Ethics*; p. 297.

2. *Ibid.*; pp. 308, 288, 261, 300, 308, 76.

3. Bonhoeffer; *Life Together*; p. 27. For a full citation of Bonhoeffer's works, see the Bibliography at the end of Book III.

4. Bonhoeffer; *Ethics*; p. 299.

Government is not necessarily concerned with the nation and national-ism, either. Many states, like the old Austrian empire and the former Soviet Union, are not nation-states. Their reality is from below. Moreover, govern-ment should not be concerned with the emancipation of the masses. The main trouble with the masses is that they are anti-personal since, "in the masses the boundary of the personal disappears, the individual ceases to be a person, and it is only a part of the mass, drawn with it and led by it."[5] In a few brief sentences, he disposes of most of these secular idealisms that have been strong forces in history. "The emancipation of the masses leads to the reign of terror of the guillotine. Nationalism leads to war. The libera-tion of man as an absolute ideal leads only to man's self-destruction. And at the end of the path which was first trodden in the French Revolution there is nihilism."[6]

Perhaps it is this ideological impoverishment that is responsible for Bon-hoeffer's lack of interest in forms of government. "Scripture offers no indi-cation with regard to the relation between people and government. ... It knows that the people grows from below, but that government is instituted from above." He does, however, offer a criterion for judging governmental forms: "That form of the state will be relatively the best in which it becomes most evident that government is from above, from God, and in which the divine origin of government is most clearly apparent."[7]

One might infer from this criterion that Bonhoeffer's favorite form of government would be monarchy in its traditional European sense. It was in the regimes of the Hohenzollerns, the Habsburgs, the Bourbons and the Romanoffs that government most clearly was seen to reach from the top down, as testified by accepted theory, monarchical titles and political prac-tice. If monarchy was indeed his preference, he refrains from saying so. Moreover, on the other side, we must notice that Bonhoeffer admired the American constitution – which is just about his only favorable comment on the United States that one can find. The source of his admiration for the United States Constitution was his belief that the framers "were conscious of original sin" and gave "due consideration of man's innate longing for power and for the fact that power pertains only to God."[8]

Having been stripped of religious functions by the mandate to the Church and of cultural functions by the mandate to "labour," the state is left with what Bonhoeffer in one place calls the "regulative" power. It is clear,

5.   Bonhoeffer; *The Communion of Saints*; p. 60.

6.   Bonhoeffer; *Ethics*; p. 38.

7.   *Ibid.*; pp. 310, 316.

8.   *Ibid.*; p. 40.

of course, that this power at the very least includes the maintenance of law and order. It has the right to legislate and wields the power of the sword. There is to be no anarchy. Beyond this, however, Bonhoeffer's thinking is vague. He shows no acquaintance with the literature of political pluralism, guild socialism and economic councils that was rather abundant in the 1920s and which, one should hasten to add, left much to be desired. Bonhoeffer, though, was a theologian and a churchman – not a political scientist or a political theorist.

The power to legislate is not unlimited. The concept of mandate in itself is a limitation. Thus, if government were to attempt to replace monogamy with polygamy or to promote sexual promiscuity, the attempt would be invalid as a violation of God's commandment and as an invasion of another God-established mandate.

Moving from the family to the social order, we again discover God-given facts that must be respected, facts that unmistakably point to inequality. Bonhoeffer is no equalitarian. "We can no longer escape the fact that the ethical calls for clear relationships in terms of superiority and inferiority. Nor can superiority and inferiority simply be interchanged to accord with the fluctuations in the value of subjective accomplishment and character."[9]

It cannot even be said that government has a monopoly on law making. There is, for instance, the question of natural law. Bonhoeffer has little to say about natural law, and what he says is somewhat equivocal. He is bothered by the fact that natural law has been used to support both revolution and the status quo, both democracy and dictatorship. Whatever we do, we must not take the position that government has a "twofold basis," one in the Decalogue and one in natural law, for "it is only because these two laws have been declared to be identical ... that natural law, reason, can be represented as the basis of governmental action." Regardless of the name used, "there is in every thing its own law of being" that must be respected. There are such things as laws and conventions that no statesman can overlook except at his own peril: "Arrogant disdain for them or violation of them denotes a failure to appreciate reality which sooner or later has to be paid for."[10]

It is the duty of government to maintain conditions under which the Christian faith can flourish or, at least, not be unduly handicapped. Bonhoeffer recognizes that there are "conditions of the heart, of life, and of the world which impede the reception of grace in a special way, namely, by ren-

---

9.   *Ibid.*; p. 241.

10. *Ibid.*; pp. 203, 277, 206, 207.

dering faith infinitely difficult" – among which are slavery, hunger, poverty, loneliness, homelessness and injustice. Measures to cope with such conditions would be regarded as "preparing the way." These measures are "penultimate" and should be preserved because of their preparatory character: "Any arbitrary destruction of the penultimate will do serious injury to the ultimate."[11]

Bonhoeffer's concept of the penultimate is not an endorsement of the social gospel. For him, the penultimate is important, but not indispensable. At least, no one penultimate measure is necessary for the achievement of the ultimate. Conditions that impede the reception of grace mean that faith is made difficult, "but not that they make it impossible."

What can be summed up as a social injustice has made the world at times more receptive to the gospel, and periods of relative social righteousness sometimes have been the very ones when estrangement from the gospel has been "especially deep-seated and alarming," with the result that the government's objective "cannot be simply the realization of a programme of social reform."

Bonhoeffer illustrates his argument by referring to the Apostle Paul's attitude toward slavery: "St. Paul did not regard the form of slavery which was practiced in his time as an institution which conflicted with the commandment of God."

Why not? Bonhoeffer says that slavery in Paul's time was "relatively mild," but that the really decisive thing was that "the slave was clearly not prevented by his actual situation as a slave from living as a Christian."[12] What Bonhoeffer is telling us, therefore, is that the connection between social conditions and spiritual conditions is tenuous, unpredictable and unmanageable.

In view of the assignment of religious functions to the Church and of the cultural functions to "labour," and in view of the narrow scope of government's "regulative" power, it comes as a surprise to discover that Bonhoeffer lays enormous stress on the obedience of the citizen to his government. A Calvinist who ascribes a moral and religious mission to the state and who, like Calvin himself, regards political power as more important than bread and air and water could not be more emphatic.

What comes through here, of course, is the traditional political subservience and social passivity of German Lutheranism. Bonhoeffer's opposition to Hitler should not lead us to forget that Bonhoeffer was a very patriotic German. When the Nazi regime prohibited him from speaking in

---

11. *Ibid.*; pp. 94, 95, 92.

12. *Ibid.*; pp. 94, 96, 298.

public, Bonhoeffer protested vehemently. What hurt him most was the reason given for the prohibition:

> "The reason given is 'disruptive activity.' I reject this charge. In view of my whole attitude, my work and my background, it is unthinkable that I should allow myself to be identified with groups which rightly bear the ignominy of such a charge. I am proud to belong to a family which has for generations earned the gratitude of the German people and state."

In one case, he was willing to work for the exemption from military service of a pastor so that his congregation might not suffer, but only "provided that this could be justified on military grounds."[13]

He was troubled about his own liability to military service. He felt that it would be "conscientiously impossible to join in a war under the present circumstances," that the military oath he would have to swear was "the worst thing of all," but that, in view of the fact that the Confessional Church had taken no stand on the war, his refusal to serve "would be regarded by the regime as typical of the hostility of our church towards the state."[14]

He solved his own personal problem – temporarily – by joining the Abwehr, a military counter-intelligence organization under Admiral Wilhelm Canaris.[15] The Abwehr, however, was engaged in a conspiracy to assassinate Hitler and overthrow the Nazi regime, which eventually is what led to Bonhoeffer's imprisonment and execution.

Speaking more generally, Bonhoeffer acknowledged that Christians differ on what the Church should do in wartime, but "no one can deny that the motivating force behind its conviction and action is love of the German people and the desire to serve it during the war in the best possible way."[16]

The obedience due to the government is "unconditional and qualitatively total" and only in extreme cases, as when the government tries to make

---

13. Bonhoeffer; *True Patriotism: Letters, Lectures and Notes*, 1939-1945; pp. 64, 218.

14. Bonhoeffer; *The Way to Freedom*; pp. 205-206.

15. Wilhelm Franz Canaris (1887-1945). German naval officer who, after Adolf Hitler's rise to power, was made head of the Abwehr. Despite his work with the military intelligence service, he worked against Hitler with the General Staff, opposed atrocities, leaked intelligence to the Allies and was instrumental in planning assassination and coup attempts against Hitler and his government. He was directly involved in the 1938 and 1939 coup attempts and, in March 1943, flew to Smolensk to meet with conspirators on the staff of Army Group Center. Hitler dismissed him from command in February 1944. Later that year, he was placed under house arrest, which prevented him from participating in the July 20 plot to assassinate Hitler, but the Gestapo discovered evidence linking him to that conspiracy. A few weeks before the end of the war, he was executed by slow strangulation at Flossenbürg concentration camp, where fellow conspirators Bonhoeffer, Hans Oster, Carl Sack and Ludwig Gehre also were executed.

16. Bonhoeffer; *Ethics*; pp. 218, 307, 315.

itself "master over the belief of the congregation," can obedience be denied "for the Lord's sake." A good case, though not an absolutely convincing one, could be made that it was not the Nazi government as such that Bonhoeffer resisted, but that government's interference with church affairs.

Only concrete, particular, and rare cases can justify disobedience, and these must under no circumstances be generalized: "Generalizations lead to an apocalyptic diabolization of government. Even an anti-Christian government is still in a certain sense government."

Bonhoeffer could hardly be more explicit: "According to Holy Scripture, there is no right of revolution."[17] In sum, his judgment is: resistance, sometimes; revolution, never!

---

17. *Ibid.*; pp. 307, 315.

CHAPTER FIVE

Church, State and Society

Bonhoeffer's apparent political conservatism should not mislead us into thinking that he was satisfied with the status quo. How could he be? He had lived through the defeat of his beloved country in World War I and in which one of his brothers had been killed, as well as the ensuing, and devastating, inflation and economic crisis that plunged a horrified middle class into the proletariat. He saw the rise, and nearly the end, of the violence and demonic behavior of the Nazi regime. He was well aware of the horrors of World War II as German cities were pulverized, and he knew that the future of Germany looked bleak.

Bonhoeffer remarked that World War II did not bring about "a radical alteration of our life," as did World War I.[1] The underlying forces of destruction before World War I were hidden, whereas they were obvious before World War II – and that war was an intensification, not a change. He undoubtedly was thinking of the period between the accession of Hitler to the chancellorship and the savagery of World War II when he wrote these words:

"Just as a speeded-up film reveals, in a more impressive concentration, movements which otherwise would not be perceptive, so the war makes clear in a particularly vivid and unconcealed form what for years has been becoming more and more uncannily clear as the nature of the world. War isn't the first thing to bring death, to reveal the sorrows and troubles of human bodies and souls, to unleash lies, unlawfulness and violence. War isn't the first thing to make our existence so utterly insecure, to make man the impotent one, who must see his wishes and plans crossed and destroyed 'by higher authority.' But war makes all this, which has already existed without it and before it, obvious to us all, however much we would still like to overlook it."[2]

---

1. Bonhoeffer; *True Patriotism*; p. 78.

2. *Ibid.*; p. 78.

Being a thinking man, Bonhoeffer probed beneath the surface of things and found an even deeper crisis. He could see the dissolution of ideologies, the impotence of philosophical systems, the dire threat of science and technology to continued existence on Earth, the breakdown of constitutional processes, the unattainability of what used to be known as peace settlements, the loosening of social ties, the erosion of moral standards, and the disappearance of religious faith. He summed it all up by observing that "we no longer worship anything" – not even false gods – but that "if we still have an idol, perhaps it is nothingness, obliteration, meaninglessness."[3] In other words, the political and social crisis is but a manifestation of a deep spiritual crisis. Without a solution of the spiritual crisis, nothing else can be solved.

To many Christians, the solution of the spiritual crisis must come from church control of – or, at least, the direction of – government. There must be reconstruction and reform by the state as dictated by the Church speaking and acting as the representative of Christ on Earth. This view, which first appeared with the Emperor Constantine, held sway for well over a thousand years and still has many supporters today. Nor are the supporters confined to those countries where the Church still is established. Indeed, many are to be found in countries like the United States, where the separation of church and state is constitutionally imposed.

On the other hand, it sometimes is in countries where the Church is established that a belief in salvation by Church pronouncements operating through governmental action is least prevalent. It is certain that, for Bonhoeffer, such a belief is a snare and a delusion.

"The first political word of the church is the call to recognize the proper limit, the call of common sense. The church calls this limit sin, the state calls it reality; both, though with different stresses, might call it finitude." For the Church to issue pronouncements on political and social questions requires "detailed knowledge" that the Church does not possess and, for that reason, Bonhoeffer says the pronouncements lack secular validity and Christian authenticity. The Church "has no right to address the state directly in its specifically political actions. It has neither to praise nor to censure the laws of the state, but must rather affirm the state to be God's order of preservation in a godless world; it has to recognize the state's ordinances, good or bad as they appear from a humanitarian point of view, and to understand that they are based on the sustaining will of God amidst the chaotic godlessness of the world."[4]

---

3. John D. Godsey; *Preface to Bonhoeffer: The Man and Two of His Shorter Writings* (Fortress Press; Philadelphia; 1957); p. 57.

4. Bonhoeffer; *No Rusty Swords*; pp. 156, 163, 222.

The lengths to which Bonhoeffer was willing to go in defending this strictly non-political position was illustrated by what he said about the Nazi treatment of the Jews: "Without doubt the Jewish question is one of the historical problems which our state must deal with, and without doubt the state is justified in adopting new methods here. ... Thus even today, in the Jewish question, it cannot address the state directly and demand of it some definite action of a different nature."[5]

Now, it is possible and even probable that, as a prisoner in a Nazi concentration camp, Bonhoeffer did not know about the systematic extermination of millions of Jews. But even after making this allowance, the fact remains that Bonhoeffer had to be well-acquainted with the announced policies of the Nazi government concerning the Jewish question (which was a question in Germany only because the Nazis themselves made it one) and with the barbarous treatment of the Jews by that government and party even before the war.

When confronted with such an extreme case, how could he take the position that "new methods" were in order, that the Church could not demand "different action," or that the Church could not even "address the state directly" on this subject? Whatever one may think of Bonhoeffer's remarks on "the Jewish question," they do show how profoundly and consistently he was opposed to any involvement of the Church in political activity.

So, we are back where we started: a godless post-Christian world in which conversation between Christian and non-Christian is almost nonexistent. With political action out as an option, how about intellectual reconstruction? Why not reformulate the Christ-faith in terms that are meaningful to modern man? Why not draft more relevant confessions of faith? Why not develop new theologies that can restore communication between Christian and non-Christian?

This intellectual approach was the one tried by Tillich, but Bonhoeffer has no confidence in it at all: "Tillich set out to interpret the evolution of the world (against its will) in a religious sense – to give it its shape through religion. That was very brave of him, but the world unseated him and went on by itself."[6] There is no power in abstractions, especially insofar as the proletariat is concerned. This is an important point for Bonhoeffer because he held that "the churchliness of the modern bourgeoisie is threadbare," and that renewal "is only possible if the church succeeds in winning the proletariat."[7]

---

5. *Ibid.*; p. 223.

6. Bonhoeffer; *Letters and Papers from Prison*; p. 180.

7. Bonhoeffer; *The Communion of Saints*; p. 191.

We are thrown back once more, then, to the central and all-important question which is, as Bonhoeffer himself summarized it, "how to claim for Jesus Christ a world that has come of age."[8] It cannot be emphasized too strongly how absolutely central this objective is for Bonhoeffer. A deep love for and faith in Jesus Christ are the very core of his thinking. Where are such a love and such a faith to be found and, once found, how can they be communicated?

The traditional answer always has been in the Church. In spite of his much-celebrated criticism of the institutional church, Bonhoeffer never offered any other answer than the traditional one, and indisputable evidence can be gathered to prove it from works written at different periods in his life. "The church is the presence of God in the world."

"The church speaks of miracles because it speaks of God, of eternity in time, of life in death, of love in hate, of forgiveness in sin, of salvation in suffering, of hope in despair,"[9] he says. "The idea of a Christian who does not attach himself to the congregation is unthinkable."[10] Christian fellowship is to be cherished and not taken for granted: "It is by the grace of God that a congregation is permitted to gather visibly in the world to share God's word and sacrament. Not all Christians receive this blessing. The imprisoned, the sick, the scattered and lonely, the proclaimers of the Gospel in heathen lands stand alone."[11]

Furthermore, no matter how secularized we become, there always will be "the so-called 'ultimate questions' – death, guilt – to which only 'God' can give an answer, and because of which we need God and the Church and the pastor."[12] The Church is God's chosen vehicle for the propagation of the Christian faith and, because this task is of primordial importance, the Church is accorded the position of being one of God's four mandates: "The Church as a self-contained community serves to fulfill the divine mandate or proclamation."[13]

Multiple quotations from several of Bonhoeffer's works, ranging from *The Communion of Saints* (which he wrote when he was only 21) to his *Letters and Papers from Prison*, had to be used at the risk of being tedious because of the misuse to which his truly devastating criticism of the institutional church has been put. It is this devastating criticism that has caused so

8.   Bonhoeffer; *Letters and Papers from Prison*; p. 189.

9.   Bonhoeffer; *No Rusty Swords*; pp. 154-155.

10. Bonhoeffer; *The Communion of Saints*; p. 156.

11. Bonhoeffer; *Life Together*; p. 18.

12. Bonhoeffer; *Letters and Papers from Prison*; pp. 178-79.

13. Bonhoeffer; *Ethics*; p. 266.

many American liberals to clutch Bonhoeffer to their bosom as one of their own. There are, of course, parallels between Bonhoeffer's criticism of the institutional church and that of American liberals. Nevertheless, anyone acquainted with Bonhoeffer's theological views would appreciate how uncomfortable he would feel in that embrace. What we have here "is simply parallelism, and this is not overcome by the knowledge that the other will is running the same course."[14]

The basic argument of American theological liberals is that the Christian faith, or the way in which it is presented, is not relevant to the social and mental conditions of modern man. The fault modern man finds with the institutional church is not that it has not been relevant, but that it has not been authentic.

Bonhoeffer's reaction to American church life as he had occasion to observe it, limited though that occasion was, makes his distaste for liberalism unmistakably clear. He had a special opportunity to know, and harshly criticize, that citadel of American theological liberalism, Union Theological Seminary in New York. He described that seminary as "notorious" and saw it as promoting "the permeation of Christian theology with pragmatic philosophy." It was preoccupied with "exclusively social needs." Moreover, he said, "The theological atmosphere of the Union Theological Seminary is accelerating the process of the secularisation of Christianity in America."[15] His opinion of the seminary professors was scathing: "They intoxicate themselves with liberal and humanistic expressions, laugh at the fundamentalists, and basically they are not even a match for them."[16]

Concerning the sermons in the famous Riverside Church in New York, his comment was: "I have no doubt at all that one day the storm will blow with full force on this religious handout, if God himself is still anywhere on the scene."[17]

His indictment of sermons in New York City generally is so sweeping, comprehensive and enlightening that it is worth quoting in full. The point of the quotation, however, is not its accuracy but its expression of Bonhoeffer's point of view:

"One may hear sermons in New York upon almost any subject, although one only is never handled or, at any rate so rarely that I never succeeded in hearing it presented – namely, the gospel of Jesus Christ, of the cross, of

---

14. Bonhoeffer; *The Communion of Saints*; p. 120.

15. Bonhoeffer; *No Rusty Swords;* pp. 86, 88, 91.

16. Mary Bosanquet; *The Life and Death of Dietrich Bonhoeffer* (Hodder and Stoughton; London; 1968); p. 83.

17. Bonhoeffer; *The Way to Freedom*; p. 231.

sin and forgiveness, of death and life. ... But what do we find in the place of the Christian message? An ethical and social idealism which pins its faith to progress, and which for some not quite evident reason assumes the right to call itself Christian. And in the place of the Church as a community of believing Christians stands the Church as a social institution. Anyone who has seen the weekly programme of one of the large New York churches, with its daily, almost hourly events, tea parties, lectures, concerts, charitable events, sports, games, bowling, dancing for people of all ages, anyone who has heard the efforts to persuade a new arrival to join the Church on the grounds that it will give him a special kind of entry into society, anyone who has observed the painful anxiety, with which the pastor advertises and presses for membership, is able to make some estimate of the character of such a Church."[18]

If the kind of liberalism that Bonhoeffer saw in America is not what he meant in criticizing the institutional church, what did he mean? In a world that he described as "come of age," he meant that terms like "religion" and "religious" would have to be so radically changed that it might be better to drop them altogether. The reason for doing so is not the irrelevance of these terms to contemporary conditions, though the irrelevance exists, but disloyalty to Christ and disobedience to God's command.

To speak of the Christian "religion" is to place the Christian faith in the same general category as other religions, however much differences of level may be stressed. But Jesus Christ is not *a* truth among many truths, but *the* truth. Moreover, the words "religion" and "religious" have the effect of splitting the world into two compartments, the sacred and the secular. The sacred is concerned with special rituals and beliefs, in special places (churches or sanctuaries), special times and days (Sundays, Christmas, Easter, etc.), and special people (church members). The secular world is the workaday world from which religion is absent – even for "religious" people in those areas not labeled "religious." When the Church constricts itself into mere religious society and allows the Christian faith to become a religion, Bonhoeffer says it violates the command of God, who demands the sanctification of the secular in the name of Jesus Christ to the point where the distinction between sacred and secular is altogether extinguished. Jesus instructed his disciples to stay in the world and redeem it, not to escape from it into sanctuaries, monasteries and other places. "The pure teaching of the Gospel is not a religious concern, but a desire to execute the will of God for a new creation."[19]

By allowing itself to become an institution, the Church became like all

---

18. Op cit; Bosanquet; *The Life and Death of Dietrich Bonhoeffer*; p. 85.

19. Bonhoeffer; *The Way to Freedom;* p. 48.

institutions – self-centered and defensive. It sought to acquire new privileges and to make old ones more secure. Its defensiveness took the form of apologetics – i.e., arguments designed to convert unbelievers and to defend Christianity against attacks from within and from without – and condemned the world for refusing to accept its claims.

Bonhoeffer scarcely could express his indignation strongly enough: "The attack by Christian apologetic on the adulthood of the world I consider to be in the first place pointless, in the second place ignoble, and in the third place unchristian."[20] The Church discredited the noblest doctrine of the Christian faith in its efforts to make itself stronger by making church membership easier. Grace, for instance, comes cheap: "Cheap grace is the preaching of forgiveness without requiring repentance, baptism without church discipline, communion without confession, absolution without personal confession. Cheap grace is grace without discipleship, grace without cost, grace without Jesus Christ, living and incarnate."[21]

This self-segregation of the Church from the center of everyday life – from "where the action is," as the contemporary catchword puts it – has robbed the Church of the power to reconcile and to redeem: "Our Church, which has been fighting in these years only for its self-preservation, as though that were an end in itself, is incapable of taking the word of reconciliation and redemption to mankind and the world. Our earlier words are therefore bound to lose their force and cease." It is easy to fall prey to the attractiveness of separation and to believe that faith can be obtained only in the sanctuary of the monastery: "I discovered later, and I am still discovering right up to this moment, that it is only by living completely in this world that one learns to have faith."

Faith is not born in the tranquility of meditation, the contemplation of the infinite, or the inspiration of a worship service. These things may cultivate, refine and deepen an already existing faith, but they cannot create it. True, God alone creates it, and it is his gift. But, for Bonhoeffer, God gives his gift in action. Faith is born in the fire of trial and tribulation, in the agony of decision, in the midst of battle. By identifying itself with religion, using the term in Bonhoeffer's sense, the Church has made it necessary for the world to be and to remain what it has become – *religion-less* – if Christ is to live and rule in the hearts and minds of men in this world come of age.[22]

So unfaithful has the institutional church become that Bonhoeffer feels even God has been compromised. Is it God himself or some false concep-

20. Bonhoeffer; *Letters and Papers from Prison*; p. 179.

21. Bonhoeffer; *The Cost of Discipleship*; p. 36.

22. Bonhoeffer; *Letters and Papers from Prison*; pp. 172, 201, 153.

tion of God that has been compromised? It is at this point that Bonhoeffer seems close to the Death-of-God "theologians," for he speaks of the necessity of learning to live on our own and "manage our lives without him." His language, at times and in places, gets fuzzy, and unfriendly critics might accuse him of calculated obscurity. In a characteristically German way, he tells us: "Before God and with God we live without God." Which way are we to take that statement? Is God with us or isn't he? Further comments make it certain that Bonhoeffer is condemning only false conceptions of God. Now, Bonhoeffer's point is not to deny that God is indeed omnipotent but that, had we looked at the figure of Christ and seen God as the Bible sees him, we would have known God as the one "who wins power and space in the world by his weakness. This will probably be the starting-point for our 'secular interpretation.'"[23] If we keep our eyes glued to Jesus Christ, we shall see that the way in which God reveals himself to us primarily is through love, suffering, weakness, sacrifice and surrender.

And, thus, we come to the positive side of Bonhoeffer's teaching concerning the relations of the Church to the state and to society. It simply is a matter of radical obedience. God commands and we obey without hesitation or reservation or evasion. As we have seen earlier, God's command is a person-to-person relation that always is concrete and usually mediated in community. Therefore, the Church must become once more what it was in New Testament times – a fellowship, not an organization or an institution. Through its members, it must identify itself with human suffering, place God at the center of life that includes the strongest and not just the weakest parts, and carry the gospel to all men. In this way, Bonhoeffer believes he has avoided the twin pitfalls of pietism and social activism: "Now otherworldliness and secularism are only two sides of the same thing, namely, disbelief in God's kingdom."[24]

He sums up in greater detail what he means as follows:

"The hour in which the church today prays for the kingdom is one that forces the church, for good or ill, to identify itself completely with the children of the earth and of the world. It binds the church by oaths of fealty to the earth, to misery, to hunger, to death. It makes the church stand in full solidarity with evil and with the guilt of the brother. The hour in which we today pray for God's kingdom is the hour of utmost togetherness with the world, a time of clenched teeth and trembling fist. It is no time for solitary whispering."[25]

---

23. *Ibid.*; pp.196-197.

24. Op cit; Godsey; *Preface to Bonhoeffer: The Man and Two of His Shorter Writings*; pp. 31, 33.

25. *Ibid.*; p. 33.

In its proclamation of the kingdom, the Church of our time will have to do what it did in New Testament times – use the language of the home, the streets and the marketplace, not the highbrow language of the seminary and the university. And so, in what may turn out to be a prophetic passage, Bonhoeffer declares:

"It will be a new language, perhaps quite non-religious, but liberating and redeeming – as was Jesus' language; it will shock people and yet overcome them by its power; it will be the language of a new righteousness and truth, proclaiming God's peace with men and the coming of his kingdom."[26]

The Church that will create this new language will be motivated by faith and hope. It will act responsibly, not because it is unconcerned with consequences, but because it is obeying God's command. In obedience to the command of God, the two main kinds of irresponsibility are overcome:

"Irresponsibility in respect to the future is nihilism, and irresponsibility in respect to the present is fanaticism. We must overcome them both, and in this task, which is also a highly personal one, we can and must finally unite, however different the background of our experience is."[27]

---

26. Bonhoeffer; *Letters and Papers from Prison*; pp. 172

27. Bonhoeffer; *I Loved This People*; p. 12. For a full citation of Bonhoeffer's works, see the Bibliography at the end of Book III.

CHAPTER SIX

Conclusion

The political implications of Bonhoeffer's theology are difficult to isolate and evaluate. Some points, of course, stand out clearly. The concept of mandate puts him in the camp of those thinkers who favor the decentralization of power, like the pluralists, the sphere-sovereignty theorists and the guild socialists.

The dangers of centralization and the consequent bureaucratization of human relationships are evident to Bonhoeffer. His consciousness of these dangers comes naturally to one who comes out of the North European historical tradition of thinkers like the German Gierke[1] and the Dutchman Althusius,[2] though there is no evidence that he was acquainted with the work of either thinker.

The crucial question we have to face is whether the dangers of centralization have not been made inevitable by science and technology. On this question, Bonhoeffer has nothing whatever to say, which is quite understandable and excusable in that he was a theologian and not a social scientist.

Bonhoeffer's emphasis on command and obedience puts him in an ambiguous position. It certainly has some very anti-individualistic and anti-intellectualistic overtones. It is anti-individualistic in that individual action is initiated entirely outside of the individual; i.e., in God's will. The individual's obligation is to obey immediately and unquestioningly. He does not discuss, justify or explain the command: He obeys it.

---

1. Otto Friedrich von Gierke (1841-1921). A leader of the Germanist school of historical jurisprudence who popularized the theories of Johannes Althusius. His books include *Natural Law and the Theory of Society, 1500-1800, Associations and Law: The Classical and Early Christian Stages* and *Political Theories of the Middle Ages.*

2. Johannes Althusius (1557-1638). Political theorist who was the intellectual father of modern federalism and an advocate of popular sovereignty. In his greatest work, *Politica,* he contends that because all power and government comes from God, civil authorities cannot use their power to serve their own ends and that government power must be limited.

From this point of view, Bonhoeffer is in the Prussian military tradition. We should remember, however, that, for Bonhoeffer, God's commands are specific and concrete. They are addressed to the individual and to him alone, even though he usually hears them within the context of his communal experience.

Bonhoeffer's position is anti-intellectual in his refusal to admit the possibility that God's commands might form a pattern and, therefore, have a general import. His dislike of abstractions, the liberal ideas of the French Revolution, and "religious" orthodoxy make him unfriendly to the idea of law. In this respect, as in so many others, Bonhoeffer was typically Lutheran. He had Luther's view of temporal law as "a rank growth" and the deep-set feeling that all law is hostile to the inner liberty of man (inner liberty being for Bonhoeffer the only kind that really counts). By denying generality to God's commands and insisting on the individual, concrete and momentary character of command, Bonhoeffer robs law of one of its most valuable characteristics – predictability. Even that great authoritarian Hobbes conceded that the sovereign should state his purpose so that his subjects could obey his commands more intelligently and effectively.

And, yet, there is in Bonhoeffer some recognition of the place of law in human life. He makes some room for natural law, talks about the law "inherent in things," and advises the statesman not to disregard positive laws and conventions. In this respect, Bonhoeffer aligns himself with the other side of the German tradition usually contrasted with the Prussian militaristic authoritarianism – namely, the *Rechtsstaat* or constitutional state. There can be personal responsibility through law. What Bonhoeffer feels about the comparative merits of personal command and general law comes out in his estimate of Gladstone[3] and Bismarck,[4] both of whom he admired:

---

3. William Ewart Gladstone (1809-1898), British Liberal politician and prime minister four times (1868-1874; 1880-1885; 1886; and 1892-1894). He was a notable political reformer, known for his populist speeches, and was for many years the main political rival of Benjamin Disraeli. He entered Parliament in 1832, and served in numerous governments in junior capacities, but also as president of the board of trade and chancellor of the Exchequer. He was responsible for Cardwell's Army reform (1868), which made peacetime flogging illegal; the disestablishment of the Church of Ireland (1869); the Irish Land Act (1870); Forester's Education Act (1870), which made elementary education available to Welsh and English children between the ages of five and 13; the Ballot Act of 1872, which instituted secret ballots for local and general elections; laws restricting the high courts (1873); and many others.

4. Otto von Bismarck (1815-1898), German statesman who is considered the founder of the German Empire. For nearly three decades he shaped the fortunes of Germany: from 1862 to 1873 as prime minister of Prussia and from 1871 to 1890 as Germany's first Chancellor; and as prime minister of Prussia when he devoted himself to the task of uniting Germany. Victories in the war of 1866 with Austria and the Franco-German

footnote 4 continued on next page

"The greatness of British statesmen – and I am thinking here, for example, of Gladstone – is that they acknowledge the law as the ultimate authority; and the greatness of German statesmen – and I am thinking now of Bismarck – is that they come before God in free responsibility. In this, neither can claim to be superior to the other. The ultimate question remains open and must be kept open, for in either case he can live only by the grace of God and by forgiveness. Each of these men, the one who is bound by the law and the one who acts in free responsibility, must hear and bow before the accusation of the other. Neither can be the judge of the other. It is always for God to judge."[5]

In spite of what he says about neither one being superior to the other, anyone who has read Bonhoeffer's discussion of personal responsibility is bound to see how heavily he leans toward Bismarck's side.

We must remember that, for Bonhoeffer, the important concept is not the individual but the person. The difference between the two is considerable. The concept of individual suggests interchangeable units that, therefore, are in no way unique or distinctive. It is a concept set opposite to collectivity, which is but the sum of individual units. If erected into doctrine, one would say that individualism is the opposite of collectivism. The concept of person, on the other hand, suggests something – or, rather, someone – unique and, therefore, never interchangeable. "The person, then, as a freely created spiritual being, can be defined as the unity of a self-conscious and spontaneous active spirit."

The concept of a person is related to and inseparable from that of community. There is no difference in kind involved here. The community "is self-conscious, and has a will of its own, though only in the form of its members. ... 'I-Thou' relations also are possible between a collective person and an individual person. For the collective person is in fact also an individual person."[6]

It is through this concept of person that Bonhoeffer avoids the usual

---

War (1870-71) instigated the kingdoms of Bavaria, Württemberg, Baden and Hesse to join the North German Alliance, an alliance of Prussia and 17 northern German states created by Bismarck in 1866. This led to the declaration of the German Empire in 1870 and the proclamation of King William I of Prussia as German Emperor in Versailles in 1871. The imperial constitution was declared in April 1871 and Bismarck was appointed imperial chancellor. His greatest achievements, however, were administrative reforms, developing a common currency, a central bank, and a single code of commercial and civil law for Germany. Bismarck also became the first statesman in Europe to devise a comprehensive scheme of social security to counter the Social Democrats, offering workers insurance against accident, sickness and old age. In foreign affairs, he was a master of alliances and counter-alliances.

5. Bonhoeffer; *Ethics*; p. 209.

6. Bonhoeffer; *The Communion of Saints*; pp. 39, 51.

antithesis of individualism and collectivism. He could have borrowed his concept from Spain, where he lived for a time, but the language he uses makes it evident that he got the term from the existentialists. He must have done this reluctantly because he had a low opinion of psychotherapists and existentialist philosophers. We should "not regard psychotherapy and existentialist philosophy as God's pioneers. The importunity of all these people is far too un-aristocratic for the Word of God to ally itself with them. The Word of God is far removed from this revolt of mistrust, this revolt from below."[7]

We must remember that, for Bonhoeffer, everything authoritative and truly real is Christocentric and, therefore, derived from Scripture – that it always comes from the top down and never from the bottom up.

It is notable that nowhere in Bonhoeffer's theology does the person stand alone. He always is involved simultaneously in each of the mandates as a father or mother, as a worker, as a subject or citizen, and as a church member. Moreover, in each of these four mandates, the person is part of a complex network of relationships. Obviously, this involvement is a denial of classic individualism. Bonhoeffer, though, would argue that it is just as much a denial of collectivism, since each mandate lies directly under God's control. Sovereignty resides solely in God. Going one step further, by his use of the concept of vocation (i.e., deputyship), Bonhoeffer achieves the same type of limitation on the claims of occupational groups.

In all these respects, Bonhoeffer is profoundly German, but he is German in the ancient medieval tradition that admitted only *group* individualism – if it could be said to countenance any individualism at all. It certainly is a conservative tradition with its emphasis on the organic nature of life and the external nature of authority in God. By the same token, it harmonizes rather nicely with contemporary political conservatism that distrusts centralized power and advocates a considerable measure of institutional autonomy, especially in the economic realm. Only in the laissez-faire overtones and the faith in the efficacy of free competition would this type of contemporary political conservatism be at odds with Bonhoeffer.

Bonhoeffer's position on the institutional church is very hostile to liberalism and social activism. He has no confidence whatsoever in church pronouncements or intervention in matters political, social and economic. It is not merely that the church has no special knowledge and competence in such matters but, rather, that church pronouncements or intervention lie outside of its mandate, which is limited to the proclamation of the gospel.

Beyond this lies the still more important point that, in any case, such

---

7.   Bonhoeffer; *Letters and Papers from Prison*; p. 193.

pronouncements could not be God's commands. God's commands do not take the form of generalized directives such as Christian programs, party platforms, legislative statutes and political ideologies. Bonhoeffer's comment about the need to reach the proletariat proves rather than disproves this point:

> "I believe that the attempt must be made to bring proletarians into the service of the church, and that the future of our church depends largely on our getting preachers from proletarian circles, in the first instance, of course, for the working-class congregations in the big cities. I also think that we should attract children from working-class families to go on in the Sunday schools to be teachers, and that schools should be established in which likely youngsters from working-class backgrounds should be prepared for service in the church."[8]

Surely, no more traditional attitude toward the problem of relating proletariat and church can be found than this one, for all the adjustments are to be made by the proletariat and none by the church. On the other hand, it should be pointed out that Bonhoeffer was only 21 years old when he wrote these words and that, in later years, he came to the conclusion that the problem was far more complex than integrating the proletariat and other non-Christian groups into the established institutional church.

All in all, Bonhoeffer is a typical Lutheran and accurately reflects Lutheranism's well-known political and social passivity. As we have seen, even in the case of the persecution of the Jews, he did not feel that the Church should speak to the government, even indirectly! Thus, in the matter of the involvement of the institutional church in political activity, it would be difficult to find a theologian who is more conservative than Bonhoeffer.

But there is another side to Bonhoeffer – namely, the vehement protest of a man, persecuted and condemned to death, against the institutional church for what he saw as nothing less than its betrayal of Christ. It is this side of Bonhoeffer that has appealed so strongly to American liberals. Nevertheless, these liberals are mistaken because Bonhoeffer actually goes much further than they do on at least one point. The liberals who control the mainline Protestant denominations, the National Council of Churches, the World Council of Churches and the World Alliance of Reformed Churches still believe that the institutional church should be deeply involved in social causes and vigorously active in politics. They still have hope for the institutional church. Bonhoeffer does not, and that is why he is not a liberal but a radical. As a Lutheran, he never believed in the involve-

---

8. Bonhoeffer; *The Communion of Saints*; pp. 192-193.

ment of the institutional church in politics anyway, so the leap to radicalism was easier.

What is so easily misleading is that, when Bonhoeffer says that the world come of age is a religion-less world in which the Church has disappeared, he does not mean the world without Christ and without the Church as God intended it to be. The entire world in all its aspects must be claimed for and won to Christ and permeated with his spirit. The institutional church must be replaced by the true Church, which essentially is a fellowship of Christian persons, independent of organization and structure. No one who wrote *Life Together* could possibly disbelieve in the Church. The mission of the Church is what it always was:

> "The Church must share in the secular problems of ordinary human life, not dominating, but helping and serving. It must tell men of every calling what it means to live in Christ, to exist for others. In particular, our own Church will have to take the field against the vices of hubris, power-worship, envy, and humbug, as the roots of all evil. It will have to speak of moderation, purity, trust, loyalty, constancy, patience, discipline, humility, contentment, and modesty."[9]

Once again, it is important to underscore the fact that Bonhoeffer's critique of the institutional church is that it lacks the Christian authenticity described in the above quotation. Relevance is a secondary consideration. A Church that authentically is Christian automatically is relevant.

How is the proclamation of the gospel in a world come of age to be made and how is it to transform that world in the light of Jesus Christ?

We have seen that Bonhoeffer reserves this task to the fourth mandate, the Church, but that he also feels that the institutional church has betrayed its trust. Who, then, is to carry out this task? The pre-millenialists would say: Christ himself, wait for the Second Coming. But this is not Bonhoeffer's answer.

Bonhoeffer's conviction is that the present world will be conquered and transformed in the same way as the Roman Empire; that is, by the personal obedience of millions of individual Christians, living in Christian fellowship, each responding to the categorical commands of God as disclosed in particular situations at particular times. As disciples of the Master, each individual Christian will identify himself with all whom he comes into contact with regardless of merit or status, serving all and lording it over none. As the occasion presents itself, he will teach, preach, heal, liberate and give.

That service will be to all men, but most especially to the poor, the sick,

---

9.   Bonhoeffer; *Letters and Papers from Prison*; p. 211.

the mentally disturbed, the crippled, the uneducated, the underprivileged, the victims of every form of exploitation and oppression and injustice. No master plan will be necessary. As each Christian, acting within the scope of his vocation, responds to the call of discipleship in complete obedience to God's commands, a general design or pattern will emerge that foreshadows the Kingdom of God on Earth. Acting through his Church, conceived as a fellowship of people responding to the call of discipleship, God brings order out of the multitude of individual personal decisions.

It is upon the collective impact of this Christian fellowship on the world come of age, as it was on the world of the declining Roman Empire, that Bonhoeffer places his hope – not on the American way of life of which he was so critical, not on liberalism or any ideology, not on governmental power, not on the institutional church, not even on the Confessional Church of Germany that he helped to form and which defied Hitler.

As we contemplate Bonhoeffer's solution to the crisis of our age, certain similarities immediately come to mind. We think of Adam Smith's "invisible hand," which supposedly brings the general welfare out of the clutches of egocentric competitors. We recall the belief of the Enlightenment that there is a mysterious and unalterable harmony in the universe that governs not only the organic and inorganic spheres, but the human sphere as well.

The similarities, however, are accidental and far removed from what Bonhoeffer has in mind. For him, the essential thing is that Jesus is Lord, as the original creed of the Church first put it. The trouble with Adam Smith's invisible hand is not that it is invisible, but that it is not the hand of Jesus. The trouble with the Deists of the Enlightenment and the Stoics of antiquity is that their god is not a person and bears no resemblance to the God of ancient Israel, who was incarnate in Jesus of Nazareth and lives on as the Holy Spirit. Only a person can create order. Curiously enough, it also is true that only a person can create disorder. Bonhoeffer's comment probably would be that this apparent contradiction is an evidence of freedom, that a world of people cannot be a deterministic world no matter how many limitations are placed upon it, that a truly human sphere is one in which personal responsibility has meaning.

How much importance will political leaders ascribe to Bonhoeffer's solution to the crisis of our age? Probably none or, at most, very little. The language and concepts are completely unfamiliar. More to the point: There is no handle for the political leader to grasp. What can you do? In the unlikely event that the politician somehow and somewhere heard of Bonhoeffer's theology, his answer probably will be: "Nothing!"

If we change the question from "will" to "should," however, we will get a different answer. Only the most enlightened politicians, whom we honor by the name of statesmen, are moved by the power of ideas. But all politicians, whether statesmen or not, are moved by *conditions*. They also are very much limited by them. Whoever or whatever can alter conditions can imprison or liberate the politician.

It is at this precise moment that Bonhoeffer's solution becomes politically relevant. If the Church as he conceives it actually turns out to have the impact on the world he believes it will have, conditions will be radically altered and, consequently, politicians will give it their respectful attention – but not before. Until and unless this happens, Bonhoeffer's solution will be ruled out of consideration (in the unlikely event it is even considered at all) as unrealistic, utopian and unscientific.

Bonhoeffer probably would be extremely displeased by a supporting reference to Rousseau, but the fact remains that it was Rousseau who said the legislator (i.e., statesman, state builder, founding father) must be able to change human nature if he is to achieve anything. In these words centuries earlier, Rousseau voiced Bonhoeffer's thought. However disagreeable and distasteful it must be to the secular mind, the missionary must precede the politician.

Major Works
of Dietrich Bonhoeffer

Creation and Fall (SCM Press; London; 1937).

No Rusty Swords: Letters, Lectures and Notes, 1928-1936 (Harper & Row, Publishers; New York and Evanston, Ill.; 1947).

Letters and Papers from Prison (SCM Press; London; 1953).

Life Together (New York and Evanston, Ill.: Harper & Row, 1954).

Ethics (New York: Macmillan, 1955).

Act and Being (Harper & Row, Publishers; New York and Evanston, Ill.; 1956).

The Cost of Discipleship (Macmillan; New York; 1955).

The Communion of Saints: A Dogmatic Inquiry into the Sociology of the Church (Harper & Row, Publishers; New York and Evanston, Ill.; 1960).

Christ the Center (Harper & Row; New York; 1960).

I Loved This People (John Knox Press; Richmond, Va.; 1964).

The Way to Freedom: Letters, Lectures and Notes, 1935-1939 (Harper & Row, Publishers; New York and Evanston, Ill.; 1966).

True Patriotism: Letters, Lectures and Notes, 1939-1945 (Harper & Row; New York; 1973).

Emil Brunner

Contents

Introduction

Emil Brunner[1] was a great theologian who has not received the recognition he deserves. During his earlier years, he was closely associated with Barth, but always it was "Barth and Brunner," with Brunner coming in second – and secondary – place. The differences that later sprang up between Barth and Brunner did not result in equality of reputation. Barth was much more radical in his challenge than Brunner, who was a moderate in comparison. But moderation is not exciting, it is not "news," and it has a tendency to conceal those who espouse it.

Nor did Brunner enjoy the reputation or exert the influence of Tillich. Tillich, of course, spent many years teaching, lecturing and writing in the United States. It was only natural that he was widely known in this country. In addition, Tillich had that snob appeal that comes to those who use "big words," deal in abstractions and indulge in fancy displays of erudition. He was attractive to the kind of person who comments: "He is so profound I don't understand a word he says."

Brunner, on the other hand, wrote simple and lucid declaratory sentences free of ponderous dependent clauses and usually free of an unnecessary display of erudition.

Unlike Bonhoeffer, Brunner did not have the advantage of being a Christian martyr or the author of catchy phrases like "religion-less Christianity." There probably was a temperamental difference between the two men, a difference accentuated by the dissimilarity of their lives and their countries. In Bonhoeffer, there was a vehement protest that was contagious and communicated an explosive quality to his language.

Brunner, on the other hand, was more calm and objective so that, even when he was making the same points as Bonhoeffer, his words did not have the same impetus or punch. There always will be a difference in quality, if not in substance, between a passionate indictment of society and a calm critique of that society. It is well to remember, too, that Bonhoeffer came out of the Lutheran tradition, whereas Brunner came out of the Reformed tradition.

In spite of differences in traditional roots, temperament and theological language, however, Brunner, Barth and Bonhoeffer stand together as the-

---

1. Emil Brunner (1889–1966).

ologians committed to the new orthodoxy. All three rejected fundamentalism and all three accepted the contributions of Biblical scholarship and, in some measure, the insights of the so-called "Higher Criticism."

Otherwise, however, the three men were united in their rejection of theological liberalism and in their commitment to salvation by grace through faith, the authority of Scripture, and the divinity and centrality of Jesus Christ. It is that commitment that justifies their being classified as neo-orthodox.[2]

---

2. Neo-orthodox is defined as being related to a 20th century movement in Protestant theology that is characterized by a reaction against liberalism and an emphasis on various Scripturally-based Reformation doctrines.

CHAPTER ONE

Brunner and Revelation

B runner takes the same position as Barth and Bonhoeffer – and anyone who is not just a philosopher or any theologian who is not just a sociologist of religion – that God can be known only through revelation.

We do not find, stumble upon or discover God. He discloses himself to us, or else we would not know him or anything about him. Our intellect cannot grasp him on its own initiative because the reality of God "is far above all human doctrinal conceptions."[1] Revelation is "not a starkly objective process" because it also is "inwardly subjective" and, therefore, should be characterized as "transitive" to include both aspects and underscore the personal nature of all revelation.[2] "Revelation and faith – this is our principal article of belief which determines all else – are personal encounter."[3]

Does this concept of revelation as personal encounter mean that Brunner's theology is Christocentric? He certainly claims that it is: "We must begin with the statement that the true, valid knowledge of God can only be gained in His revelation, in Jesus Christ."[4] But there are other forms of revelation. God reveals himself in his creation.[5] Thus, to say that pagans "have no knowledge of God at all" is "a foolish statement, and one which is utterly contrary to experience," and which "does not occur anywhere in the

---

1. Brunner; *The Christian Doctrine of God: Dogmatics I*, 14. Hereinafter cited as *Dogmatics I*. For a full citation of Brunner's works, see the Bibliography at the end of Book IV.

2. *Ibid.*; p. 29.

3. Brunner; *The Christian Doctrine of the Church, Faith, and the Consummation: Dogmatics III*, 11. Hereinafter cited as *Dogmatics III*. For a full citation of Brunner's works, see the Bibliography at the end of Book IV.

4. Brunner; *Dogmatics I*; p.168.

5. Brunner; *The Christian Doctrine of Creation and Redemption: Dogmatics II*, 6. Hereinafter cited as *Dogmatics II*. For a full citation of Brunner's works, see the Bibliography at the end of Book IV.

Bible."[6] On the other hand, all revelation of God "is to be understood 'Christologically.' There is no other revelation in creation save that which derives its being from the Eternal Son or the Logos." It is true that there always will be much in revelation as reflected in creation that Christians are incapable of understanding Christologically in the full sense of the term. And, of course, pagans who have never heard of Christ could hardly be expected to think Christologically at all. However: "We have indeed no right to assert, as some pessimists do, that sinful man as such cannot know *anything* aright. This kind of pessimism is out of touch both with the Bible and with experience."[7]

It follows, therefore, that there is such a thing as natural theology, since it is "an anthropological fact, which no one can deny."[8] Brunner, though, is careful to add that natural theology is kind of a mixed bag: "Natural Theology is therefore not, as that medieval doctrine believes, a reliable basis for Christian theology, but a very contradictory phenomenon, in which both truth and error, divine revelation and human delusions are involved."[9] Neither is he enthusiastic about comparative religion: "To try to discover an 'original moral common sense' behind these influences of the various religions is simply a wild-goose chase."[10] His skepticism extends to those efforts that seek to distill and combine the essence of different Christian creeds, which he describes as "cloudy ecumenism" and "supra-eclecticism."[11]

In spite of all these qualifications and reservations that are designed to safeguard the personal nature of revelation and the indispensability of Jesus Christ, Brunner parts company with Barth by seeing the revelation of God in Nature; i.e., the orders of creation. Brunner says, "There is an order in 'Nature' which we can naturally perceive. There are regular happenings, laws of nature and the like. ... There would be no human activity at all without a knowledge of these constants, and without confidence in their constancy." This constancy is the great preservative force of the universe by which, "whether we are aware of it or not, we are relying on God's faithfulness." It follows that "just as there is a 'natural revelation' so there is a 'natural grace:' that is, a grace which is given to all existence, which must be

---

6. Brunner; *Dogmatics I*; p. 121.

7. Brunner; *Dogmatics II*; pp. 29, 27.

8. Brunner; *Dogmatics I*; p. 133.

9. Brunner; *Dogmatics II*; p. 23.

10. Brunner; *The Divine Imperative: A Study in Christian Ethics*; p. 33. For a full citation of Brunner's works, see the Bibliography at the end of Book IV.

11. Brunner; *Dogmatics I*; p. 82.

distinguished from the grace of redemption."[12]

The difference essentially is that between a reprieve and a pardon. It is an adaptation or reformulation of Calvin's dictum that natural revelation is enough to convict us, but not enough to save us, and of his distinction between common grace and redeeming grace.

The supreme revelation of God in Jesus Christ is mediated to us through Scripture, Brunner says. "As in the case of the Reformers, we must express our first principle thus: the Scriptures have the authority of a norm, and the basis for this principle is this: The Scriptures possess this authority because they are the *primary witness* to the revelation of God in Jesus Christ."

The Bible has many peculiarities: It is a message both divine and human, with characteristics from each; it is a narrative, rather than being doctrinal in approach; it is the source of authority, rather than authority itself; it is confessional, rather than propositional in nature; and it has no "teaching authority" in matters of secular knowledge. Obviously, Brunner is no fundamentalist, since he sees the Bible as being "coloured by the frailty and imperfection of all that is human."[13] Admitting human imperfection, and adhering to the Protestant principle of *sola scriptura*, presents Brunner with something of a difficulty. He stated the difficulty thus:

> "We cannot believe in Jesus the Christ without the Bible; but we should not believe in Jesus the son of God because the Bible says so."[14]

No more than Barth does Brunner intend this concept of "witness" to undermine the authority of Scripture and draw a wedge between the Word-in-the-flesh and the Word-in-the-script. But how do you accept the findings of Biblical scholarship and, at the same time, remain faithful to the teaching of the Great Reformers of the sixteenth century? Brunner answers this question with a striking analogy that is worth quoting in full:

> "Is everything true that is to be found in the Bible? Let me draw a some-what modern analogy by way of answering this question. Everyone has seen the trade slogan 'His Master's Voice.' If you buy a gramophone record you are told that you will hear the Master Caruso. Is that true? Of course! But really his voice? Certainly! And yet – there are some noises made by the machine which are not the master's voice, but the scratching of the steel needle upon the hard disk! For only by means of the record can you hear 'the master's voice.' So, too, is it with the Bible. It makes the real Master's voice audible – really His voice, His words, what He wants to say. But

---

12. Brunner; *Dogmatics II*; pp. 151, 152, 153.

13. Brunner; *Dogmatics II*; pp. 151, 152, 153.

14. Brunner; *Dogmatics II*; p. 342.

there are incidental noises accompanying, just because God speaks His word through the voice of man."[15]

A Christ-centered faith is necessarily a Bible-centered faith: "Christian faith is faith in Christ, and Christ meets us and speaks to us in the Bible. Christian faith is Bible faith."[16]

Another rather lengthy quotation is needed to show how Brunner conceived the relation of revelation in nature and revelation in the Bible and the connection of both to Jesus Christ:

"The book of Nature does not suffice to reveal the Creator aright to such unintelligent and obdurate pupils as ourselves.

"The Creator has therefore given us another, even more clearly written book in which to know Him – the Bible. In it He has also drawn His own portrait so that we must all perceive that He is truly the Creator. The name of this picture is Jesus Christ. In Him we know the Creator for the first time as He really is. For in Him we know God's purpose for His creation."[17]

It is obvious from his discussion of Scripture that Brunner finds many more scratchings and background noises in the Old Testament than in the New Testament. How does he explain this? By making a distinction between word and deed, therefore rejecting Barth's idea that when God speaks, he acts. "The fact that He Himself takes the place of the spoken word is precisely the category which distinguishes the Old Testament revelation – the revelation through speech – from the New Testament revelation, the revelation in Christ."

Brunner's position also could be stated this way: When God gave us the Ten Commandments, he spoke; when he became incarnate in Jesus Christ, he acted. This position has the advantage of disposing of the doctrine of verbal inspiration,[18] a doctrine that has had "disastrous results" for all to see.[19] But the New Testament is not one whit less verbal than the Old Testament. The point is obvious, but Brunner disregards it nonetheless. Why?

---

15. Brunner; *Our Faith*; p. 19. For a full citation of Brunner's works, see the Bibliography at the end of Book IV.

16. *Ibid.*; p. 17.

17. *Ibid.*; p. 25.

18. Doctrine of verbal inspiration. The belief that the Bible is the verbally inspired word of God – i.e., that God directed the writing of the Bible on a word-by-word basis, which meant that the writers were protected from putting down even as much as one word that might inadvertently mislead readers or incorrectly communicate the truths God wanted known. This belief in the Bible is different from that which sees it as a book with only concepts and ideas that were divinely inspired.

19. Brunner; *Dogmatics I*; pp. 27, 28.

The explanation appears to be that he wants no social, economic and political model to be constructed from Old Testament materials by some overzealous and misguided Christian.

"Not only the political order in the narrower sense of the word, but the economic, social and family order of the people of Israel is unique in history. Hence any possibility of revival, or direct borrowing, is ruled out."

We also should not look for such a model in the Ten Commandments:

"When we wish to know what is just in the State, in economics, in society, marriage and the family, we receive no help from the Decalogue, but can only attach to its commandments what we have learned in other ways."[20]

Unfortunately, Brunner says mistaken views of Scripture "are still bearing their own fruit."[21] His attitude toward the Old Testament again is illustrated in his comment that the study of Christian doctrine should begin with the Prologue of the fourth Gospel and not the Book of Genesis.[22]

---

20. Brunner; *Justice and the Social Order*; pp. 110, 112. For a full citation of Brunner's works, see the Bibliography at the end of Book IV.

21. Brunner; *Dogmatics I;* p. 28.

22. Brunner; *Dogmatics II*; p. 6.

CHAPTER TWO

The Will of God

The idea of the will is a central aspect of Brunner's theology. It is a consequence of God being a person: "God is pure personality; man is not." A person is a living being because he acts; i.e., has a will. Principles, rules, concepts, conditions and things have many properties, but they have no will. Only people have will. That is why Brunner does not hesitate to say of God, very categorically and very succinctly: "He is will."[1]

The idea of command is included in that of will and cannot be separated from it. At many points, what Brunner says about command follows Barth very closely: "God's command is wholly personal, therefore it is wholly concrete."[2] It comes at a particular time and cannot be confined to it: "Here, too, there is only one consideration – the command of the hour."[3] We recognize here one of Barth's favorite phrases, but Brunner makes no reference to this connection, nor does he use quotation marks. The parallel, however, is unmistakable. On the other hand, Brunner is careful to warn us that there are no gaps between commands: "The Divine Command is imposed on every moment; there are not moral holidays. The command is constant in intent and variable in content."[4]

God's will is "the foundation of all true morality," and he says there is no such thing as "an 'autonomous' ethic … independent of the will of God."[5] That values are "independent entities" is nothing but a "phantasmagoria."[6]

---

1. Brunner; *Dogmatics I*; pp. 140, 159.

2. Brunner; *The Divine Imperative*; p. 198.

3. Brunner; *God and Man: Four Essays on the Nature of Personality*; p. 100. For a full citation of Brunner's works, see the Bibliography at the end of Book IV.

4. Brunner; *The Divine Imperative*; pp. 119, 134.

5. Brunner; *Dogmatics I*; pp.166-167.

6. Brunner; *The Divine Imperative*; p. 194.

God's will is the source of natural law: "What we call the 'laws of nature' are God's orders of creation." And natural law is the "divine thread of preservation above the abyss of nothingness."[7]

Contrary to the teaching of St. Thomas Aquinas,[8] however, there is no such thing as eternal law. The reason Brunner gives for rejecting this concept is that, unlike its Creator, the created world is not eternal and "all laws, whether natural or moral, belong to the created world."[9]

God's will also is the source of the civil law, though not directly, since we receive it from the state. Brunner describes this law as a "rude, arbitrary, coercive, external authority" made mandatory by God to preserve "life in the created order tainted by sin" and for which we should be grateful. The civil law, therefore, "is necessary for the sake of love, because it is necessary for the sake of life."[10]

If God's will is the source of all morality, law, values and life itself, the discovery of that will assumes an overriding importance. In answering this question, one of the first things Brunner does is to reject conscience, that "flaming sword which drives us away from the presence of God and ourselves and hides Him from us."[11] His rejection is startling enough, in the sense of being unconventional for a Christian, to deserve an extended quotation:

> "Conscience is something far more sinister than all these images employed by rationalizing methods of interpretation. For the sinister thing about conscience is precisely that it has nothing to do with God at all, that it attacks man like an alien, dark, hostile power, as it has been represented in ancient myths and by the great poets of ancient and modern times – who in this respect are so much wiser than the philosophers."[12]

How does Brunner explain conscience, which, after all, is a universal fact of experience? Interestingly enough, he offers a thoroughly secular

---

7. Brunner; *Dogmatics II*; pp. 25, 34.

8. St. Thomas Aquinas (1225 or 1227-1274); Catholic philosopher and theologian and one of the 33 Doctors of the Church. His work gave birth to the Thomistic school of philosophy, which shifted the influence of medieval philosophy away from Plato and toward Aristotle. This philosophy long was the official dogma of the Roman Catholic Church, which considered Aquinas to be its greatest theologian. His major works include *Summa contra Gentiles, Summa Theologica, The Principles of Nature, On Being and Essence and On Truth.*

9. Brunner; *Christianity and Civilisation*; Vol. I; p. 24. For a full citation of Brunner's works, see the Bibliography at the end of Book IV.

10. Brunner; *The Divine Imperative*; pp. 142, 143.

11. *Ibid.*; p. 157.

12. *Ibid.*; p. 156.

answer – an answer that is quite standard today among Christians and non-Christians:

> "If guilt, responsibility and obligation are objectively explained, namely as the product of mere social convention, then conscience too is 'recognized' as a mere product of education. It is then nothing more than the experience which human society has had of what is useful to it, and which now confronts me as what society demands of me. But when I 'recognize' that, I am set free from its imperative, because now I know how this imperative came into being. Because I have discovered the mechanism, hitherto unknown to me, through which so-called conscience originates, it has lost for me its normative and mysteriously imperative power."[13]

Though Brunner's answer is quite secular, he does not see its consequence as secular at all – quite the contrary. The deliverance of man from the tyranny of conscience means that he is free to live in accordance with the will of God.

With conscience out of the way, we are brought back to the original question: How do we know the will of God? Brunner's answer is: The Christian knows it by faith and the non-Christian knows it by reason, though the two avenues are not mutually exclusive. It is true that Brunner does not put it quite so bluntly or in those words, but that is what his answer amounts to. It is made possible by his concept of revelation, which makes room for revelation in nature and history, as well as in Jesus Christ. To be sure, revelation in Jesus Christ alone is final and completely sufficient, but revelation in the orders of creation also is authentic and valid, albeit partial and insufficient for salvation. Thus, Brunner parts company with Barth, who rejects any and every revelation other than or outside of Jesus Christ. Barth takes his stand with Calvin. For Brunner, there really are two worlds which, while they overlap and commingle, nevertheless are distinct. Both worlds are ruled by the will of God, but that will takes two different forms. One takes the form of love and is perceived by the believer through reason.

When we think of the first world, the believer's world in which God's will is expressed and understood as love, it is important to remember this: "God is not primarily the lawgiver, but the lifegiver."[14] The connection between law giving and life giving is love. As previously noted, law "is necessary for the sake of love, because it is necessary for the sake of life." The whole of the law was summarized by Jesus himself as love: Thou shalt *love*.[15] All the specific commandments prescribed in the Old Testament "are

---

13. Brunner; *Dogmatics III*; p. 255.

14. Brunner; *Our Faith*; p. 54.

15. Matthew 5:43.

authentic 'expositions' of the One Command. It is part of the condescension of God towards our weakness that He does not merely tell us to do *one* thing, but a variety of things. 'The Commandments' are the god-given example of what His will and His love mean in the concrete situations of life."[16] Law in the Old Testament is given "in order to educate men for the reception of the Ultimate, and to make them ready for it."[17] The same kind of interpretation applies to the New Testament: "It is of the utmost importance to note how unsystematic, how 'casual' are all the commandments which are scattered through the New Testament."

Scattered through the New Testament and condensed in parts of the Old Testament, "The Law is the 'schoolmaster to bring in Christ.'"[18] In using such descriptive terms as exposition, example and schoolmaster, Brunner is pointing to what the law is intended to achieve. The law also is intended to protect what already has been achieved and, in that respect, is "like a wall thrown about a glorious garden."[19]

It is when we consider what Brunner says about love that we understand why he does not identify will with command. Will includes command, of course, but goes beyond it. Actually, it is a misnomer to call Jesus' summary of the law a commandment – even as the sole or greatest commandment – if we use that word in the sense of compulsion. "In itself compulsion is contrary to love; it is sinful."[20] Love cannot be commanded: "Enforced love is not love at all. ... Love is the most freely willed of any activity of which we are able to think."[21]

To understand the commandment "Thou shalt love" as law or duty would be to negate the whole experience of personal encounter because the "effect of 'law' is to make God's will impersonal"[22] and, whenever love is understood in that sense, "confusion and anarchy result."[23] Love is a gift,[24] it means identification,[25] and it transcends justice because justice is "a kind of

16. Brunner; *The Divine Imperative*; pp. 143, 135.

17. Brunner; *Dogmatics II*; p. 228.

18. Brunner; *The Divine Imperative*; pp. 136, 143.

19. Brunner; *Our Faith*; p. 56.

20. Brunner; *The Divine Imperative*; p. 445.

21. Brunner; *Truth as Encounter;* p. 98. For a full citation of Brunner's works, see the Bibliography at the end of Book IV.

22. Brunner; *Dogmatics II*; p. 222.

23. Brunner; *Dogmatics III*; p. 310.

24. Brunner; *Dogmatics II*; p. 224.

25. Brunner; *The Divine Imperative*; p. 326.

interior morality."[26] When love appears, "something visible begins to break forth from invisible faith."[27] Love is "the essence of man's personality," greater than reason and creative spirit, and experienced only in communion – communion with God and communion with man.[28] Love is also the ultimate purpose of creation: "The love of God is the *causa finalis* of the Creation. In Jesus Christ this ideal reason for the Creation is revealed."[29]

It should be pointed out that Brunner is not denying that God is Love when he says that God is Will because, at the divine level, the two are one and the same. The initially hostile reaction that Brunner's statement is likely to provoke comes from an erroneous identification of love with emotion or sentimentality. Love in the sense of *agape* is essentially good*will* toward all mankind, deserving and undeserving. The Gospel of John says that God so loved the world that he gave his only begotten Son that the world through him might be saved.

Giving is an act of will – not a sentiment, emotion, philosophical disposition, attitude, or instinct. Furthermore, giving is free. It neither is internally nor externally imposed. For man, love is a response to a "command" that no longer is an act of necessity, but an act of will. For God, of course, the question does not arise, for who could command him anything?

But, with man, the question always arises for the reason that what man does never is purely an expression of love and, thus, an act of will, but a mixture of will and necessity. It is Brunner's insistence on will, interpreted as love, that purges his concept of the unpleasant military flavor it has in Bonhoeffer's usage.

---

26. Brunner; *Justice and the Social Order*; pp. 116, 22.

27. Brunner; *Our Faith*; p. 84.

28. Brunner; *The Scandal of Christianity: The Gospel as Stumbling block to Modern Man*; p. 59. For a full citation of Brunner's works, see the Bibliography at the end of Book IV.

29. Brunner; *Dogmatics II*; p. 13.

CHAPTER THREE

Sin and the World
of Law and Politics

Before entering the world in which the will of God is understood as law perceived through reason, it is necessary to inquire why there has to be such a world at all. The answer, of course, is sin.

What is sin? "Moral evil, understood as sin, is not that which is not yet good, but that which is no longer good. Sin is not underdeveloped good, but spoilt and perverted good."[1] What causes good to become spoilt and perverted? Essentially, it is rebellion, "for sin means turning away from God."[2]

In another place, Brunner identifies sin with godlessness and alienation from God. It is not solely deliberate: "His sin is deeper than his awareness of it." Although sin, in its effects, "extends far into the unconscious,"[3] we cannot understand it or cope with it "by psychological introspection. It is part of the nature of sin that it darkens our view, that we always try to excuse ourselves."[4]

Where does sin come from? What causes it? Bad qualities (and good qualities, too) are inherited, but sin "can never be inherited." It is not, therefore, to be accounted for biologically. Neither can it be equated with mental illness, though medical science has come to recognize a relationship between the two.[5] Is society, then, responsible? The answer here also is negative, in spite of the fact that Brunner lays great stress on social factors. The following passage illustrates both points vividly and clearly:

"For is it not true that we are all connected with one another by hidden

---

1. Brunner; *Christianity and Civilisation*; Vol. I; p. 54.

2. Brunner; *Dogmatics I*; p.17.

3. Brunner; *Dogmatics II*; pp. 105, 95, 130.

4. Brunner; *The Scandal of Christianity*; p. 67.

5. Brunner; *Dogmatics II*; pp. 105, 130.

roots, like the runners of a strawberry patch, all of whose plants have developed from the one parent stock? We are not only connected with each other in our life-root but our connection is precisely evil. There is a kind of common 'sin fluid' that flows through the whole root system, and yet each individual knows it to be his own guilt."[6]

The fact that the social aspects of sin are not the cause of individual sin is no reason to minimize them. They most are readily visible in the state: "Every State represents human sin on the large scale; in history, in the growth of every State the most brutal, anti-divine forces have taken a share, to an extent unheard of in the individual life, save in that of some prominent criminals."[7] In fact, Brunner goes even further and says: "Evil which takes shape in social wrong, or is incorporated in institutions, or as a mass phenomenon, is worse than evil in any individual form, in isolation." In any case, whether in its social or individual aspects, "sin is a source of corruption, an element of social disintegration, of conflict, of destruction."[8]

Shall we then put the blame on Satan? That idea and the associated idea of exorcism have achieved considerable popularity in recent years, but Brunner would have rejected these ideas had he lived to observe their popularity. He does, however, take Satan seriously, for "there are also extraordinary phenomena ... which do suggest the notion of the Diabolic, the Satanic, or at least of the Demonic." This kind of evil is no subjective figment of the imagination: "As a force of a super-human kind it stands over against man. It is an 'objective reality;' that is, it is a reality which is objectively encountered, not merely a reality within the mind."

But we are not to blame Satan for sin. He does not create or cause sin, he merely exploits it: "Since man is dominated by sin he stands under demonic influences. But this order is never reversed. The dominion of demonic forces is never the reason for sin." The "Satanic element" wears "a numinous halo ... which fascinates and allures by the magic of its attraction," but which still is largely "a *terra incognita*,[9] waiting to be explored." The sinner is disarmed and defenseless against the onslaught of Satan, which is as deadly as it is alluring. Jesus Christ alone was invulnerable because, being sinless, the onslaught came exclusively from the outside and "not from within."[10]

---

6. Brunner; *Our Faith*; p. 43.

7. Brunner; *The Divine Imperative*; p. 445

8. Brunner; *Dogmatics II*; pp. 96, 130.

9. *Terra incognita* is defined as unknown territory; an unexplored country or field of knowledge.

10. *Ibid.*; pp. 142, 143, 108, 144, 141.

Since, for Brunner, sin cannot be blamed on biology, psychology, sociology or demonology, he assigns the blame to the individual person. "Sin is an *act* – that is the first thing to say about sin." Again, he says: "Sin is the total act of the person." What makes it possible for Brunner to adopt this position is the conception of the will that he developed in connection with his doctrine of God. To be alive is to will. The will is the objective and subjective evidence of life.

But, as we have seen, to will is to act freely and not out of necessity. The result is clear: "Sin and guilt are inseparable. Where one begins the other begins; where one ends, the other ends too. Sin and guilt are co-extensive."[11] Our sins and our guilt are recorded as automatically as the speedometer of an automobile registers the number of miles traveled – and no used car dealer can turn the speedometer back! "Make no mistake about it, on that register is written our death sentence."[12] And this death sentence is not the worst part of man's predicament, since "sin deprives him of that eternal life for which he has been destined."[13]

How can man prevent his deprivation of eternal life?

Brunner's answer is the traditional Protestant one – by the grace of God through faith in Jesus Christ. What is at stake is this:

"Through Jesus Christ, for the believer Time acquires an otherwise unknown quality of decision; decision between Heaven and Hell, between being saved and being lost forever, between the absolute fulfillment and meaning and the absolute loss of all meaning. This decision took place in Jesus Christ, in the 'fullness of the time.' But that which has taken place once and for all in Jesus Christ as a universal event of History, must be 'appropriated' by the believer. He, too, is placed within the sphere of decision, and this decision is faith."[14]

Faith is the grateful response of a person's encounter with and acceptance of Jesus Christ.[15] It should be emphasized that, for Brunner, this response is indispensable and explains why he rejects Barth's universalism in vehement terms. "If there is no possibility of being lost, then the danger is not grave," and it becomes impossible "to maintain the real necessity for decision." On the other hand, Brunner just as vigorously rejects double pre-

11. *Ibid.*; pp. 109, 94, 106.

12. Brunner; *Our Faith*; p. 70.

13. Brunner; *Dogmatics II*; p. 69.

14. Brunner; *Dogmatics I*; p. 317.

15. Brunner; *The Theology of Crisis*; p. 79. For a full citation of Brunner's works, see the Bibliography at the end of Book IV.

destination[16] as a "foreign body" that is inconsistent with Calvin's otherwise "clearly Biblical" theology.[17] But if God does not control the individual's decision, who or what does? Brunner does not answer this question, other than to classify it as a mystery that only God could clear up and, so, does not dwell upon it.

The consequences of sin are not limited to the next world. They affect the present world and involve us in law and politics. The first thing to single out concerning this world of time and space that functions as a stage for law and politics is that it is sustained by the orders of creation whose existence is independent of sin, but which sets bounds to sin. These orders of creation mostly are the laws of nature, in the sense of the course of the stars and the regular seasonal changes. Physical objects obey the law of gravity, which "even the free Swiss burgher can do nothing about," and the year consists of 365 days so that "everyone knows that too – even the most inveterate Swiss Democrat."[18] For the gift of the orders of creation, he says, we should be grateful: "At every moment God 'upholds' the world above an abyss of nothingness, into which it could fall at any moment, and into which it would fall, if God were not holding it."[19]

In addition to the orders of creation, there also are orders of preservation. Unlike the former, the latter exist only because of sin. The consequences of sin must be held in some check so that life may continue and individual persons are given an opportunity for redemption in Jesus Christ. Another way of making the same point is to say that sinful man is incapable of living by the "law" of love, that he is unable to live in a world consisting wholly of personal relationships, and that he, therefore, needs the orders of preservation to circumscribe and contain his evil propensities.[20] For Brun-

---

16. In his *Institutes of the Christian Religion* (Book 3, chapter 21), John Calvin writes of double predestination: "In conformity, therefore, to the clear doctrine of the Scripture, we assert, that by an eternal and immutable counsel, God has once for all determined, both whom he would admit to salvation, and whom he would condemn to destruction. We affirm that this counsel, as far as concerns the elect, is founded on his gratuitous mercy, totally irrespective of human merit; but that to those whom he devotes to condemnation, the gate of life is closed by a just and irreprehensible, but incomprehensible, judgment. In the elect, we consider calling as an evidence of election, and justification as another token of its manifestation, till they arrive in glory, which constitutes its completion. As God seals his elect by vocation and justification, so by excluding the reprobate from the knowledge of his name and the sanctification of his Spirit, he affords an indication of the judgement that awaits them."

17. Brunner; *Dogmatics I*; pp. 314, 336, 323.

18. Brunner; *Our Faith*; pp. 52, 44, 45.

19. Brunner; *Dogmatics II*; p. 153.

20. *Ibid.*; p. 218.

ner, a few areas of human relations, notably sex and marriage, belong to the orders of creation, but most of these belong to the orders of preservation. The first order of preservation is natural law;[21] i.e., that part of it which deals with human relations. Brunner says it is perceived by the unbeliever through reason. The Christian perceives it through reason, too – wherein, of course, he has a common bond with all non-Christians – but also in the light of revelation in Jesus Christ. Because natural law is law, its effect "is to make God's will impersonal, and this corresponds to the process of breaking up 'the law' into several laws, into many 'works of the law.'" Unlike some theologians who try to make natural law and revealed law antithetical, Brunner argues that much of the revealed law "is simply the *lex naturae*[22] illuminated by the Covenant-revelation."[23] Brunner is one of the few 20th-century Protestant theologians who lay stress on natural law as an essential gift of God for the maintenance of a modicum of justice on Earth:

"Either there is a valid criterion, a justice which stands above us all, a challenge presented to us, not by us, a standard rule of justice binding on every state and every system of law, or there is no justice, but only power organized in one fashion or another and setting itself up as law. Either there exist eternal, indefeasible rights of man, or there are merely the opportunities of the lucky and the lack of opportunity of the unlucky. Either there is a sacred law, which can be appealed to against every inhuman, unjust social order, against any caprice or cruelty on the part of the state, or that sacred law is a mere dream and law is nothing but another name for the chance products of the actual elements of power in a political field of force.

"But if there is no sacred, eternal, divine, absolute law, there is no possibility of denouncing any form of law or policy or national act as unjust. If the positivistic theory of law is right, there is no possibility of waging war against the totalitarian state as a monster of injustice. Nor can we even say – it is unjust – but only it does not suit me, I do not like such things."[24]

It is hard to see how a stronger defense of natural law could be given.

The civil law is another part of the order of preservation. Like all law, it originates in the will of God, but only indirectly and, hence, "it must be made plain, particularly to the man who has sinned, that the will of God is

---

21. Natural law is defined as a body of law or a specific principle that is held to be derived from nature and binding upon human society in the absence of or in addition to positive law, or that law established or recognized by governmental authority.

22. *Lex naturae*; i.e., natural law.

23. Brunner; *Dogmatics II*; p. 228.

24. Brunner; *Justice and the Social Order*; p. 8.

also a social law, and a legal system, and indeed a political law as well."[25] In a direct sense, the state is the author of civil law: "It is the State which creates the legal system, without which human civilization would be unthinkable."[26]

Why do we have this distinction between direct and indirect authorship? Because God wants man to have a measure of freedom, without which it could not rightly be said that man was made in the image of God. "God wills to rule, but He does not wish to overwhelm us."[27] Because sin is social and individual, the civil law never is more than a partial embodiment of justice. The degree to which justice is achieved is determined by reference to natural law. Even perfect justice still would belong to this world – the world tainted by sin – and, therefore, be a part of the order of preservation because love and justice essentially and ultimately, though not immediately, are incompatible. "Justice belongs to the world of systems, not to the world of persons."[28]

Another part of God's order of preservation is the state. Brunner's attitude toward the state is rather ambivalent, a curious mixture of condemnation and sanctification. As to the first, he says categorically that "the State will never, never be governed by the Word in the sense of the Gospel," and that "the State is an institution of compulsory Law. The nature of the State is in opposition to the nature of the *Agape* of Jesus. ... The true dominion of Christ, and what we call the State, are fundamentally opposed."[29] He heaps pejorative adjectives like "rude, coercive, arbitrary, external" upon the state to describe it. "In the State, we human beings see our own sin magnified a thousand times," and the Christian "must take an active part in politics because there, if nowhere else, he learns that we are poor sinful human beings, who with the best will in the world cannot do the real good."[30] Surely, Karl Barth himself scarcely could be more denunciatory!

On the other side, Brunner goes far in the direction of Calvin, who held the state to be the gift of God's providence and more important to us than air and bread and water. "Therefore the Christian recognizes the State, which exists whether he will or no, and whose peace and security he 'inherits' as a gift of God, as a divinely salutary means of discipline; to adjust oneself to the state and to accept it is both an act of discipline and an act of

25. Brunner; *Dogmatics II*; p. 218.

26. Brunner; *The Divine Imperative*; p. 445.

27. Brunner; *Dogmatics II*; p. 216.

28. Brunner; *Justice and the Social Order*; p. 116.

29. Brunner; *Dogmatics II*; pp. 318, 302.

30. Brunner; *The Divine Imperative*; pp. 142, 445, 480.

repentance." Compulsion, while evil in itself, is nonetheless indispensable because "without this daemonic, violent power of compulsion we cannot imagine how any unity of a people could have come into existence." If Brunner's state does not quite have the exalted moral and religious missions of Calvin's state, it still is related to both and must partake of both to some extent. "It forms part of the A B C of all true statecraft that without moral foundations the State must fall to pieces."

The purpose of the state is to achieve the good of the people, a good that "must not be conceived in the narrow terms of material prosperity."[31] The good of the people includes the safeguarding of natural rights: "The state is created for the protection of those human rights which man has not from the state but from the Creator."[32] Moreover, we must recognize "that morality only grows on the foundation of religion, although it may preserve its life for a time in isolation."[33] Although Brunner denies sovereignty to the state because that belongs to God alone, he does grant it the power of life and death because, without this power, the state would cease to exist and society "would become the plaything of those who by no means abrogate their desire to kill, and there are such in every nation."[34]

That there be a state recognized as God's gift to a sin-infested humanity is a basic consideration for Brunner, but what kind of state exists is a relative consideration. In his eyes, the worst possible state is the totalitarian, "the worst and most dangerous social evil which we can conceive. It is the Satanic incarnation of our time."[35] It "bears its own logical fruit in the negation of original human rights and in the non-recognition of the dignity of man." Monstrous as the Nazi regime was, Brunner found the Soviet regime even worse because, to him, it was "the most consistent of all embodiments of the totalitarian principle."[36]

He denounced Barth for failing to take the same strong stand against communism that he had taken against Nazism. Barth, however, was not alone in being singled out by Brunner:

"It is a frightening sign of blindness that many theologians, pastors, and church leaders do not recognize this as anti-Christianity but see in Communism a very unpleasant but nevertheless discussible phenomenon. Here the word of our Lord to the Pharisees applies: 'You know how to interpret the

---

31. *Ibid.*; pp. 446, 445, 463.

32. Brunner; *Christianity and Civilisation*; Vol. II; p. 111.

33. Brunner; *The Divine Imperative*; p. 464.

34. Brunner; *Justice and the Social Order*; pp. 71, 188.

35. Brunner; *Christianity and Civilisation*; Vol. II; p. 121.

36. *Ibid.*; Vol. I; p. 115.

appearance of the sky, but you cannot interpret the signs of the times.'"[37]

At the other end of the scale, the best state is one that is both democratic and federal. Other state forms lie somewhere in between. Democracy, however, is not everywhere and always the best form of government; i.e., "the one which provides the best guarantee of justice." It demands that the people be "ripe" for it and that society not be so "disorganized" as to require a strong, authoritarian hand to prevent anarchy. "Democracy presupposes a living insight into political necessities on the part of the individual citizen."

Furthermore, even if these conditions are met, we are not justified in insisting that the democratic principle be applied throughout society in a doctrinaire fashion. Thus, Brunner finds that "the hierarchically constituted army is a legitimate institution of the Swiss democracy." Moreover, he is not in favor of extending the democratic principle to industry because the owner or manager is "not responsible to his workers, but for his workers" – though he should share his responsibility as much as possible. The extension of the democratic principle to industry, he says, would be "futile" and "ruinous."[38]

Brunner's endorsement of federalism is much more sweeping and enthusiastic than his endorsement of democracy. "The bulwark against the totalitarian State," he says, "is not democracy, but federalism. Federalism is the just order of the State, and federalism is the State built up from below. That is the order of creation." Brunner's Swiss patriotism may have overreached itself in thus classifying federalism as an order of creation, inasmuch as the state belongs to the order of preservation and federalism is a form of the state. But this classification does show the importance that he attaches to federalism. The choice is between federalism and totalitarianism, and he describes that choice as "the burning issue" that confronts our age.[39]

Brunner's federalism is broader than the classic territorial conception, since it is not merely a matter of having a number of autonomous and semi-autonomous provinces, "states," Swiss cantons or German *Laenders*. It is spatial also in the sense of being anti-urban, and points to the "dissolution of the monstrous agglomerations of people, which are so destructive of personality and community."[40] "There is nothing more ugly, soulless and inhuman on the face of this earth than a gigantic mushroom city built up by the

37. Brunner; "Intellectual Autobiography" in *The Theology of Emil Brunner*; p. 15. For a full citation of Brunner's works, see the Bibliography at the end of Book IV.

38. Brunner; *Justice and the Social Order*; pp. 177, 178, 169, 172, 171.

39. *Ibid.*; pp. 120, 125.

40. Brunner; *Communism, Capitalism, and Christianity*; p. 14. For a full citation of Brunner's works, see the Bibliography at the end of Book IV.

accidental conflux of large masses at a place of industrial opportunity."[41] The state ought to leave as many functions and decisions as possible to such social units as families, parishes and unions, and "State intervention must always be the *ultima ratio*."[42] Though he nowhere uses the word, it is clear that Brunner's political thought points in the direction of pluralism.

Brunner gives the form of the economy the same moderate treatment as he gave the state. There are a number of passages that indicate a sharply critical attitude toward capitalism. He accused capitalism of having produced "devastations of the soul" and "deformity of human life" that are "indescribable."[43] He goes so far as to assert that, "Capitalism is economic anarchy; therefore the Christian is obliged to fight against it, and to fight for a better order."[44] It will not do to argue that we should keep capitalism in order to avoid the worse evil of communism, he says. That is a "false alternative."[45]

These sharp criticisms of capitalism are greatly modified by what Brunner says elsewhere, especially in his book *Justice and the Social Order*. In that book, he comes out unequivocally for private property because, he says, private property is presupposed by the Bible as "normal" and because, without it, "there is no free personal life." He approves of interest earnings for bank accounts, making the point that it "is unearned income, but not undeserved income." He is against monopolies and for labor unions and collective bargaining.[46]

On the balance, in spite of all its faults, capitalism is preferable to any other economic system. Socialism certainly is not a desirable alternative because it is incompatible with liberal democracy. Referring to the British Labour party and its supporters, Brunner remarked: "I should call them fools who have not learned the lesson of history."[47] Even religious socialism, which he once espoused, became "a beautiful illusion."[48]

With regard to society, Brunner's emphasis is on tradition. "It is the conviction of the traditionalist that the wisdom of past times, embedded in tra-

---

41. Brunner; *Christianity and Civilisation*; Vol. II; p. 32.

42. Brunner; *Communism, Capitalism, and Christianity*; pp. 12-13. *Ultima ratio* is defined as the final argument or, in the case of force, the last resort.

43. Brunner; *Christianity and Civilisation*; Vol. I; p. 156.

44. Brunner; *The Divine Imperative*; p. 426.

45. Brunner; *Communism, Capitalism, and Christianity*; p. 11.

46. Brunner; *Justice and the Social Order*; pp. 59, 58, 143, 150, 151.

47. Brunner; *The Church in the New Social Order*; p. 18. . For a full citation of Brunner's works, see the Bibliography at the end of Book IV.

48. Brunner; "Intellectual Autobiography" in *The Theology of Emil Brunner*; p. 7.

dition, is greater than the wisdom of the present generation, taken by itself."[49] He speaks of tradition as "the very essence of the Christian Church," and this fact makes her "the legitimate guardian of all natural and cultural tradition." But he does not want to limit reverence for tradition to the Church: "Tradition is not merely keeping alive the spiritual heritage of the past. Even more important, because more slowly connected with the personal and social character of man, is the continuity of social values, such as custom, law, civil institutions, family tradition, public spirit and virtue."[50]

Brunner's truly Burkean attitude toward tradition, combined with his emphasis on the personal nature of revelation, makes him militantly hostile to ideologies or any other form of abstraction. His hostility is eloquent and colorful. Ideologies "are really dangerous because they acquire their control over life surreptitiously." He compares them to mighty monsters, "which are like the pestilence that walketh in darkness."[51] In the form of idealistic progressivism, "It is the bastard offspring of an optimistic anthropology and Christian eschatology."[52] His most sweeping condemnation of all is probably the following:

> "When the other day I was asked what the real trouble with the German nation and the real cause of its corruption, I replied without much reflection, 'Abstraction.' Perhaps I should have added, 'But that abstraction is also, perhaps in a lesser degree, the evil of all western civilization."[53]

In accordance with Brunner's hostility toward abstractions, what one might call social ideals do not receive very favorable or extended treatment. They all, most definitely, are relative values. He has little to say about liberty beyond the following lukewarm endorsement: "It is true that within the New Testament message reference is made to freedom, but no one would claim that this idea holds a key position."[54] In view of this statement, it is probable that Brunner would have been surprised and disapproving if he could have watched the 1972 proceedings of the World Council of Churches in Bangkok in which salvation was identified with liberation.

Brunner shows considerably more concern with the idea of equality, perhaps because it so often is associated with socialism and communism. He

---

49. Brunner; *Christianity and Civilisation*; Vol. I; p. 122.

50. Brunner; *The Scandal of Christianity: The Gospel as Stumbling Block to Modern Man*; pp. 91, 32.

51. Brunner; *The Theology of Crisis*; pp. xv, xvi.

52. Brunner; *Christianity and Civilisation*; Vol. I; p. 55.

53. Brunner; *The Scandal of Christianity*; p. 91.

54. Brunner; *Christianity and Civilisation*; Vol. I; p. 127.

says flatly: "Human beings are never equal." But this does not mean that there is no place for equality. Both equality and inequality are rooted in Scripture.[55] "As created in the Image of God, all men are equal; created as individuals, they are unequal. The need for completion, due to inequality, is the natural form of that true community, of *agape* which belongs to the truth that man has been made in the Image of God. These statements contain the characteristic principle of Christian social ethics."[56] The fact, he says, is that being talented or a genius is "something bestowed" and that "either you are one by birth, or you will never be."

God did not create all people alike or endow them equally, Brunner says, because people require community and there can be no community without individual differences and, therefore, inequality. "The idea of equality, taken by itself, dissolves all essential communion which is based on a primordial togetherness of men."[57] Pursuing this thought further, he writes: "Equality in society creates mechanism, not organism. Our natural feeling tells us that nothing would be more intolerable than equality. Without the difference arising from inequality, there would be no social 'incline,' no current, no flow of intercourse."[58]

For Brunner, it is justice – not freedom, equality or progress – that comes nearest to being the social ideal that he is willing to affirm. Even in this case, we must remember that justice is the highest value in the order of preservation, and that order is tainted by sin. Relative justice is the best that man can achieve in a corrupt social order and, were justice to be absolute rather than merely relative, it still would be inferior to love. "Looked at from the standpoint of love, it presents the appearance of a kind of inferior morality, of a mere preliminary stage of the good."[59]

Justice, therefore, is important as a stepping stone that we can use as a guide, and yet know well enough not to treat it as an idol. It does not fall under the ban against abstractions because it is recognized as such and accorded its proper relative character.

Justice, Brunner says, also is important as a bond with non-Christians: "Justice, then, is a topic where Christian and non-Christian thinking meet, where they have a common ground without being identical."[60]

---

55. Brunner; *Justice and the Social Order*; pp. 30, 63.

56. Brunner; *Dogmatics II;* p. 66.

57. Brunner; *Christianity and Civilisation*; Vol. I; pp. 142, 112.

58. Brunner; *Justice and the Social Order*; p. 138.

59. *Ibid.*; p. 22.

60. Brunner; *Christianity and Civilisation;* p. 108.

CHAPTER FOUR

The Christian Witness to the World

As we have noted, Brunner sees the world as a corrupt society in which sinful men must live in accord with the commandment of love. It is a corrupt world in which evil is checked, but not extinguished, by the orders of creation and preservation.

In this corrupt world, both the Christian and the non-Christian live. The Christian has a higher allegiance and, therefore, is not of this world, but Christ instructed him to be in this world and to stay in it for the purpose of redeeming it. Jesus told his disciples collectively that they were the salt of the earth and the light of the world.[1] In short, this whole position may be summarized thus: Christians, both individually and collectively, must be witnesses to Jesus Christ in this corrupt world in which all of us, Christians and non-Christians, live. How is that to be done? What does that entail?

Brunner approaches these questions from two standpoints – that of the individual and that of the Church. The first of these takes the form of his doctrine of vocation, and the second is handled as a contrast between the concepts of Church and *Ekklesia*.

In a Christian context, the doctrine of vocation requires the individual to look upon his position in life (i.e., his social status, his associations and – especially – his occupation) as an assignment from Almighty God. He is to accept this position simply, single-mindedly, whole-heartedly and with no reservations or regrets. The purpose of this assignment is to glorify God by witnessing to Jesus Christ.

As Brunner recognizes, the immediate effect of the doctrine of vocation is to severely limit a person's pretensions. The Christian is not called upon to "clean up" everything, and he must not yield to "the mania for reforming other people" wherever he finds them. In any case, it is not for him to "be a

---

1. Matthew 5:13-14.

reformer of the world as a whole. Rather, his call to the work of reform is determined by his 'class and calling.'"[2] To the extent to which his occupation and station in life call him to be a reformer, the first thing he must do is to accept – just as it is – the situation in which he finds himself:

"Anyone who is really called to be a reformer must prove his worth by showing that he has learned first of all to respect that which now exists, and to adapt himself obediently to it. Our neighbour and his world are not material which we have to mould first of all. It is presented to us already shaped, in the shaping of which we have to honour the Creator's Hand and Work, in spite of all that human sin may have added to this shape."[3]

Whether or not he is a reformer, the Christian must provide a Christian witness to his neighbor and, in doing so, there is no need to be a globetrotter or an occupation hopper. For "your neighbour is given to you; you do not need to hunt for him, therefore you do not need to search for your sphere of service." Neither does the Christian have to think up what to do: "A particular calling implies particular duties."[4]

Adhering to the doctrine of vocation frees the Christian from "feverish haste," from "bitterness," and from "hopeless resignation." He does not live a whole life longing for greener pastures and in restless discontent. He is happy in his lot. In all this, however, he should remember that to glorify God is the underlying and overriding purpose of life. For that reason, there are occupations "which a Christian can scarcely exercise" and "there may be political groups and programmes where the probability is too slight that a man could take part in them as a Christian without betraying his Lord."[5]

This important requirement of witnessing for Christ has been forgotten or ignored by some people who claim to be Calvinists, by some students of Calvinism, and by some critics of the so-called Protestant work ethic as they interpreted the doctrine of vocation. Brunner follows Calvin very closely in the way he applies the doctrine of vocation to politics. Calvin specifically prohibited private individuals from dabbling in or interfering with public affairs, except when expressly commanded to do so by those who have the right to issue that command. Public affairs and politics are the exclusive concern of the magistrates, a term by which Calvin designates all officials in all branches and units of government. Brunner's idea is just as restrictive, a rather surprising fact for a patriotic Swiss who lived in and admired a democracy in which voting and access to public office was open to all.

---

2.   Brunner; *The Divine Imperative*; pp. 202, 216, 229.

3.   *Ibid.*; p. 214.

4.   *Ibid.*; pp. 208, 203.

5.   *Ibid.*; pp. 203, 481.

The only duty of a Christian statesman is to govern well, he says. The sole standard is excellence. In saying this, Brunner has in mind secular criteria that unbelievers, as well as believers, can subscribe to. He apparently thinks there is something like a theologically neutral science of government since he compares the statesman to the "Christian engineer" who "does not build 'Christian bridges' but solid bridges." There can be no doubt about this: "A Christian who is called to be a statesman is not called to 'govern as a Christian,' but – and just because he is a Christian he ought to know this – as a good statesman."

This same standard of non-theological excellence applies to the Christian statesman's choice of co-workers, who are to be chosen without inquiry into their religion, "only from objective motives" and "from the point of view of their effectiveness for the accomplishment of a particular end."[6] If this secular view of the function of magistrates seems strange coming from a Christian theologian, we must remember that Brunner ascribes the redemption of man to the Church and not to the state.

Brunner, however, recognizes that a Christian in office can run into situations that are exceedingly painful just because he is a Christian. Being a Christian does not subtract from, but adds to, the woes of the magistrate. The Christian magistrate is caught between "the requirements of the order and the command of love" and, in this situation, "he cannot help being horrified" at the necessity of choosing. Which one? Why?

As to which one, Brunner unequivocally says that the Christian magistrate must choose the first – the "official," "harsh" and "objectively technical" duty, in spite of the fact that this duty is "wholly opposed to love." As to why, Brunner replies that there is a duty to succeed. Any action that does not aim at success is nothing but a "fantasy," and success "is not – as so often is said – a dubious ethical concept, but one which is indispensable for ethics in particular."[7] Success is the price of statesmanship, and a heavy price it is for the Christian:

> "The contrast between that which God wills and what we do ourselves, in our 'official' capacity, remains culpable and terrible ... We never see the real meaning of 'original sin,' we never perceive the depth and the universality of evil, or what evil really means in the depths common to us all, until we are *obliged* to do something in our official capacity – for the sake of order, and therefore for the sake of love – which, apart from our 'office,' would be absolutely wrong."[8]

---

6. *Ibid.*; pp. 263, 265.

7. *Ibid.*; pp. 226, 225, 236.

8. *Ibid.*; pp. 227, 225.

Surely, no one has exceeded Brunner in delineating in a more merci-
lessly clear light the predicament of the Christian magistrate. But his pro-
posed solution looks like pure Machiavellianism.[9] Brunner is aware of this
objection, and tries to meet it in this way: "As a rule the notorious proposition, 'the end justifies the means,' conceals great confusion of thought
whether it is defended or rejected as a principle. To make it absolutely valid
and unassailable we might word it like this: the necessary end hallows the
necessary means."

Brunner's defense, however, helps him not at all because Machiavelli
never advocated the indiscriminate use of such means as murder and breaking faith, but stressed that they should be used only when necessary. It is
true that Brunner tries to shed any possible Machiavellian label in the following statement: "The will to witness says: 'if an end makes it necessary
to use dubious means, then this end ought not to be desired.' The necessary
end, we said, hallows the necessary means. But whether an end can be said
to be 'necessary' always depends on the means which it requires for its realization."[10]

Brunner's attempt to extricate himself from the charge of Machiavellianism does put him in the position of rejecting the proposition that the end
justifies the means, but what about the practice? If the means to be used are
unnecessary because they are dubious, what makes them dubious? Brunner
does not say. The effect of his silence is to leave the Christian magistrate
exactly where he was before Brunner tried to shed the label of Machiavellianism – namely, the Christian magistrate must put his official duty first
and perform it, however much it horrifies him and makes him culpable.

The Christian magistrate is bound, but not immobilized, by the office he
holds. Official life never is the whole of life, Brunner says, no matter how
demanding and engrossing it sometimes may be. There always is a private
sector as well. In making this point, he says that the office "is the shell
which contains life, but not the life itself. Actual life consists in meeting
another person in love."[11] There is no set of regulations so tight as to leave
no room for personal encounter, no legal net so closely woven as to prevent
the flow of Christian witness, no job description or administrative organization chart so comprehensive and rigid as to extinguish Christian resource-

---

9. Machiavellianism is defined as the political theory of Niccolò Machiavelli (1469-
    1527), Italian political philosopher best known for his work *Il principe* (The Prince),
    which details his theory of government and the maxims of practical statecraft. He
    viewed politics as amoral and believed that any means, however unscrupulous, justifi-
    ably can be used in achieving political power.

10. *Ibid.*; pp. 246, 277.

11. *Ibid.*; p. 228.

fulness and resiliency. Brunner describes this ineradicable element of flexibility:

> "And therefore also, in quietness, and in small things – or if it is granted to him, publicly and in a larger circle – he will remember his priestly duty, and at the right time and place he will say something 'amazing,' something which does not simply belong to the subject at hand, something unexpected, about God and eternal things, something which, just because it is said at an unusual time and in an unusual way, will have more demonstrative, attractive, and awakening power than the majority of sermons."[12]

The Christian magistrate, he says, is aware of the fact that there is "a 'private' way of working behind the established institutions of public life."[13]

Nor is it always necessary that he should work behind these established institutions. He may, on occasion, use these institutions as launching pads or, as Theodore Roosevelt once said about the presidency, as a "bully pulpit." But, even in such cases, the Christian witness still is unofficial in the sense that there is nothing in the office of president of the United States as established by the Constitution and constitutional practice that makes a Christian witness mandatory. For Brunner, therefore, the Christian witness in politics always is a qualified one:

> "It is indeed our duty to try to make the power of Christ operative in the sociopolitical realm as well as in others. However, in this particular area the love commandment will, at best, find expression in a very indirect sense. This can take place much more immediately on the level of direct interpersonal relationships.
>
> "This insight has become decisive for my whole thinking."[14]

The time has now come for us to move from the individual witness to the collective witness, from the doctrine of vocation to the doctrine of the Church.

What, according to Brunner, is the function of the Church in the corrupt world in which we live? The Church has one fundamental and overriding function, which "is to preach the Gospel of Jesus Christ, the Kingdom of God which transcends all social orders, the good and the bad alike."[15] The Church must follow in the footsteps of its Lord and Master, Jesus Christ, who came "to lead us from the lie to truth, from damnation to salvation,

---

12. *Ibid.*; p. 259.

13. *Ibid.*; p. 277.

14. Brunner; "Intellectual Autobiography" in *The Theology of Emil Brunner*; p. 4.

15. Brunner; *The Church in the New Social Order*; p. 7.

from perdition and death to life and blessedness."[16]

Brunner's description of the ultimate aim of the Church – i.e., the fulfilled Kingdom of God – reproduces accurately, without parroting, the Biblical teaching:

> "Life without cessation, joy without sorrow, power without limitations, fellowship with God without disturbance, time without passing away, physical life without the flesh, sight without the pale cast of thought, without the paradoxes of faith, knowledge no longer 'as in a glass darkly' or in a riddle, but 'face to face, even as we are known' – all this might be expressed in one sentence: God will be there, and we shall be with Him. He will be our God, and we shall be His people."[17]

If it be objected that this is highly pietistic and other-worldly language far removed from the rough and tumble, stresses and strains, perplexities and pressures of practical politics, Brunner's reply is that the connection is closer than most people think and that our failure to see it and act accordingly has cost us dearly. In a way, the distinction is not unlike that between pure science and applied science when we recognize that the latter would not even exist without the former – except that, in the case of theology and politics, we are dealing with life and death, reality and illusion, sense and nonsense. "Our life," Brunner says, "is 'superficial,' without depth or meaning so long as it does not have its roots in eternity. Either it has eternal significance or it has no significance at all. Temporal sense is nonsense."[18]

To summarize Brunner's thought in more conventional terms, the main function of the Church is evangelism. Brunner shares with Tillich, Barth and Bonhoeffer the realization that evangelizing in the 21st century is an arduous, uphill struggle.

One approach to the task of evangelism is intellectual. The traditional concepts of Christian theology in which the Christian message has been expressed are true, but irrelevant, to modern man because he does not understand them. If modern man is to understand them, the Christian message must be "thought out afresh and re-formulated in intellectual terms." To do this job, Tillich dedicated his entire life and built his monumental theological edifice. But one great danger in this approach to evangelism – a danger to which Tillich very largely fell victim – is that of betrayal.

Brunner was well aware of this danger: "Certainly this demand for a 'contemporary' presentation of Christian truth contains a danger – the dan-

---

16. Brunner; Our Faith; p. 59.

17. Brunner; *The Mediator: A Study of the Central Doctrine of The Christian Faith*; p. 571. For a full citation of Brunner's works, see the Bibliography at the end of Book IV.

18. Brunner; *Our Faith*; p. 33.

ger of betrayal of the central concern of the Bible. This is the danger of every translation: *Toute traduction est une trahison*[19] is a witty remark, but it has been put still more strongly in the phrase *traduttore-traditore.*[20] Nevertheless, the danger is unavoidable and should be faced with courage and intelligence. Brunner, though, did not expect a great deal from the intellectual approach.

Although he valiantly and often brilliantly stated and explained Christian truth, he made no attempt to coin new terms as Tillich did at such great length and as Bonhoeffer did to some extent. Why not?

"The spirit of the typical 'modern' man is relativistic and sceptical; he is weary of all systems, averse to all doctrines, and contemptuous of all creeds."[21] Again, he comments: "The modern man no longer believes in an absolute, in whatever form it may be offered, whether that of the Christian faith, of idealism, or of mysticism. If he believes in anything it is in absolute uncertainty."[22]

What we must seek in evangelism is a "point of contact" – a phrase used by the translator of Brunner's "Intellectual Autobiography" to render the German *anknuepfung*. Actually, it is a poor translation that does not convey the force of the German word, which means not merely touching, but being hitched, locked or tied together. Brunner used this word to denote the problem he faced when he taught in Japanese universities and had to deal with students who knew nothing whatever about Christianity. "Now in this strictly missionary situation where I had to teach students who had not the slightest knowledge of the Christian faith, it became of primary importance to find 'the point of contact.'"[23]

Where does one find this point of contact, this hitching point of believer and unbeliever with which evangelism begins? True to his doctrine of revelation, Brunner asserted that this point is a common encounter with God. Sometimes, there is no such point because there has been no such encounter. The usual reason is that men "fix their eyes on man, his personality and culture, and not on God."[24] There must, therefore, be a "real encounter with the God who reveals Himself to us in the opened scripture," always bearing in mind "that the reader of the Bible can never know before-

19. *Toute traduction est une trahison* (French) means "Any translation is a treason." *Traduttore-traditore* (Italian) means "translator-traitor."

20. Brunner; *Dogmatics I*; pp. 10, 71.

21. Brunner; *The Divine Imperative*; p. 17.

22. Brunner; *The Theology of Crisis*; p. 8.

23. Brunner; "Intellectual Autobiography" in *The Theology of Emil Brunner*; p. 19.

24. Brunner; *The Theology of Crisis*; p. 73.

hand at what passage in the Bible this encounter will take place."[25] Speaking from his experience in Japanese universities, Brunner writes: "The most important way of leading to Christ is, of course, the transparency of Christ's spirit in the character, in the life, and in the face of the one who presents the Christian doctrine."[26]

Preaching the gospel of Christ is the one fundamental, overriding, indispensable and immediate task of the Church. Believers in Christ must be won now and, in the fullness of time, the Kingdom of God must be established on earth as it is in heaven. Nothing else must be allowed to take precedence over this task or cause it to be minimized. Brunner's position here is very traditional and conventional, not to say conservative, which is why his handling of the relation of the Church to politics had to be postponed. Describing the development of his theology, he said: "But my deepest concern was not so much with the problems of social ethics as with the more fundamental question about God."[27]

This matter of priorities, however, should not cause us to neglect his interest in political and social questions. It is fair to say that he was more deeply interested in these questions and devoted more of his writing to them than Tillich, Barth and Bonhoeffer. Brunner showed a familiarity with the literature of German political theory that is impressive, and certainly unmatched by any of the other three. German or German-Austrian political theorists such as Jellinek,[28] Spann,[29] Kelsen[30] and Meinecke[31] are cited fre-

---

25. Brunner; *Dogmatics II*; p. 240.

26. Brunner; "Intellectual Autobiography" in *The Theology of Emil Brunner*; pp. 19, 6.

27. *Ibid.*; p. 6.

28. Georg Jellinek (1851-1911). German legal and political philosopher best known for the theory of the "two-sided" and "self-binding" character of the state offered in his *Allgemeine Staatslehre* (1900). In his book *Die sozialethische Bedeutung von Recht, Unrecht und Strafe* or *The Social-Ethical Significance of Right, Wrong, and Punishment* (1878; 2nd ed., 1908) he defined the law as an ethical minimum – i.e., as a body of normative principles essential to civilized existence. Other works include *The Declaration of the Rights of Man and the Citizen*.

29. Othmar Spann (1878-1950). Conservative Austrian philosopher, sociologist and economist whose radical anti-liberal and anti-Socialist views helped antagonise political factions in Austria during the interwar years. Repeatedly, Spann tried to draw the ruling powers' attention to his authoritarian theory of a corporate state which, as he saw it, could – and should – be introduced immediately for the benefit of all.

30. Hans Kelsen (1881-1973). Austrian jurist and political theorist. He was tasked with writing the new Austrian constitution after the breakup of the Habsburg monarchy, and sat on the new state's constitutional court. His work concentrated on the concept of sovereignty, international law and international institutions such as the United Nations. His books include *Pure Theory of Law, Peace through Law* and the *General Theory of Law and State*.   footnote 31 on next page

quently and relevantly. His chief reliance in economic thought is on Werner Sombart[32] because of that economist's classic work on capitalism.

There is, therefore, a clear connection in Brunner's mind between the Church and politics. But he does not become weary of warning us that the connection is very indirect. It is well to remember "that social ethics and the doctrine of the State play a very small part in the New Testament."[33] Anyone who looks to the New Testament for instruction in matters political and social "cannot fail to be astonished, bewildered and even disappointed." Jesus himself was interested "unambiguously, not to say one-sidedly" in the Kingdom of God, which is "the be-all and the end-all" of his Gospel; and "there is no room in it for anything else, for all these important but temporal and secular things like art, education, science, social and political order." And, thus, "we know that we do not know what a Christian civilisation is and can be. We know that we do not have in our hands a ready-made programme which has simply to be applied."[34]

Brunner finds it "necessary to state that the interest of the Church for the social order can only be an indirect one. It is not the primary, not the essential task of the Church to create, to change, to improve the social order."[35] Of course, the Church should not join, form, identify itself with, or support any political party – Christian or otherwise. Brunner's castigation of the involvement of the Church in political activity could hardly be more vehement: "Almost without exception the worst that could befall would be the formation of 'Christian' parties; for this would bring in a disastrous confusion between the spheres of Church and State. ... The curse of the betrayal of the Name of Christ broods over the 'Christian' social organization for this struggle. We cannot tack this Name on to any of our little political banners."[36]

In the light of this stand on the relation between the Church and politics,

---

31. Friedrich Meinecke (1862-1954). A leading German historian and political philosopher, he was a pioneer of what came to be known as "historicism." His books include *Cosmopolitanism and the National State* and *Machiavellianism: The Doctrine of Raison d'Etat and its Place in Modern History*.

32. Werner Sombart (1863-1941). German economist and sociologist, and one of the leading Continental European social scientists during the first quarter of the 20th century. His major work was the six-volume *Der moderne Kapitalismus* (1902), which coined the word "capitalism." It is a systematic history of economics and economic development through the centuries.

33. Brunner; *Dogmatics II*; p. 318.

34. Brunner; *Christianity and Civilisation*; Vol. I; pp. 6, 7, 10.

35. Brunner; *The Church in the New Social Order*; p. 7.

36. Brunner; *The Divine Imperative*; p. 432.

we can imagine what Brunner would think about social activism. Indeed, we do not have to imagine it at all – he condemns it unequivocally, categorically and extensively. In view of the highly controversial nature of social activism in our day, it would serve well to quote Brunner at some length, lest someone should suspect misrepresentation and remain unconvinced:

> "Our present danger is the activism of the West, as one finds it perhaps most typically represented in the 'socialized' church of America. Christian faith is here jeopardized by submergence in mere social ethical idealism and pragmatism. This means that the spiritual reserve, the capital of faith which previous generations have stored up, is thoughtlessly wasted by a merely expansive activity. Bent on work, one forgets the source of works. Full of good will to do something, one immediately loses the keen sense of *what* ought to be done. The Church, which has no conception of what it means to stand on the word of God alone, is in the process of being dissolved into the world, of first becoming a great social-welfare trust and then wholly disappearing. The socialized form is the Church in the beginning of its dissolution."[37]

In another passage, Brunner singles out Protestant activism:

> "It is characteristic of modern Protestant activism that it has lost its feeling for the absolute contradiction, the eschatological gulf, between the world of God and the world as it is. The word of God is toned down, reduced to religious literature and moral programs, so as to harmonize it with present thought and life. Theology is changed into philosophy, history, and psychology of religion."[38]

One more passage is aimed at individual ministers who have succumbed to social activism:

> "The pastor's study, once the room in which a man humbly subjected himself to the Eternal Word, has become transformed into an office for numerous social agencies; and the sermon is a piece of applied popular ethics as the day requires it. The birthright of the gospel of the kingdom of heaven is sold for the pottage of practical success and immediate influence."[39]

Brunner accuses ecclesiastical social activists of "terrible arrogance," which leads them to think "they understand everything, and that they can and should interfere with everything 'in the name of the Church,' even where they understand and know nothing at all."[40]

---

37. Brunner; *The Theology of Crisis*; p. 87.

38. *Ibid.*; p. 88.

39. *Ibid.*; p. 89.

40. Brunner; *Dogmatics II*; pp. 320-21.

One might think that Brunner's condemnation of social activism means that he has no social conscience, that he is giving an uncritical approval of the status quo. This would be an erroneous conclusion. Brunner is not devoid of a capacity for righteous indignation, and he has that sense of "the eschatological gulf" that he accuses many ministers of lacking. His power in this respect is well-reflected in the following passage:

> "In the light of revelation we see the whole curse of historical life: injustice within the system of law, lack of peace in and through the State, lack of truth in science, triviality and idolatry of beauty in art, and the deification of culture, slavery in civilization. We see above all – and this is the real point I want to emphasize – how the real purpose of life is being thwarted at every turn in all the 'orders' which constitute the framework of human life: the 'ends' sought are so futile and empty, and the 'means' used to achieve these ends are utterly contemptible."[41]

It is realizations such as this one that cause Brunner to say that there is a duty "to resist, to protest, not to be 'conformed to this world.'"[42]

Can the Church resist and protest without yielding to social activism? Brunner thinks it can. The answer depends on a proper analysis of the factors that determine culture and civilization. These factors are: (1) natural factors like topography and climate; (2) "the physical and spiritual equipment of men within a given area;" and (3) "the spiritual presuppositions of a religious and ethical nature which, not in themselves cultural, we might call the culture-transcendent presuppositions of every culture." The first two factors are "inaccessible to human determination and freedom," but "assuming equal natural data and equal physical and spiritual forces, two cultures will develop differently if this third factor, the culture-transcendent presuppositions, is different."[43] It is on this third factor that the Church can have an impact capable of transforming political and social conditions. This is because "the really shattering changes in the social structure take place as changes in the system of values, which, for its part, depends on faith and unbelief."[44]

At this turn in the argument, it is Brunner's judgment that the Church has failed in its primary task of evangelizing the world and in its secondary task of changing political and social conditions by transforming the value systems upon which they rest. He gets at the problem by distinguishing between the Church and the *Ekklesia*.

---

41. Brunner; *The Divine Imperative*; p. 255.

42. *Ibid.*; p. 217.

43. Brunner; *Christianity and Civilisation*; Vol. II; pp.10-11, 217, 11.

44. Brunner; *The Divine Imperative*; p. 274.

The Church that we know is not the *Ekklesia*; i.e., the Church that existed in New Testament times. "For what we call the Church is not a brotherhood but an institution; not the Body of Christ but a corporation in the juristic sense of the word." The Church as we know it is only an instrument. It is not anything Jesus wants: "Jesus Christ wills to have a people – a people, but certainly not an institution." Institutions have a way of becoming ends in themselves, of growing imperialistic and defensive, of confusing their existence with their message. For that reason, Brunner has no interest in church mergers in the institutional sense. Indeed, he is suspicious of them, and he goes so far as to say: "It would certainly be a misfortune if there were only one Church in the U.S.A."[45]

On the other hand, "the *Ekklesia* is a thoroughly uncultic, unsacred, spiritual brotherhood, which lives in trusting obedience to its Lord Christ and in the love to the brethren which He bestows."[46] It is characterized by such words as fellowship, brotherhood and community. Its members are united by love instead of law, which means that their relationships are personal and not official and that they are communal because they are shared in freedom and reciprocity. Because it is deeply personal and communal, it is "more social than any Socialism" and "more communal than any Communism."[47]

The *Ekklesia* is charismatic because it is controlled exclusively by the Holy Spirit and, therefore, entirely unstructured. That is the way the Church was in the days of Peter and Paul, Brunner says, and that is the way it can be again in our day. He observes: "This may seem fantastic to us. We cannot repress the question: Did this charismatic order actually work?"[48] Answering his own question affirmatively, Brunner admits that it was something "which certainly Paul and the other Christians themselves regarded with ever-renewed astonishment as a miracle."

For Brunner, the fact that it was a miracle then and would be one now is no objection because "to deny the reality of miracle would be to deny the freedom of God, of the God who is the Lord of the whole world."[49]

---

45. Brunner; *Dogmatics III*; pp. 22, 80.

46. *Ibid.*; p. 33.

47. Brunner; *The Church in the New Social Order;* p. 12.

48. Brunner; *Dogmatics III*; p. 45.

49. *Ibid.*

CHAPTER FIVE

Conclusion

Brunner's political thought can be best characterized as moderate and conservative. It certainly is reasonable in his teaching on law. It is true that, for him, the essence of the Christian life is love and not law, and that he shares with Tillich and Barth a distrust of excessive intellectualism and a refusal to absolutize law. But he leaves a great deal of room for law, both natural and civil, in the world as it is.

Brunner's essentially moderate and reasonable attitude toward law is made possible by his conception of revelation, which is closely akin to that of Calvin and far removed from Barth. Because law cannot do everything, one is not warranted in concluding that it can do nothing. We are protected by God's orders of creation and preservation, and magistrates who strive to use these orders to promote justice are not wasting their time.

The calling of a statesman or a jurist is an honorable calling in itself, and it allows love and personal encounter to shine through the exigencies of politics and the technicalities of the law. Because of his broader conception of revelation, Brunner's thought makes it possible for Christian and non-Christian to be partners, without one's giving up the unique claim of Christianity or getting mired down in religious eclecticism.

Brunner's position on the state is the conventional Western democratic one. He is in favor of democracy, federalism, pluralism, checks and balances, and majority rule. It is true that he qualifies his endorsements in several ways – e.g., that majority rule requires a politically mature electorate and should not be understood to mean popular sovereignty. But these qualifications could be arrived at on purely secular grounds, and it is difficult to prove that Brunner has given them an original and adequate theological foundation.

Most Western thinkers probably would think that his position on capitalism is sound, but neither original nor profound. Of course, he realizes the serious flaws of capitalism and forthrightly denounces them, as we have seen when he criticized Protestantism for its failure to see and feel the "eschatological gulf." His endorsement of capitalism is partly based on a very strong conviction that capitalism is much preferable to either socialism or communism, and that it is the only practical alternative to those other economic systems.

In a more positive way, he praises capitalism for providing an economic foundation for individual liberty and fostering independent nuclei of power in society capable of checking governmental abuses of power. He says nothing about the concept of profit, either negatively as an instrument of exploitation or positively as an incentive and reward for creative imagination and courageous risk-taking.

Viewed as a whole, then, Brunner's thought places him in the conservative camp. His stand on law, tradition, capitalism, democracy, federalism, and checks and balances clearly is conservative. So are his distrust of Church pronouncements on political and social matters, and his fervent denunciation of social activism as a betrayal of the gospel. So is his giving a rather low rating to liberty and equality as social ideals, as well as placing a rather Platonist concept of justice ahead of them.

The one great exception to Brunner's conservatism is his concept of the *Ekklesia*. In that concept, he becomes astonishingly radical. Although he himself devoted his life to theology, he sees no need for it in the *Ekklesia* because the Holy Spirit will supply the doctrinal elements as needed. He shares with Tillichian liberals a deep distrust of institutions, and he places the *Ekklesia* under unstructured charismatic leadership. The presence of the Holy Spirit is all that matters to him.

Brunner once wrote a very favorable presentation of the Buchmanite, Oxford Group[1] in terms that suggest he would have favored many of the lay renewal and charismatic movements that flourish in our day, had he lived to see them. All of this is speculative, of course, as we do not know whether his Calvinistic background would have caused him to frown on these instances of irrationalism. However that may be, his thinking about the *Ekklesia* does not harmonize with the rest of his theology. There is contradiction and dissonance here. Though quite unlike Tillich in almost every respect, Brunner is like him in that he, too, awaits for the new *kairos*.

---

1. Buchmanite, Oxford Group; Named after Frank Buchman (1878–1961), an American Lutheran minister whose ideas veered in an occult direction after World War I. The religious principles and methods of the 'group movement' included open confession and testimony. The Buchmanite, Oxford Group or Moral Rearmament movement flourished here and there in the 1920s and early 1930s, but had little lasting effect, and many people in both secular and sacred traditions looked on it as slightly eccentric.

Major Works of Emil Brunner

The Mediator: A Study of the Central Doctrine of The Christian Faith (Lutterworth Press; London; 1934).

The Theology of Crisis (Charles Scribner's Sons; New York & London; 1935).

God and Man: Four Essays on the Nature of Personality (SCM Press; London; 1936).

Our Faith (SCM Press; London; 1936).

The Divine Imperative: A Study in Christian Ethics (Lutterworth Press; London; 1937).

Justice and the Social Order (Lutterworth Press; London; 1945).

Christianity and Civilisation; 2 vols. (Nisbet & Co.; London; 1948 and 1949).

The Christian Doctrine of God: Dogmatics I (Lutterworth Press; London; 1952).

Communism, Capitalism and Christianity (Lutterworth Press; London; 1949).

The Christian Doctrine of Creation and Redemption: Dogmatics II (Lutterworth Press; London; 1952).

The Church in the New Social Order (SCM Press; London; 1952).

"Intellectual Autobiography," in *The Theology of Emil Brunner* (Macmillan; New York; 1962).

The Christian Doctrine of the Church, Faith, and the Consummation: Dogmatics III (Westminster Press; Philadelphia; 1962).

Truth as Encounter (SCM Press; London; 1964).

The Scandal of Christianity: The Gospel as Stumbling Block to Modern Man (John Knox Press; Richmond, Va.; 1965).

Book V

The Impact of Theology on Political Thought

Contents

Introduction

The time has come to pull together the political implications and teachings of the theologies of Tillich, Barth, Bonhoeffer and Brunner to see what those thinkers have to offer us in the 21st century.

This is not simply a matter of reviewing and summarizing what these four theologians have said in their work. It also is a matter of evaluating and adding to what they have said, often pushing their thought beyond its furthest point and sometimes contradicting what they probably would have said if they were still alive.

CHAPTER ONE

The Christian, the Church and the Public Philosophy

The term *the public philosophy* is borrowed from Walter Lippmann,[1] and so is its meaning – i.e., it is the philosophy of life and politics that underlies the functioning of government and society, which is the product of a long tradition of civility and which is shared by nearly all members of a community.

Without the public philosophy, the necessary underpinning of constitutional government – perhaps all government – would be gone. The complete erosion of it would produce anarchy or despotism. If this statement sounds too Hegelian, it might suffice to say that you cannot alter one – either the public philosophy or the government – without altering the other. It will be recalled that the public philosophy was the one factor that Brunner said was capable of bringing about a radical change in culture and civilization.

Now, if there is a message common to all four of the theologians whose thought we have analyzed, it would be a profound distrust of all ideologies and philosophical systems. For them, truth is not to be apprehended propositionally to any appreciable extent – and certainly not to a saving extent.

The source of this distrust is a dual one. In the case of Tillich, for exam-

---

1. Walter Lippmann (1889-1974). American writer, journalist and political commentator. In 1913, Lippmann, Herbert Croly and Walter Weyl became the founding editors of *The New Republic* magazine. During World War I, Lippmann became an advisor to President Woodrow Wilson and assisted in the drafting of Wilson's *Fourteen Points*. Lippmann agreed with the Platonic view that the population is a great beast, a herd, that has to be controlled by an intellectual specialist class. It was Lippmann who first identified the tendency of journalists to generalize about other people based on fixed ideas, and he was the first to use the phrase "Cold War" in his 1947 book by the same name. In addition to his newspaper columns, he published several other books, including: *Essays in the Public Philosophy* (1955); *A Preface to Politics* (1913); *Public Opinion* (1922); *The Phantom Public* (1925); *A Preface to Morals* (1929); and *The Good Society* (1937).

ple, one suspects that his distrust has secular roots and is part of the general disillusionment of Western culture with ideologies and philosophies. There has been a confusing multiplicity of them and, in recent times, practically all have failed to command the common/popular allegiance. Communism in its various forms has been an exception, and it has produced tyranny. In the case of Barth, the root of distrust lies in his conception of God as "wholly Other" and of the consequent seriousness with which he takes the commandment against idolatry. But whether the source of this distrust be secular or theological, the message of these theologians is the same – beware of everything that is doctrinaire.

It would be easy to dismiss this message because it is not needed in a world in which propositional truth is held in contempt and denounced *ad nauseam*. To do so, however, would be to ignore some areas which, even in an anti-intellectual age such as ours, are dominated by doctrinaire attitudes. We see this attitude among some civil rights champions who are willing and eager to sacrifice everything for the idol of equality. In the field of race relations in the past 50 years, we have seen segregationists and integrationists ready and willing to disregard all moral and constitutional considerations: The ends they sought were opposite, but the doctrinaire spirit was identical. In the field of politics, we find some advocates of what has come to be known as participatory democracy erect the rule of the numerical majority into an arrogant absolute.

In these and other instances, the message of our theologians is a salutary warning that ought to be heeded, particularly when we remember that our skeptical and relativistic age is not eternal and might be succeeded by another in which a doctrinaire spirit is predominant.

But for our time, despite such pockets of doctrinaire intolerance, the need of the moment is rather the opposite of what these four theologians are teaching us. Reason is a great deal more than a Bergsonian[2] tool for the adjustment of rational means to non-rational ends: It is a God-given faculty for the perception of truth. Objective facts, ideas external to ourselves, and logic independent of our wishes are essential to life. That is why the Church has developed creeds and theologies. That is why political life has developed ideologies. That is why universities have developed educational philosophies. When churches have discarded creeds and theologies, Christians have become the victims of heresy and nonsense. When ideologies

---

2. Henri Bergson (1859-1941). French philosopher who was awarded the Nobel Prize for Literature in 1927. He argued that the intuition is deeper than the intellect. His *Creative Evolution* (1907) and *Matter and Memory* (1896) attempted to integrate the findings of biological science with a theory of consciousness. Bergson's work was considered the main challenge to the mechanistic view of nature.

have waned, political life has become an unstable arena for meaningless personality conflicts and factional fights. When universities have lost a philosophy of education, the result has been curricular monstrosities and a loss of institutional identity.

There has to be a source of order in every society and community, and that source is a public philosophy. There must be principles for the classification of facts and ideas, priorities must be assigned, intellectual discipline must be imposed, and definite procedures must be spelled out and obeyed. The importance of a public philosophy as a source of order perhaps is most easily seen in the contrast between national and state constitutions in the United States. The national constitution is a lucid, orderly, logical and polished instrument because those who made it had – and followed – a clear public philosophy.

Some of the state constitutions, on the other hand, were made by people who had no public philosophy at all. The results of this lack of a public philosophy are evident: the fettering of legislative power by a host of paralyzing restrictions; the dispersion of executive power among numerous mutually irresponsible officers; the cluttering up of the constitutional document with statutory materials and purely local matters. The inclusion of provisions that should be made by state legislatures, municipal councils and county commissioners is an especially convincing indication that the state constitution makers had lost all sense of the relative importance of things. With no philosophy to guide them, they are tossed to and fro by every political faction, pressure group, vested interest, and personal consideration.

The four German and German-Swiss theologians analyzed in this book make a heavy demand on the political leader and his following by insisting that the validity of every public philosophy is relative and should be so considered, consciously and publicly. It takes a great deal of maturity to allow one's self to be guided by propositions and rules that one knows are time-bound and marred by imperfection. The point is most prominent in Tillich, who posits not only maturity, but courage, as an indispensable requirement of statesmanship.

It should be observed, however, that a realization of the relative character of a public philosophy is not necessarily a specifically Christian experience. It can be found in Aristotle's *Politics*, where he advises constitution makers not to make their work "too perfect" and to understand that not every measure that is most purely democratic or oligarchic makes these regimes most successfully democratic or oligarchic. It was Aristotle, too, who argued that the middle-class state is best because rational behavior requires an emotional balance between the desire to gain something on the one hand and the fear of losing something on the other.

Aristotle taught that every form of government has its own characteristic system of values, and he went into great detail in advising the statesman on how to keep the system stable and intact. At the same time, he was able to cleave to doctrine without being doctrinaire about it. Thus, Aristotle exemplified one of the greatest virtues of the Greek mind at its best – namely, wisdom. If a non-Christian philosopher like Aristotle can achieve such wisdom, what has a Christian thinker got that is different; i.e., specifically Christian? What is different, and what the Christian thinker has, is something called judgment.

Now, that word *judgment* can be misleading. It is not used here in the sense of condemnation or exclusively negative criticism, nor is it used in the sense of a wise choice among alternative courses of action – some or all of which leave much to be desired. Judgment includes these meanings, of course, but it goes beyond them in two essential respects.

The first is the element of distance. Just as no one can judge a painting with his face to the canvas, so he who would judge a public philosophy must do so from a distance. The second element is that of standing outside of the thing to be judged. He who would know the full scope of a valley cannot do so from within the valley but, instead, must do it from a mountain peak, an airplane or some other point outside the valley. So it is in judging a public philosophy. It is impossible to evaluate a particular philosophy from within; only from a point outside can one successfully judge. Also involved in this necessity of standing outside is the power to move people. Just as he who would move a heavy object cannot be a part of that object, but must get leverage on it, so must whoever would judge a public philosophy. Without some detachment, there can be no leverage to carry through the judgment and, therefore, nothing can be moved.

It is this quality of judgment, understood in the sense just explained, that the non-Christian lacks. He is the prisoner of his culture, and sees things from the perspective of his particular public philosophy. Even so great a mind as Aristotle could not emancipate itself from this limitation. He adhered to the Greek-barbarian dichotomy that caused him to say that no Greek could be a slave by nature, though barbarians could be; and that no Greek city-state should wage war on another Greek city-state, though war against non-Greeks would be legitimate. In spite of his having been the tutor of Alexander the Great, Aristotle had no appreciation of empire and its possibilities, so he could write his entire *Politics* without even mentioning empire. The reason was that Aristotle judged everything from within the framework of the *polis*[3] and was unable to go outside of it.

---

3. *Polis* is defined as the Greek city-state of Aristotle's time that was characterized by a sense of community.

The Christian, by comparison, has this quality of judgment because he has that sense of distance and that ability to stand outside of his culture and public philosophy, without which there is no judgment. He judges cultures, institutions and philosophies from the standpoint of God, who is outside as well as inside these things – which means that the Christian looks at the temporal from the perspective of the eternal.

Using philosophical language to make the same point, the Christian is aware of both the immanent and the transcendent. This necessary sense of distance is especially strong in Barth. We see it in Bonhoeffer's simultaneous emphasis on what he calls the ultimate and the penultimate. We see it in Tillich's distinction between the finite and the infinite. We see it in Brunner's distinction between the order of redemption and the orders of creation and preservation. We see it in Calvin's contrast between common grace and saving grace. What these theologians are telling us, therefore, is that the Christian is liberated from the fetters that bind the natural man and partakes of the freedom of God to the extent to which he receives, accepts and appropriates (modern jargon would say "internalizes") the revelation of God in Jesus Christ.

This concept of judgment has practical political consequences. The Christian is able to judge the strong and weak points in every public philosophy with a good chance of being successful. He can make his approval and disapproval acceptable because the recipient feels that the Christian is not an enemy, but a friend and brother. The Christian's criticism, both positive and negative, is likely to be accepted because he also identifies with the ones to whom the criticism is addressed. This is what Jesus meant when he told his disciples to be in the world, but not of the world. This is what the Apostle Paul meant when he instructed us to tell the truth in love. In the Christian attitude, there is no naked and sterile truth that destroys, but a living truth made flesh in love that redeems.

No doubt, this claim of the Christian distinctiveness of judgment will seem unwarranted to the secular mind. Modern secular man is well-informed when it comes to pointing out past and present instances of bad judgment on the part of Christians. He, quite correctly, observes that Christians are not necessarily better people and better judges than non-Christians – indeed, sometimes neither as good nor as right. No Christian should deny the validity of this secular indictment. But this indictment misses the mark because no Christian has any business saying that he, and other Christians, are perfect people. Christians are sinners, too. Someone very rightly said that every church door should have a sign on it that reads: "For sinners only!" What, then, is the difference between the Christian sinner and the non-Christian sinner? It is this: The Christian sinner knows that he is a sinner and, further, also knows that he has resources and a destiny that Christians alone possess.

There is a view of liberty – which is as popular as it is false, and which is abetted by current conceptions of democracy and enshrined in the American *Declaration of Independence* – that holds that all men are born free. It is a false view. If all men were born free, they would not be a blessing but a menace. Freedom is an achievement and not a natural right. Once again, Thomas Jefferson and those who agree with him are the prisoners of their public philosophy – in this case, that of the 18th century Enlightenment. But man must be made fit for freedom, and this is a process that is the off-spring of Christian maturity or, as the Apostle Paul expressed it:

> "Now the Lord is that Spirit: and where the Spirit of the Lord is, there is liberty."[4]

---

4. II Corinthians 3:17.

CHAPTER TWO

The Doctrine of Vocation

The doctrine of vocation is one of the most significant contributions of theology to the Christian witness in politics. As we have seen, it played an important role in the thought of Barth, Bonhoeffer and Brunner. Its classic statement, however, is to be found in Calvin's *Institutes*:

> "Lastly, it is to be remarked that the Lord commands every one of us, in all the actions of life, to regard his vocation. For he knows with what great inquietude the human mind is inflamed, with what desultory levity it is hurried hither and thither, and how insatiable is its ambition to grasp different things at once. Therefore, to prevent universal confusion being produced by our folly and temerity, he has appointed to all their particular duties in different spheres of life. And that no one might rashly transgress the limits prescribed, he has styled such spheres of life *vocations*, or *callings*. Every individual's line of life, therefore, is, as it were, a post assigned him by the Lord, that he may not wander about in uncertainty all this days. ... He that is in obscurity will lead a private life without discontent, so as not to desert the station in which God has placed him. ... Hence also will arise peculiar consolation, since there will be no employment so mean and sordid (provided we follow our vocation) as not to appear truly respectable, and be deemed highly important in the sight of God."[1]

It is regrettable that anthologies in the history of political theory always confine themselves to reproducing the last chapter of the *Institutes* on civil government because that chapter cannot be fully understood without reference to Calvin's doctrine of vocation, which is spelled out elsewhere in the book. This is especially true of his discussion of the nature and limits of resistance to constituted authority. Even his insistence on obedience to bad rulers makes sense only in the light of his doctrine of vocation. What Barth,

---

1. John Calvin; *Institutes of the Christian Religion*; 2 vols. (Presbyterian Board of Christian Education; Philadelphia; n.d.); Vol. I; Book III; pp. 790-91.

Bonhoeffer and Brunner have done with it is to pick it up, give it fresh for-
mulations, and apply it to the conditions of their time.

The doctrine of vocation is part of the teaching of the Church, especially
in that part of the Church that belongs to the Reformed and Presbyterian
communions. That doctrine is both narrower and broader than the teaching
of the Church. It is narrower in that there are many elements in the teaching
of the Church that deal with matters other than vocation. It is broader in its
application to politics because the Christian witness of government officials
is wider and more specific than the witness of the Church as a whole; i.e.,
Christian government officials have the right and the obligation to speak
and take action on many issues about which the Church as a whole, if it is
wise, would do well to maintain silence. On this point, Tillich, Barth, Bonhoeffer and Brunner are all agreed. Social activists are not likely to be
favorably disposed toward the doctrine of vocation because it has the effect
of cutting down on Church pronouncements on political issues and should
provoke them, if they are logical, to regard that doctrine as an escape from
responsibility.

Let us remember, and here we're limiting ourselves to the doctrine of
vocation as it applies to magistrates – i.e., those who wield governmental
authority over us – that there are rigidities, or what Bonhoeffer called technical requirements, that apply from the most menial to the most exalted
positions. These rigidities can confront magistrates with "horrifying" decisions, as Brunner noted, and circumscribe the scope of their discretionary
power in any case.

There are jobs in which routine is so intractable, technical requirements
are so specific and numerous, and options are so few and far between that
the magistrates who fill them are likely to feel hemmed in, caught in a
treadmill, and dehumanized. How can a magistrate, if he is a Christian, give
a Christian witness in such exiguous[2] quarters? While this, indeed, is a
problem, and one that extends to far more than governmental positions, we
would do well to remember the point that Bonhoeffer and Brunner made –
that there always is some room for a Christian witness.

Let us take Brunner's own example: "I just behave differently to my
neighbour in my capacity as a judge, a policeman ... from the way in which
I would behave towards him in a 'private' relationship – as man to man."[3]
Now, Brunner undoubtedly is right in saying this, since there is a difference
that goes with the office, but it would be wrong to conclude that either the
judge or the police officer is an automaton and that we have a situation in

---

2. Exiguous; that is, excessively scanty or inadequate.

3. Brunner; *The Divine Imperative*; p. 225.

which, to paraphrase Cicero,[4] every magistrate is a speaking law and every law is a silent magistrate. No job is that simple. A judge, for example, often has wide discretion in imposing a sentence on someone convicted of a crime. Whether he will be lenient or "throw the book at him," and what he chooses to say in passing, are discretionary matters in which a strong Christian witness is possible – and, for a Christian judge, mandatory. He also may use the prestige and the contacts that go with judicial office to obtain a change in the law that binds him and which his Christian conscience says is unjust.

Who could be in a better position than a judge in securing changes in a law that applies to situations with which he is thoroughly familiar because they keep coming up in court? His position gives him a professional knowledge and special opportunities that are unique and not available to people in other walks of life.

The case of the police officer is not essentially different. True, he does not stand as high in the public esteem as a judge, and there are places and times in which he is vilified. Nevertheless, his job is by no means automatic. Where is the line between firm enforcement of the law and police brutality? Where does common courtesy end and official impartiality begin? There is room for a Christian witness in answering such questions, room for something that goes far deeper than the mere avoidance of corruption, indispensable as that is. There is nothing in his official capacity that prevents a police officer from reacting as a Christian to charges that he is nothing but a fascist pig, or worse. Indeed, as Brunner suggests, he may say "something amazing" that will have a Christian impact then or later.

There is another way in which a Christian witness may be effective, even for bureaucrats who find themselves far down in the official hierarchy. That is the way of constitutional resistance. This way, perhaps, is questionable, and certainly has been much debated because it involves the refusal to apply a law or to carry out an official order. It does, however, have the sanction of no less a theologian than John Calvin, who regarded it as legitimate resistance (not revolution). This way does not bring outside meddling or irresponsible claims to a right to disobey by private people. For Calvin, a preacher or a doctor or a business person who chose such a course would be stepping outside his vocation. But the magistrate is staying within his vocation. The French Huguenots, who were followers of Calvin, unsuccessfully tried to resort to constitutional resistance by having the courts (then

---

4.   Marcus Tullius Cicero (c. 106 B.C.-43 B.C.). Roman orator, lawyer, politician and philosopher. In his writings, he placed politics above philosophical study, seeing the latter as being valuable in its own right, but even more valuable as the means to more effective political action.

called *parlements*) refuse to register those royal edicts that violated the fundamental law of the realm. Constitutional resistance lies at the heart of our system of judicial review, whereby a judge may annul a law that conflicts with the U.S. Constitution. It makes a great deal of difference, of course, if a judge is a member of the U.S. Supreme Court or one of the lower courts, but the principle of judicial review is intact. The judge is not an interloper, meddler or busybody, but an official acting in the line of duty.

Questionable, but nonetheless sometimes very effective, is passive resistance; i.e., foot dragging by lesser bureaucrats. Resistance of this sort takes the form of repeated postponements, a proliferation of frustrating procedures, a failure to implement decisions, or just plain inaction. This resistance is hard to get at because it is not open, and an almost impenetrable cloak of anonymity protects it. The old Spanish empire did not recognize any right of resistance by colonial or any other officials, however highly placed, and obedience was an absolute requirement. Nevertheless, Spanish colonial officials adopted a formula for dealing with unenforceable and clearly unwise orders from the Council of the Indies[5] in faraway Spain. That formula endorsed the substance of resistance by foot dragging without the name: *Obedezco, pero no cumplo* ("I obey, but I do not execute"). That formula was a marvelous tribute to the ingenuity and resourcefulness of government officials in meeting the seemingly insurmountable obstacles of absolute authoritarianism. The lesson to be drawn from these instances of resistance by lesser magistrates, whether passive or official, is that a governmental position is not without some elements of flexibility in spite of the strictest and most rigid rules.

Going from one extreme to the other in this matter of flexibility, let us move to consider those magistrates who have the greatest possible amount of discretion – namely, the members of an unlimited national constitutional convention. It would be pointless, of course, to suppose that the members of such a body are sovereign in the sense of omnipotence. They are subjected to many pressures and have to worry about ratification. But they are in a unique position as compared to the members of a congress or parliament because, whereas the latter are legally limited by the constitution, the former are the *makers* of the constitution. Bounded on all sides by many pressing realities, constitution makers come closest to an unfettered discretionary power as is given to any person (e.g., a dictator) or a group of peo-

---

5. Council of the Indies (1503), presided over by Rodríguez de Fonseca who earlier supervised preparations for the second voyage of Columbus (1493), was designed to administer the Spanish colonies and exercised supreme authority over the Indies and the Casa de Contratación, which was established in Sevilla to control colonial commerce, emigration and maritime enterprise. With the advent of the Bourbon dynasty (1700), the Council of the Indies declined in importance.

ple (e.g., a constituent assembly). The first and main task of constitution makers is that of deciding what form of government should be adopted. Should it be democratic, republican, oligarchic, socialistic, federal, unitary or some other of the many forms known to history and politics? (This is the task that faced the new states of Asia and Africa at the end of European colonial rule. It also is the task that faced older states like France under Charles de Gaulle, Portugal after the death of António de Oliveira Salazar, and Spain after the death of Francisco Franco.) Deciding what form of government should be adopted is an extremely difficult task that requires (1) the choice of a public philosophy; and (2) an understanding of the facts of national life that is realistic, objective and scientific. The first requirement looks to what is desirable, the second to what is possible, and statesmanship consists in reconciling the desirable with the possible.

Toward the accomplishment of this task, Tillich's contribution is minimal, if non-existent. He does indicate a preference for democracy, but it is slight and much qualified. In his opinion, the form of government is not a theological question. Barth's position is almost the same as Tillich's, except that he does rule out two extreme situations – anarchy and despotism. These extremes no Christian should tolerate, since they contradict the will of God. But the wide spectrum between these two extremes is a matter of indifference. Christians can accommodate themselves and give an effective witness in any of the intermediate forms. It might be said that Barth's position is not quite so latitudinarian[6] as his several very explicit statements would lead one to believe when we take note of his comments on specific topics like the family, capital punishment, war and work. Still, his general position is clearly latitudinarian, and offers no help to constitution makers in determining what form of government their nation should have.

The situation is different with Bonhoeffer. His concept of mandate leads him to favor limited government whose function is "regulative" rather than "constitutive," and to recommend a federalism that is more functional than territorial. Like Barth, he believes that a Christian can accommodate himself to, and give effective witness under, any form of government – even, as he personally demonstrated, in a jail or a concentration camp. But, unlike Barth, Bonhoeffer does not consider forms of government between anarchy and despotism to be a matter of indifference on which the Christian has nothing to say.

Brunner is the most explicit and specific of the four theologians. There is no question as to where he stands – strongly in favor of a form of govern-

---

6. Latitudinarian is defined as a person who is broad and liberal in standards of religious belief and conduct.

ment that is federal and democratic. In taking this stand, he remarks: "It is apparent that I am here showing my colors as a Swiss citizen."[7] Brunner is too modest. It only would be natural for him, of course, to find support for his opinion in the constitution and politics of his country, but his position rests on a well-developed theological foundation. His preference for a form of government that is federal and democratic is rooted in his concept of the orders of creation and preservation. On this foundation, he does not say that democratic federalism is the Christian form of government outside of which no Christian can or should live, but that it is the form of government that is most compatible with a Christian point of view and under which a Christian feels most comfortable.

With respect to the first requirement that constitution makers have to fulfill in deciding upon a form of government – i.e., choosing a public philosophy – we should not assume that the choice is entirely free. The choice is seriously modified by the political, social and economic conditions that characterize the nation. Nevertheless, there is some room for innovation that may be large or small, depending on the times. In any case, a fairly coherent public philosophy is indispensable if a constitution is to make any sense, as we have seen by contrasting the national and state constitutions in the United States.

All four of the theologians agree that there can be no such thing as the Christian public philosophy and, therefore, no one constitution can be considered to be *the* Christian constitution. To conclude otherwise would be to violate the First Commandment and yield to idolatry. Public philosophies are constructs of human reason, and human reason is finite. The Christian contribution in such matters largely is negative (in the sense of nay saying), but certainly not unimportant. The public philosophy usually is implicit in the provisions of a constitution (e.g., checks and balances or bill of rights – or the lack of them) and explicit in the preamble and, most of all, in the sections that the framers of the short-lived Spanish Republican constitution of 1931 called the *parte dogmatim* (dogmatic part). In this way, the public philosophy receives a considerable degree of visibility and becomes the point of contact with the Christian witness. What can a Christian constitution maker do with this point of contact as he exercises his vocation?

For one thing, Christian constitution makers should oppose any endorsement of the secular dogma of sovereignty, whether sovereignty be ascribed to one man as in an absolute monarchy, to a political party as in fascism, to the workers as in socialism and communism, to the nation as in nationalism, or to the people as in a democracy. Of all these species of idolatry, this

---

7.   Brunner; "Intellectual Autobiography" in *The Theology of Emil Brunner*; p. 4.

last one is the most tempting in the Western world – especially for the advocates of participatory democracy and the one-man, one-vote formula.

Bonhoeffer argues that Scripture condemns the secular dogma of popular sovereignty: "It knows that the people grows from below, but that government is instituted from above."[8] Brunner makes exactly the same point. In spite of his commitment to democracy, he says: "Every Swiss knows what a law is, but no man, I fear, has as much trouble in understanding what the Bible calls 'law' as the Swiss." The trouble is that the Swiss believe in popular sovereignty and, therefore, find it hard to understand that, in the Bible, law does not have its source in the will of the people and "is not what comes from man but what is given to man."[9]

Political theorists such as Thomas Hobbes and John Austin[10] are fond of saying that a political system cannot work unless ultimate authority is vested in a determinate person or group of persons. But ultimate authority is vested in God alone. Sovereignty as it generally is understood means anarchy in international politics and despotism in domestic politics. If it is to be retained at all in a way compatible with Christian thinking, we must redefine it in the more restricted sense it has received in American constitutional usage: A discretionary power under, and limited by, established law. It is in this sense that we speak of individual states in the United States as sovereign states. In the American commonwealth, state action is sovereign in the sense of being final, so long as it does not violate the federal and state constitutions.

The same restricted concept of sovereignty should be applied to nation-states. Admittedly, this is much more difficult because of the absence of a world constitution to draw the bounds and of a world government to enforce them. But there is such a thing as international law and there is such a thing as natural law.

In spite of the many imperfections of international law and the vagueness of natural law, the necessities of civilized international life demand that Christians support both kinds of law, just as the ancient Romans did in

8.   Bonhoeffer; *Ethics*; p. 38.

9.   Brunner; *Our Faith*; p. 44.

10. John Austin (1790-1859). English legal philosopher noted for providing the terminology necessary to analyze the interrelationship between ethics and proper law that has evolved into the modern field of analytical jurisprudence. He is considered by many to be the creator of the approach to law known as "legal positivism," which argues that law, as opposed to moral imperatives, should be viewed simply as a form of command, made by an acknowledged and legitimate ruler. His work, such as *The Province of Jurisprudence Determined* (1832), provided an easily understandable ethical framework that established the rule of law as distinct from the rule of God and Christian morality.

recognizing the *jus naturale*[11] and the *jus gentium*.[12] Perhaps these necessities, and the legal realities to which they point, someday will be embedded in national constitutional documents, as was begun in the pioneering Spanish Republican constitution of 1931. (The Spanish Republicans were too far ahead of their time and too remote from the realities of Spanish political and social conditions.)

The great foe of Christian constitution makers in these matters is legal positivism. By its denial of any validity or even reality to international law and natural law, legal positivism delivers humankind to enslavement at the hands of every psychopathic dictator or group of dictators engaged in a futile but bloody search for the omnipotence of God.

Another contribution that Christian constitution makers can offer is to support as much decentralization as is compatible with stability and efficiency. This means territorial and functional federalism, separation of powers, checks and balances, a bill of rights and other initiatives. Obviously, it is impossible to tell in advance how much and how far government should be decentralized in these ways. There are nations for which the adoption of federalism would be suicidal because it would encourage, if not unleash, deep-seated centrifugal tendencies. Other nations would be threatened with political immobility by checks and balances, thus inviting anarchy – with despotism as the final outcome. Nevertheless, to the extent to which conditions make a choice possible in this direction of decentralization, that choice should be made. Many thinkers, both Christian and non-Christian, recognize bigness as one of the greatest dangers of our time – big government, big business, big labor, big universities. In this country, revenue sharing is perhaps the most obvious recognition of the need to decentralize.

At this point, it is only fair to note that there is a long history of non-Christian political thought reaching as far back as Polybius[13] and Cicero that advocates the same thing we are advocating here. There are strong secular grounds for defending the main lines of the American constitutional system, so long as this is done with due regard for the country's own problems; with respect for the institutions and ways of other peoples; and with adaptability and inventive resourcefulness in coping with quite different

---

11. *Jus naturale.* Latin meaning "natural law."

12. *Jus gentium.* Latin meaning "the law of nations."

13. Polybius (c. 203 B.C.-120 B.C.). Greek historian of the Mediterranean world, especially the rise of the Roman Republic, which he attributed to Roman fitness and the excellence of Roman civic and military institutions. He is most valued for his account of the Second and Third Punic Wars between Rome and Carthage. Polybius's account endeavoured to provide a universal history (his *Pragmateia*) of the period between 220 B.C. and 146 B.C., along with a prologue on Roman history from 264 B.C, that recorded the rise of the Roman hegemony.

conditions and backgrounds. In this respect, the Christian constitution maker should be the ally of his secular colleagues who belong to the same constitutionalist tradition. But can he contribute anything here that his secular colleagues cannot contribute? The answer is "Yes" – he can contribute a theological foundation for their common position. This is precisely what Bonhoeffer, Brunner, Kuyper and Dooyeweerd have done or, perhaps more accurately, have begun to do. Bonhoeffer did it with his concept of mandate. Brunner did it with his concept of orders of creation and preservation. Kuyper and Dooyeweerd did it with their concept of sphere sovereignty. The importance of a theological foundation for constitutionalism is not immediately apparent to most Americans. The reason is not merely that this country has become so lamentably secularized. More to the point is that Americans are accustomed to living under a constitutional system that largely embodies and protects the kind of decentralization advocated here.

Thus, if an American is asked why private property, vested rights, religious liberty and academic freedom should be respected, he almost certainly will point to provisions in the federal and state constitutions that protect them. Because an American has civil rights, he finds it unnecessary to believe in natural rights and divine imperatives. But what would be his position if these civil rights and the existing allocations of power between the nation and the states and among the three branches of the federal government are swept away? This is exactly where a theological foundation becomes crucial. It is not necessary to assume that America's constitutional heritage is likely to be swept away, since this is very unlikely. Less unlikely, however, is a legal and political erosion of that heritage – and some would argue that activist judges and government officials arbitrarily declaring that same-sex marriages are legal would be one example of such an erosion. To prevent such a development, a theological foundation is invaluable.

If constitutionalism is to be safeguarded, Christian constitution makers must oppose any declaration that affirms the inherent goodness of human beings and any assumption that presupposes an optimistic view of human nature. The Christian doctrine of the total depravity of human nature gives the lie to any such declaration or assumption. When it describes that depravity as total, this doctrine does not assert that man is totally bad, but that all his faculties – reason not excepted – are affected by sin. From this fact arises the need for constitutional restraints.

The contribution of Christian constitution makers is positive, as well as negative. When Bonhoeffer calls the family a mandate and Brunner calls it an order of creation, they guarantee the integrity of the family as an institution and confer upon it a sanctity that undergirds and transcends its status as a civil right. When Brunner classifies private property as an order of preservation, he assigns to it rights and responsibilities that go beyond the practical arguments on behalf of private property by Aristotle and other non-Christian thinkers. When Bonhoeffer places culture and education under the mandate of "labour," he is giving academic freedom a base that is much stronger than the constitutional status given by state constitutions to universities and the provisions of the U.S. Constitution concerning copyrights and patents. It also is a firmer base than that which Daniel Day Williams[14] gives academic freedom because Williams derives it only from the medieval tradition.

What these examples of theologically-based political decentralization mean is that the constitution makers guarantee and promote the right to witness not only to themselves, but to people in all walks of life. If a Christian is to fulfill his destiny, which is to glorify God, he has to have a measure of freedom – and this is what constitutionalism gives him. It is true, of course, that a Christian can survive and witness under despotism and even in a state of near-anarchy, but the matter of degree should not be underrated. The fact is that some regimes are more conducive to the flourishing of the good life as understood by the ancient Greeks and of witnessing as the Christians understand it than other regimes. Insofar as the Christian constitution maker is concerned, what we must remember is that, as he threads his course through the complexities and perplexities of shaping the fundamental institutions of his country, the Christian is in a unique position not shared by others and he, therefore, is acting wholly within his vocation.

We may recall the second requirement for the adequate fulfillment of the difficult task of constitution making – namely, an understanding of the facts of national life that is realistic, objective and scientific. This is a requirement that applies with equal force to Christian and non-Christian alike. It often has been disregarded, and the consequences have been what one would expect.

The Weimar Constitution is an example of the failure to meet this requirement. It imposed proportional representation for the legislative bodies of the Reich (nation) and the *Länder* (states), thus accentuating the deep and numerous cleavages among the German people. It provided for cabinets responsible to the legislature, ignoring the multi-party system that produced a weak executive in a country long accustomed to a strong authoritarian executive. It retained the disproportional relationship between Prus-

---

14. Daniel Day Williams (1910-1973). Longtime teacher and writer at Union Theological Seminary in New York. His books include *The Minister and the Care of Souls, God's Grace and Man's Hope, The Advancement of Theological Education, The Ministry in Historical Perspective* and others.

sia and the rest of the country, with the result that federalism was little more than a mask for Prussian domination and easily crumbled under the onslaught of Nazism.

Argentina is another example of the same sort of thing. In 1853, it adopted a constitution modeled after that of the United States and which has been the formal constitution of the country off and on, between dictatorships, ever since. It, too, ignored the political, social, economic and geographic realities of national life. To take just one illustration: The Argentine constitution follows the pattern of the American constitution by providing that the nation shall guarantee to every province a republican form of government. Argentine practice, however, has been totally unlike the American. When an Argentine president did not like one of the provincial governments, usually because it had fallen into the hands of an opposition party, he simply removed that government from office under the pretext that it was not "republican" and appointed an official known as an "interventor" to rule the province until a government acceptable to the president could be elected. What Juan B. Alberdi, who was the architect of the constitution of 1853, overlooked was the different attitude of the Argentines toward the law, the Hispanic tradition of *personalismo* (favoritism), and the preponderance of Buenos Aires.

The trouble with the architects of the Weimar and Argentine constitutions was that they were jurists trained in the continental European tradition, which has been legalistic and has ignored sociological, historical and geographic factors. To attempt to impose a public philosophy on recalcitrant facts is utopianism, not statesmanship. The necessary realism is not a specifically Christian trait. The most that one can expect of Christian constitution makers is that they match the very best secular thinking and avoid settling for the second best, indulging in wishful thinking and being satisfied with less information than is available.

It could be argued that a Christian concept of objectivity is a special asset, inasmuch as it requires total involvement in the sense of knowing how people feel, as well as what they think, and being sympathetic to all participants in a dispute, instead of total detachment and dis-involvement. This argument usually is valid with respect to academic people. It is not nearly as valid, if at all, with respect to politicians because the necessities of getting elected in heterogeneous districts have an educational effect on politicians. In meeting the requirement of realism, therefore, the Christian constitution maker is the ally – and not the teacher – of his non-Christian colleagues.

In our discussion of the doctrine of vocation, we have deliberately moved from one extreme to the other; i.e., from the lowly bureaucrat to the constitution maker. There is, of course, a very wide range of intermediate positions – each of which has its own difficulties and opportunities for a Christian witness, and all of which could be developed interminably. It may suffice to recall Theodore Roosevelt's remark that the American presidency is a "bully pulpit" and that the president may, to use Brunner's phrase again, say "something amazing." This is just what Abraham Lincoln did in his Second Inaugural Address when he pleaded for malice toward none, charity for all, and healing the nation's wounds.

What made this plea amazing was its deeply Christian spirit, which we usually do not expect in our chief executive, and it was made at a time when the air was filled with hatred and a spirit of revenge – similar to the post-9/11 atmosphere. This kind of witnessing is open to highly-placed officials, such as senators, governors and presidents.

The great peril in this kind of witnessing is hypocrisy – an evil that does more damage to Christian witnessing than outright hostility. Nevertheless, in political life as elsewhere, we must run the risk of being wrong if we are to be right.

CHAPTER THREE

The Meaning of Encounter

Before dealing with this topic, a few remarks about terminology are necessary. The crudest meaning of the word *encounter* is "collision." This, obviously, is not the sense in which it is used here. We shall refer to encounter, for ease of discussion, as a concept with the understanding that encounter is a relationship between persons – it even could be called an event. And the word "person" is not used here out of deference to feminists or women's liberationists, but to avoid the word "individual," which is used in contradistinction with "collective." A person is unique; an individual merely is a type or category.

The word *encounter* as used by theologians is borrowed from the philosophy of existentialism,[1] and all four of the theologians discussed in this book have been influenced by that philosophy. On a more popular level, the word has become tied up with sensitivity training (also known as interpersonal relations). Some aspects of it have had an impact on the lay renewal and charismatic movements. Though this usage of the word is new, some of its substance is much older, as we can see in Baptists' testimonials. The popularization of the word encounter has had good and bad effects. It has been good in that it meant a rediscovery of the senses – especially touch – as a means of communication and in that it has the therapeutic value of confession. It has been bad in that it has meant an invasion of privacy, encouraged a morbid concentration on introspection, and promoted irrationalism. And, yet, encounter has a noble and fruitful meaning and its substance, though not the word, can be found in the Bible.

An encounter is not something discovered and grasped by the intellect. Neither is it an empirical reality perceived by the senses, though it may be conveyed through the senses, like a touch of the hand, the expression on a

---

1. Existentialism. Chiefly, a 20th-century philosophical movement embracing diverse doctrines, but centering on the analysis of individual existence in an unfathomable universe and the plight of the individual who must assume responsibility for his acts of free will without any certain knowledge of what is right or wrong or good or bad.

face, an inflection of the voice. It belongs to the dimension of the spirit, of person-to-person relationships, and is a fact of experience. It does not belong to the realm of things, and it transcends the subject-object dichotomy.

An encounter always involves the perception and appreciation of a presence – the presence of another person. This presence may be physical, but it need not be. If another person, though physically present, is not seen but ignored, overlooked or regarded as an object, there is no encounter. Presence can exist when another person is physically absent. For the man whose beloved wife is away, she is present: a multitude of little objects and relationships to other people bear the unmistakable imprint of her presence. There was an old woman in a small town in North Carolina whose nickname was "Miss Poppadie" because, for her, everything dated back to the time when Papa died. For very old people, it often happens that persons long dead are more vividly and truly present than those now living with them. Being in the realm of the spirit, presence is independent of time and space.

An encounter may take place through a conversation in depth, by the mutual sharing of a sorrow or joy, or by the mutual facing of an impending crisis. But it may be much less direct, as in the case of letters. Some letters are factual, objective, colorless, impersonal and unrevealing. Other letters are so revealing of the one who wrote them that the writer's presence is all-encompassing and almost palpable.

Another characteristic of an encounter is that the persons who experience it incorporate something of each so that neither one ever is quite the same again. Each person takes in some of the other self and assimilates some of the other person's world – hopes and aspirations, loves and hates, view of life, personal background, loyalties and allegiances.

When theologians speak of an encounter with Jesus Christ, it is well to keep these characteristics of presence and encounter in mind; otherwise, the theologians are speaking nonsense. Those who look at an encounter in the light of rationalism and positivism will admit that there was an encounter between Jesus of Nazareth and his disciples, but they will deny it to present-day Christians because they hold that the "Christ of faith" is not present in the sense that the historical Jesus was. But if we look at an encounter with Christ in the light of the dimension of the spirit and as a fact of experience, this encounter is not only real, but crucially so. The question properly may be asked, "How it is possible to have an encounter with Christ in the absence of his physical presence in the everyday sense of the term?" There are two answers to that question – through reading the Bible and through the observation of the lives of Christians.

The first, most important, and most reliable avenue toward encountering Christ is through reading the New Testament, which is the only record we have of the teachings and deeds of Jesus, the only account we have of his death and resurrection. We also have the Old Testament, which is the background of everything Jesus said, did and was. It is because of these facts that the Bible is the cornerstone of Protestantism and the motivating force behind the translation of the Bible into a multitude of languages.

How can the reading of the Bible be the source and occasion of an encounter with Christ? There is no mystery about this, other than the mystery that accompanies the reading of anything. It was John Milton who said that "books are not absolutely dead things but do contain a potency of life in them to be as active as that soul whose progeny they are; nay, they do preserve as in a vial the purest efficacy and extraction of that living intellect that bred them." So seriously did Milton mean this that he concluded that he "who kills a man kills a reasonable creature, God's image; but he who destroys a good book, kills reason itself, kills the image of God, as it were in the eye."[2] Surely, no more eloquent testimony to the power of the written word ever was made, and we must bear in mind that Milton was speaking of the classics of literature and other "good books." How much more applicable this testimony is to the power of Scripture!

This power of the written word is recognized in the case of the great secular writers. Thus, it is impossible to read the works of Nietzsche[3] and ever look at life in the same way again, and this is true even of those who vigorously reject his philosophy. The same thing could be said of W.W. Crosskey's fat tomes,[4] since no one who read them ever again could think

---

2. John Milton; "Areopagitica" (Harvard Classics; P.F. Collier & Son Company; New York; 1909–14); Vol. 3; p. 192.

3. Friedrich Nietzsche (1844-1900). German philosopher and writer. Best known for quasi-philosophical and anti-religious works, including *Human, All Too Human* (1878), *The Gay Science* (1882), *Thus Spoke Zarathustra* (1883), and *Beyond Good and Evil* (1886). Reliance on abstract concepts in a quest for absolute truth, Nietzsche believed, merely is a symptom of the degenerate personalities of philosophers like Socrates. He concluded that traditional philosophy and religion are both erroneous and harmful for human life; enervating and degrading our native capacity for achievement. Progress beyond the stultifying influence of philosophy, then, requires a thorough "revaluation of values." In *On the Genealogy of Morals* (1887), he decried the slave morality enforced by social sanctions and religious guilt. Only rare, superior individuals can rise above all moral distinctions to achieve a heroic life of truly human worth.

4. W.W. Crosskey; *Politics and the Constitution in the History of the United States*; 3 vols. (University of Chicago Press; Chicago; 1953-1980; vol. III completed and edited by Murray Dry); Crosskey, according to Peter Linzer, put forth an idiosyncratic history of the Constitution, arguing (1) that the Constitution was intended to give Congress general legislative powers, not limited to those enumerated in Art. I, sec. 8; (2) that the limitations on federal power over the next 150 years were illicit; and (3) that the expansion of federal powers beginning in 1937 achieved the historically correct result, if by an artificial and circuitous route of using the effect, direct or indirect, on commerce to reach matters that courts over the years had incorrectly deemed not to be "commerce" itself.

of the Constitution in quite the same way, though not necessarily because he agrees with Crosskey's controversial conclusions. If we concede that, how much more power should we ascribe to Scripture as exemplified again and again, sometimes spectacularly, in human lives over the ages!

The other answer to the question of how it is possible to have an encounter with Christ is that it occurs through the observation of the lives of Christians – or, at least, of some Christians. There is no mystery about this either, other than the mystery that occurs every time one human being influences another. We constantly are encountering persons through other persons. Students who have been molded by great teachers – such as, in my generation, the political theorist Leo Strauss[5] – can be spotted immediately by their vocabulary, their attitudes, their foes, their commitments, and their points of view. Sometimes, the influence of great teachers shows through even in little things like facial expressions, gestures and mannerisms. If we grant this phenomenon, as we must if we are to heed the common universal experience of mankind, it is not hard to see how the person of Jesus Christ – from whose birth all history is measured – can be encountered in the person of his followers.

It will be objected that many people have read the Bible and not been gripped by it. That is undeniable. It also can be objected that encounters between Christians and non-Christians not always have been encounters and, therefore, have not led to an encounter with Christ. That, too, is undeniable. Even in Christ's own day there were many people, such as the Pharisees and Sadducees, for whom confrontation with Jesus himself did not amount to an encounter. This is why theologians are careful to point out that a true encounter with Christ, and its concomitant faith, is a gift which, for reasons we do not understand, is accepted by some and rejected by others. We are dealing here with revelation, a fact that is as indisputable as it is unexplainable.

When theologians like Barth, Bonhoeffer and Brunner assert that Jesus Christ was God incarnate and that, without an encounter with him, no one knows what man is or what one's very self is, the assertion sounds unduly extreme and arrogantly dogmatic. But is it really so difficult to understand, if not to believe?

Academic people find it especially difficult. And, yet, there is in their

---

5. Leo Strauss (1899-1973). German-Jewish émigré political philosopher and political historian, who wrote more than a dozen books and 80 articles on the history of political thought from Socrates to Nietzsche. In his writings, he contrasted the wisdom of ancient philosophers such as Plato and Aristotle with the foolhardiness of modern philosophers such as Hobbes and Locke. He thought that the loss of ancient wisdom was the reason for the "crisis of the West."

own experience something that should help them. If a graduate student compares himself with other graduate students, even on the level of encounter, he very well may come out with a favorable estimate of his capabilities and achievements. True, some are superior and some inferior, but the differences are not so considerable as to make him feel uncomfortable. But let that graduate student compare himself with a professor who has a lifetime of scholarship behind him, and the reaction will be entirely different. Only then will the graduate student realize how little he knows. He will see the depth of his ignorance, but he also will see the heights to which he can aspire.

The same experience is felt by the professional musician, who listens to one of the world's greatest performers. The same experience is felt by the politician on the local and state level, who contemplates the presidency of the United States and has a sense of the distance that separates him from the magnitude of the presidential office. Without the summit, one cannot have an appreciation of what height and depth mean.

It is this kind of experience, only carried to its very maximum, that the theologians have in mind when they say that human beings know their true selves only when they encounter the person of Jesus Christ. Modern Man beholds one who healed lepers by the touch of his hand, who stilled the waves by a mere command, who restored paralytics to the full use of their limbs by his spoken word, and who raised a man from the dead. Of course, Modern Man is unlikely to be impressed by these deeds because he does not believe in miracles, being convinced as he is that everything in the organic and inorganic universe is governed by inexorable laws which no one – not even God – can suspend or revoke.

Modern Man, however, may be more impressed by other facets of the personality of Jesus. He beholds one who was assailed by temptation and, yet, never yielded – not even once. He beholds one who was brutally beaten, spat upon, ridiculed, insulted, maligned, misunderstood, and misrepresented without the slightest justification – and who, nevertheless, did not hold these things against his tormentors. He beholds one who, in the agony of his crucifixion, was surrounded by callous bystanders, fanatics, curiosity seekers, disciples paralyzed by fear and despair, morally obtuse and spiritually blind people – but, nevertheless, asked his Father to forgive them. Surely, no mere man could react in this manner.

A Modern Man, if he is almost universally loved and admired, might well wonder if those same people would continue to love and admire him if they could see his entire life as an open book; if they knew his secret desires and standards that are hidden in the recesses of his conscious and subconscious self; if they knew the sins that he did not commit only because the opportunity did not present itself. Probably no one would. The only answer to Modern Man's question – if he is honest enough to ask it – is that only God himself can continue to love him in spite of it all and seek to redeem him, justifying and sanctifying him. How can Modern Man know this? By looking at Jesus Christ, who reacts in precisely this way. And that is why Barth, Bonhoeffer and Brunner are right in asserting that all Christian theology must be Christocentric.

We also see Christ in our fellow men and women who are not Christians. This may seem surprising, indeed, until we take note of Barth's observation that, because all people are sinners, we see in others – and, therefore, in ourselves – what it is that crucified Christ. We become aware of our solidarity, which far transcends the concept of brotherhood as we find it in stoicism and deism. The brotherhood of men without Christ always has been spectral and remote, insufficient to create the solidarity that brotherhood should bring with it.

The relevance of encounter to Christian theology is obvious, but does it have any relevance to politics? When we pause to reflect on how painfully impersonal so much of modern life has become; when we hear the great chorus of thinkers who complain of alienation and lost-ness; when we see the lack of understanding and concern that blights so many human relationships; when we listen to philosophers and psychologists who stress – indeed, overstress – the subjective, we realize that encounter has enormous possibilities for politics. Enormous though these possibilities are, they also are likely to be indirect and of low visibility. This is because encounter largely is a person-to-person relationship and, therefore, must be repeated innumerable times.

There are exceptions to this very personal – and, therefore, highly individualized – species of revelation we call encounter, and it is precisely in political life that we most likely should be able to find them because of the availability of radio, television and the Internet. No one who heard Franklin Roosevelt's first fireside chat and Winston Churchill's first speech as prime minister will ever forget them. These were real cases of encounter since, behind the words of these men, their personal greatness showed through, liberating and ennobling the listener.

Unfortunately, such instances are rare, and the rarity usually is deliberate. Presidential speeches and messages often are written by staff members so that the personality of the president is concealed. Televised appearances exemplify the same characteristic concealment as presidents are carefully coached and makeup artists go to work on them. And what do we say about these addresses and appearances? Significantly and appropriately, we say that they are unrevealing, that they have not resulted in an encounter between the speaker and the audience. There is little left by which an encounter can take place, with the possible exception of press interviews that are more difficult to control. Some of the most glaring examples of the unrevealing and revealing presidential communications are the contrast between Dwight Eisenhower's speeches and his press conferences (syntax and all), Richard Nixon's speeches and his tapes (expletives and all), and George W. Bush's speeches and his press conferences (mangled words and all).

It was the French naturalist Georges-Louis Leclerc De Buffon[6] who said "*Le style, c'est l'homme*,"[7] a truth that was so brilliantly evident in the speeches and messages of Woodrow Wilson. And it was Nietzsche who said that language was invented to conceal thought, rather than to express it. We can see that it is Nietzsche, and not Buffon, who most consistently is followed by so many of our presidents, governors, senators and other major public figures.

Speech may conceal more than ignorance, malice, mediocrity and stupidity: It also may conceal emptiness. In one of his perceptive comments, Barth said: "Most of our words, spoken or heard, are an inhuman and barbaric affair. ... It is not the words that are really empty. It is the men themselves."[8] When a man runs for public office and does not reveal himself, we are disappointed – and should be shocked. We have become so concerned with the unrevealed finances of our public officials that we forget the still greater offense of unrevealed persons.

The possibilities of encounter in political life are by no means limited to our highest officials. They are capable of transforming official life far down the hierarchy, as well. Here, again, the possibilities are largely ignored. How are we going to have a sacramental relation, as Barth called it, with a typical bureaucrat? The very word *bureaucrat* suggests something formal and impersonal. It is a French invention describing a functionary who hides behind his desk (*bureau*), which underscores this formal and impersonal behavior and which is made still more vivid when a Frenchman derisively speaks of *Monsieur le Bureau*.

There is no reason why a bureaucrat could not be responsive and warm, show humor and compassion, give a human touch to the most ordinary official transaction. The objection that to behave in this way would be too time-consuming has no validity. The personal touch can make itself felt in an

---

6. Georges-Louis Leclerc De Buffon (1707-1788). French naturalist best remembered for his 44-volume comprehensive work on natural history, *Histoire naturelle, générale et particulière*.

7. *Le style, c'est l'homme* (French). "The style, it is the man."

8. Barth; *Church Dogmatics*; Vol. III-2; p. 260.

instant – something overlooked by Harvey Cox[9] when he said he could not have an "I-thou" relationship with the milkman. By means of encounter, the Christian bureaucrat could exert a great influence by the force of his example, provided he looked upon his position as a vocation and not just a job. It is impossible to predict what the experience of encounter would do to the functioning of bureaucracy, but it is safe to say that it would transform the attitude of the general public toward bureaucrats.

9. Harvey Cox Jr. has been teaching at Harvard University since the early 1960s, both at Harvard Divinity School and in the Faculty of Arts and Sciences. Earlier, as an American Baptist minister, he was the Protestant chaplain at Temple University and the director of religious activities at Oberlin College, as well as a professor at Andover Newton Theological School. He served as the Victor S. Thomas Professor of Divinity before being named Hollis Professor of Divinity in 2003. He is the author of such books as *Common Prayers: Faith, Family, and a Christian's Journey Through the Jewish Year; The Secular City; The Feast of Fools* and others.

CHAPTER FOUR

Spirit and Politics

The word *spirit* is a difficult and ambiguous word, and the realm of the spirit is unknown territory for almost all political scientists. In a profession so heavily dominated by behaviorism as political science is, spirit fits as tightly as a square peg in a round hole because spirit is not quantitative, does not lend itself to statistics, and cannot be fed into a computer. Neither was spirit at home in an earlier rationalist age because it is not something that can be fully grasped by the intellect. Our understanding of it resembles the average person's understanding of electricity: He does not know what it is, cannot define or describe it, but knows that it gives light, yields power, is communicable, and can be lethal.

The literature of political science and political theory is a barren desert on this subject. For an understanding of what spirit is, we must turn to theology – and, especially, to the New Testament. Only then can we be in a position to see its relevance to politics.

In the minds of the New Testament writers, there are many spirits who constitute a veritable world. There is very little about that world that we understand in this life. The New Testament speaks of spirits who are unclean, foul and evil. These spirits are living beings that are capable of taking possession of a human person, stripping him of his humanity and driving him to insanity and perdition. These unclean, foul and evil spirits have a family resemblance that points to a common origin, and they produce similar results. They have a name, Satan, who is evil personalized. In one place in the New Testament, it is said that his name is legion – which means that, although he is one in essence, he can take many forms and disguises.

Is there a world of evil spirits? Does Satan exist?

There is no doubt that the disciples and the apostles and Jesus himself believed so. But, until very recently, the world of evil spirits was dismissed as a remnant of a superstitious pre-scientific age in great need of demythologization, and Satan was tossed out into limbo with his medieval tail, horns, pitchfork and fires. Now, however, demons have become popular –

we hear of satanic cults, and there is much talk of exorcism. This relatively recent development may well be a belated realization that there are forms of evil that cannot be explained away as mental illness or understood as maladjustment. These are forms of evil that are not amenable to reason, which the most severe punishment cannot rend, which psychiatry cannot touch, and which only death can stop – until they take possession of some other human being. They are alive, elusive, resourceful, recalcitrant. No wonder the Lord's Prayer includes the petition "deliver us from evil," which some translations render "deliver us from the evil one."

The New Testament does not say that all evil is the result of possession by an evil spirit. It teaches that sin is our responsibility. It does not even say that all illness, mental or physical, is the result of sin. It recognizes that much evil and illness has psychological and sociological causes, thus leaving plenty of room for the physician, the psychiatrist and the social scientist.

What the New Testament does say is that illness and sin make the human being vulnerable to Satan, who exploits them – just as lowered bodily resistance is an invitation to the deadly germs that always are part of one's environment, but that healthy bodies are able to fend off. The demythologizers to the contrary, the New Testament is eminently realistic in its understanding of suffering, simultaneously recognizing both the utility and the limitations of the available human means to deal with it.

The world of spirits is not, of course, a monopoly of evil spirits. There also are good spirits, usually described in the New Testament as angels. Here, again, the modern mind bristles with skepticism. It cannot accept angels any more than it can accept demons, and for the same reasons: they are non-material, they cannot be fed into a computer, etc. Barth has an elaborate doctrine of angels, but it is not necessary to follow him there. Suffice it to say that angels are non-material messengers of God. Most important of all, let us not forget what the Apostle John said: "God is a Spirit."[1] And the New Testament has much to say about the Holy Spirit, who is the third person of the Trinity.

The New Testament teaches that the Holy Spirit is personal (a "he," never an "it"), brings light, power and comfort. Because he is spirit, we find it lamentably easy to think of him as a holy spook and get lost in irrational aberrations like spiritualism and some of the excesses of the charismatic movement. That is why we need what Carl Henry[2] has called "scriptural

---

1. John 4:24.

2. Carl F. H. Henry (1913-2003). was an evangelical Christian theologian, who founded the magazine *Christianity Today* as a scholarly voice for evangelical Christianity and as a challenge to the liberal *Christian Century*. The new magazine soon outdistanced
footnote 2 continued on next page

controls" and why the presence of the Holy Spirit has to be authenticated by his relationship to the historical Jesus of Nazareth and by his identity with the Christ of faith.

The analogy with electricity once again comes to mind: The presence of the Holy Spirit is evident in its manifestations. This presence is expressed in the reaction of those who experience it by such words as reverence, illumination, radiance, transluscence, wonder, awe and transfiguration. When the New Testament writers refer to it, they speak of the light of his countenance, the brightness of his glory, the light of life, and other fervent terms that attempt to express the inexpressible and somehow get through to other people nonetheless. The presence of Christ transforms whatever and whomever it touches by glorifying them, but never by denaturing them. This is the great difference with the story of King Midas – everything he touched turned to gold and, thus, was denatured. Not so with Jesus: In the story of the transfiguration, it is said that his raiment was "exceeding white as snow; so as no fuller on earth can white them."[3]

Scripture affirms that God is omnipotent, omniscient and benevolent. He loved the world so much that he gave his only Son to save it. Why, then, the skeptic asks, does God allow Satan to exist and evil spirits to interfere with human lives? No absolutely conclusive answer can be given to this question. There always will be an aura of mystery about it. An answer that denies the existence and activity of either God or Satan is unrealistic, leading to an optimism or a pessimism that is unwarranted by the facts.

Scripture does assert the sovereignty of God and tells us that Jesus Christ overcame the world. The Apostles' Creed[4] tells us that Jesus descended into hell, so that his resurrection and ascension demonstrate that he overcame not only the human world of sin, but the world of evil spirits, as well. The nearest answer to the skeptic's question is to be found in the

---

its competitor in readership, though it was not without its critics. At a luncheon of 200 Christian leaders held to honor neo-orthodox theologian Karl Barth, Henry rose and identified himself as "editor of *Christianity Today*" before asking Barth about his views on the historical fact of Jesus' resurrection. Barth retorted, "Did you say *Christianity Today* or Christianity Yesterday?" As the audience howled with laughter, Henry countered, "Yesterday, today, and forever."

3.   Mark 9:3.

4.   The Apostles' Creed. "I believe in God, the Father Almighty, the Creator of heaven and earth, and in Jesus Christ, His only Son, our Lord: Who was conceived of the Holy Spirit, born of the Virgin Mary, suffered under Pontius Pilate, was crucified, died, and was buried. He descended into hell. The third day He arose again from the dead. He ascended into heaven and sits at the right hand of God the Father Almighty, whence He shall come to judge the living and the dead. I believe in the Holy Spirit, the holy catholic church, the communion of saints, the forgiveness of sins, the resurrection of the body, and life everlasting. Amen."

story of Job, who was visited with one affliction after another to test his loyalty to God. This answer – that both suffering and evil are a punishment for sin and a test of virtue – was taken and developed by St. Augustine,[5] who said that it is not what happens to a person, but to whom it happens that matters. Adversity can make or break a person. But, here again, we run into another mystery – the mystery of predestination.

What is the political significance of the spiritual world? Because there are good and evil spirits, one obvious point of contact is the ability to discern spirits. The Apostle Paul speaks of it as a gift that should be used and respected. When the disciples wanted Jesus to have a Samaritan village consumed by fire from heaven because it would not receive him, Jesus said: "Ye know not what manner of spirit ye are of."[6] The spirit of man is his quintessence, so to speak, the living reality that underlies and activates his thought, feeling and action. We sometimes speak of "catching the spirit" of a man or a woman and, as we do catch it, we know that we have gotten hold of the most essential part of that person's self. It is not the result of rational calculation or based on quantitative data: It is the direct perception of the truth, something more like revelation than prediction.

The discerning of spirits is a great political asset. It is important because we know that words, whether ghost-written or not, often are intended to conceal and to deceive. Nor can we always tell much from appearance and manner because the politician may be a good actor or may have been well-coached. And a record, usually the most reliable basis we have for judging a person, also can be deceptive. It has happened, for instance, that a judge in one of the lower courts had a conservative record, but turned out to be a liberal after he was appointed to the U.S. Supreme Court. The reason for such a turnabout is that a lower court judge does not like to have his decisions reversed by a higher court because it is regarded as a reflection on his craftsmanship as a jurist. Once on the highest court, however, this worry no longer applies, and he takes the position he really believes in. Such facts as these make it difficult to have a reliable idea as to what is the true meaning of the present and what is going to happen in the future.

---

5. St. Augustine of Hippo (354-430). Considered to be one of the most outstanding theologians in the history of the Catholic Church. Besides the *Confessions*, Augustine's most celebrated work is his *On the City of God*, a study of the relationship between Christianity and secular society, which was inspired by the fall of Rome to the Visigoths in 410. Among his other works, many are polemical attacks on various heresies: *Against Faustus, the Manichean; On Baptism; Against the Donatists*; and many attacks on Pelagianism and Semi-Pelagianism. Other works include treatises *On the Trinity; On Faith, Hope, and Love; On Christian Doctrine*; and some early dialogues. He stands as a powerful advocate for orthodoxy.

6. Luke 9:55.

On the secular level, we have extensive factual surveys, analyses of speeches and addresses, calculations based on statistics, opinion polls, and the careful weighing of evidence. These techniques are important, of course, and should be mastered and heeded by political leaders. No Christian political leader should ignore the findings thus obtained since, as Calvin observed, he then would be guilty of neglecting some of the means that God has placed at his disposal.

But it is a narrow-minded, positivistic view that will not admit of any other means of understanding the present and foreseeing the future. Those who were able to discern the spirit of Hitler and Stalin knew what to expect long before those who confined themselves to conventional methods. Those who deride the whole idea of discerning spirits often misinterpret the process, trying to make it appear ridiculous. "Prophetic does not mean ecstatic, enthusiastic or violent."[7] There could be a bit of jealousy in this derisive attitude caused by seeing someone leap to the right conclusion without going through laborious, costly and time-consuming methods that sometimes fail anyway. Social scientists do not like shortcuts, even – and perhaps especially – when they lead to the right conclusion. The Christian, however, will insist that the gift of discerning spirits is one of the most important assets a political leader can possess. As the Apostle Paul said, the great truths are spiritually discerned.

Another characteristic of the realm of the spirit is its ability to transform where reform is not possible. A key verse on this point is to be found in the Epistle to the Romans: "And be not conformed to this world: but be ye transformed by the renewing of your mind, that ye may prove what is that good, and acceptable, and perfect, will of God."[8] This verse is especially relevant to us Americans because we have a marked tendency to believe that reform always is possible. There was a saying current on the Pacific front during World War II that expressed this tendency: The difficult we do in a jiffy, the impossible takes a little longer. The saying may be inspiring, but it is thoroughly unrealistic. There are conditions under which reform is out of the question, and the only recourse is to accommodate oneself to them and survive them victoriously.

The institution of slavery was precisely one of those conditions in New Testament times. It would have been futile for a small band of Christians to embark on an abolitionist program. Slavery was something they had to live with. So, the Apostle Paul urged slaves to obey their masters, not only out of necessity, but as a matter of conscience. What the early Christians did,

---

7. Barth; *Church Dogmatics*; Vol. IV-3; p. 897.

8. Romans 12:2.

however, was to transform the situation among themselves. Slaves were full members of the Church. Slaves were treated as brothers in Christ. Christians acted as though slavery did not exist and, among them, it *did not* exist. As more and more people joined the Christian community, the range of freedom broadened accordingly, thus showing the Roman Empire what is that good, and acceptable, and perfect will of God.

Let us take a contemporary and more modest example of the power to transform where reform is not possible. This example deals with the fact of hierarchy in a state university. The university has the usual hierarchical administrative structure with president, vice president, chancellor, vice chancellor, various deans and assistant deans, and a large number of departmental chairmen. It also has the usual academic hierarchy, reaching down from full professor to instructor.

Now, these structures present a problem for Christians. Jesus said to his disciples: "Ye know that they which are accounted to rule over the Gentiles exercise lordship over them; and their great ones exercise authority upon them. But so shall it not be among you: but whosoever will be great among you, shall be your minister."[9] Jesus uttered these words because his disciples were having a dispute as to who should be first among them – that is to say, the quarrel was about hierarchy.

Jesus was not condemning hierarchy in all circumstances, but only among Christians. In a world marked by competition and selfish ambition, hierarchy is necessary. Brunner would probably classify it as an order of preservation. Nevertheless, there is something repugnant about hierarchy from a Christian point of view because it puts rank above personal merit and encourages selfish ambition. How is a Christian to give his witness within a hierarchical structure?

There was a departmental chairman who took Jesus' words seriously. It was evident that no single departmental chairman could hope to abolish the administrative and academic hierarchies of the university. Reform was out of the question. What he did was to act as if the hierarchy did not exist in his department. He issued no orders, consulted every member without regard to age and rank, made decisions on the basis of consensus. Assignments were made in accordance with the logic of circumstances that all could see. Intradepartmental relationships were personal, not formal or official. This mode of operations worked successfully during almost the whole of that departmental chairman's long tenure. We are not suggesting that this mode of operation will work successfully everywhere and always, but simply to show what a Christian witness can accomplish through the

---

9.   Mark 10: 42-44.

power of transformation.

Some people may object to the assertion that reform is not possible within a university's administrative structure. It is true that some reforms have been made in response to faculty demands for participation in decision-making. In some universities, the chairmanship has been made elective or rotated among department members. It cannot be said that these reforms have always worked well. They often have led to politicking and infighting. The lesson to be drawn from this reform is that all structures – whether hierarchical or not – must have a spiritual basis, and that basis naturally grows out of the Christian faith. All four of the theologians whose political thought we have analyzed agree that no social order can be maintained or reformed in terms of structure alone.

It will be recalled that Barth, Bonhoeffer and Brunner all put great stress on obedience to constituted authority. It is almost trite to point out that obedience to constituted authority is seriously threatened nowadays. We see it in the disregard for constitutional processes manifested in the resort to violence and the so-called "direct action" techniques. We see it in the lack of good manners exhibited during political campaigns, not to speak of the "dirty tricks" we have heard so much about in connection with political scandals.

Here, again, the spiritual dimension is of crucial importance. Reverence is the root of obedience to constituted authority, of decent and civilized dissent, of being a member of an opposition that is loyal and constructive instead of destructive and subversive, of regarding nature as God's handiwork to be tended and preserved rather than something to be exploited and desecrated. But reverence also is an appreciation of the holy, whereby man becomes humble and aware of his limitations without losing his dignity and the will to act.

Reverence has another effect that goes beyond obedience to constituted authority – namely, that of raising the level on which disagreements and conflicts of interest are handled. On a low level, many problems are insoluble. On a high level, the same problems can be resolved. The authors of *The Federalist Papers*[10] were well aware of this fact, and correctly predicted that national officials generally would be morally and intellectually superior to state and local officials. The greater the magnitude of a challenge, the greater one needs the invisible resources of the spirit that reverence confers, and woe to the one who is confined to visible resources.

---

10. *The Federalist Papers* were a series of newspaper articles published in 1787-1788 and written under the pen name of Publius by Alexander Hamilton, James Madison and John Jay. The purpose of *The Federalist Papers* was to gain popular support for the then-proposed U.S. Constitution.

We have seen the power of this matter of levels in several of our presidents whose past gave no clue to their greatness, but who rose and grew in stature as they met the challenge of the presidential office. We also have seen it in the televised hearings of the Judiciary Committee of the House of Representatives, both for Richard Nixon and Bill Clinton. These elected politicians responded to the magnitude and awesomeness of impeachment proceedings, and their decision (at least in the Nixon case; arguments can be made for either side in the Clinton case) was made in the context of a reverence for the presidential office and the welfare of the country that freed them from vindictiveness and pettiness. Reverence, therefore, is a liberating factor that prevents obedience from degenerating into a narrow and blind adherence to the status quo.

One last observation is that the realm of the spirit is that in which the identity and creativity of the human being reside. No man is pure intellect, however brilliant. No man can be restricted to emotions, however intense. No man can be judged solely in terms of will, however good. No man can be identified with his body, however superb.

Behind intellect, emotions, will and the body lies the spirit, traditionally called the soul, which is one's identity – the magnetic center that gives cohesion to the personality. That is what we mean when we say that we have "caught the spirit" of a person. By saying this, however, we are not falling into the trap of spiritualism, which denies the reality of the body. As Barth so truly observed, "In sum, if materialism with its denial of the soul makes man subject-less, spiritualism with its denial of the body makes him objectless."[11]

Creativity is another characteristic of the realm of the spirit. Truth without the spirit that gave it birth and sustains it is lifeless. Without the spirit, there is no transluscence, and the most apt formulation or phrasing is dead, "for the letter killeth, but the spirit giveth life."[12]

It is the spirit that gives birth to the great masterpieces of art, and it is the source of hypotheses without which the finest laboratory techniques and the most accurate mathematical reasoning could not exist – and would be useless if they did.

The creativity of the spirit would be politically irrelevant if we lived in a petrified and perfect social order. But we do not live in such an order. We are in constant need of innovation and criteria for the right innovation. The art of statesmanship, as distinguished from mere political skill, must draw on the realm of the spirit for both the innovation and the criteria for it. We

---

11. Barth; *Church Dogmatics*; Vol. III-2; p. 392.

12. II Corinthians 3:6.

sometimes give that quality the name of vision and, as the Bible says, without vision, the people perish.[13]

---

13. Proverbs 29:18.

CHAPTER FIVE

The Church and Political Activity

W e must now turn to the question of the proper relationship of the Church, particularly the institutional church, to political activity. Is there or should there be a Christian witness in politics by the Church as distinguished from that of individual Christians?

This is an issue that sorely divides Christians in our day. The conflict is between the pietists and the social activists – or, though not quite so clear cut, between conservatives and liberals. The leadership of the mainline denominations and of the National and World Councils of Churches is committed to social activism. At the same time, large numbers of Christians within the mainline denominations strongly dissent from social activism and speak through some of the smaller denominations and through organizations usually described as evangelical. This is not to say that the conservative-versus-liberal division accounts for all differences of opinion among church members. There are other currents that blur any clear-cut dichotomy by encompassing some in both groups and groups that are interested in other issues. Among these currents, the most notable is probably the charismatic movement, sometimes known as neo-Pentecostalism.

Social activism[1] has its roots in the social gospel of the 1920s. The social gospel demanded that ministers devote their sermons to political issues and that church bodies make pronouncements on these issues to guide the conscience of their members and influence public policy. Social activism, however, is new in that it demands that the involvement of the Church in political activity be pushed much further. The demand is that the Church move from words to deeds. The topics emphasized by social activists are mainly racism, sexism, economics, globalization and war. They also are concerned with other issues – less sweeping perhaps, but nevertheless important and

---

1. For a detailed analysis and critique of social activism, see René de Visme Williamson, 'The Institutional Church and Political Activity" in *Modern Age*, XVIII (Spring 1974); pp. 163-74.

very controversial – such as abortion and homosexuality. The position of social activists on all these matters is that sermons and pronouncements are not enough. There must be active lobbying, petitions and demonstrations.

Some social activists have been profoundly sympathetic to pacifism, and some are outright pacifists. Many, however, are not, probably because social activists in the past supported the so-called liberation movements in Africa and revolution in South America, as well as present-day movements for what they call economic liberation from the World Bank and the International Monetary Fund. They have moved, therefore, from traditional pacifism to selective pacifism, whereby civil disobedience is recommended in some instances (e.g., the Vietnam War and the General Agreement on Tariffs and Trade talks) but not in others (e.g., World War II and the ongoing civil war in Chechnya).

With regard to racism and sexism, social activists advocate what is known as "compensatory action" (plans for "affirmative action"), which means quotas must be set for women and ethnic groups. The ultimate aim is to reach "balance" that is to be achieved by a kind of discrimination in reverse throughout government agencies, private business, universities and churches.

The push for compensatory action is accomplished by something called "corporate responsibility," which is designed to apply financial pressure to achieve the ends sought by social activists. Churches are urged to show the strength of their convictions by investing their vast funds in enterprises they approve of (e.g., high-risk minority businesses) and withdrawing these funds from enterprises they do not approve of (e.g., industries with defense contracts with Israel). Nor is pressure applied only to the disposition of denominational funds and to domestic affairs. It also is applied to private business corporations and banks in an endeavor to get them to get rid of their investments (such as the campaigns against apartheid in South Africa). It is obvious that compensatory action and corporate responsibility owe much of their impetus, if not their birth, to the civil rights movement, the Vietnam War, and the women's liberation movement.

Being unable to find a Scriptural basis for their programs in the New Testament, social activists fall back on the Old Testament, particularly the prophet Amos. The Church, they urge, should speak with a "prophetic voice," by which they mean the adoption of their stands against racism, sexism, war and other issues. But the Old Testament basis does not fit their claims. When the Old Testament prophets spoke, they did so under divine duress, spoke reluctantly, did not enjoy their message, and paid a high price for their mission. By contrast, the would-be prophets of our day voice personal opinions, rarely run any risks, and luxuriate in denunciation. The most serious defect in the social activist demand that the Church strike a "prophetic note" is that, in the Old Testament, a prophetic voice always is attributed to an individual. There is no instance in either the Old Testament or the New Testament in which a prophetic voice is ascribed to either the Old Israel or the New Israel.

Our analysis of the political implications of the theologies of Tillich, Barth, Bonhoeffer and Brunner shows that not one of them is a social activist. On the other hand, every one of these theologians shows some concern for political and social issues, and they point to instances when the Church should speak out, albeit always negatively, on these issues. Evidently, a line must be drawn somewhere.

The first and foremost mission of the Church for Barth, Bonhoeffer and Brunner (but not Tillich) is evangelism. The Great Commission must be taken with the utmost seriousness:

> "And Jesus came and spake unto them, saying, All power is given unto me in heaven and in earth. Go ye therefore, and teach all nations, baptizing them in the name of the Father, and of the Son, and of the Holy Ghost: Teaching them to observe all things whatsoever I have commanded you: and, lo, I am with you always, even unto the end of the world."[2]

Current trends in the thinking of mainline denominational executives and the leadership in the National Council of Churches and the World Council of Churches, as well as the World Alliance of Reformed Churches, make it imperative that the word *evangelism* be clearly defined. These trends are most visible in the deliberations and pronouncements of past conferences. By the term *evangelism*, they mean interfaith "dialogues" in which adherents of the world's many religions speak on equal terms with no interest in converting anyone, and they mean the change of all social structures that they deem unjust, oppressive and exploitive. Salvation is interpreted as liberation in a political, social and economic sense – which is to be achieved by revolution, if necessary. This view of evangelism is not, of course, the historic view. Neither is it the view of Barth, Bonhoeffer and Brunner.

The historic view rejects the interpretation of evangelism enunciated at these conferences. Neither liberty (liberation) nor equality is the objective of the Christian faith, and all three theologians make this point absolutely clear. Liberty and equality are secular ideals. Even if understood in the light of the Christian faith, rather than in the light of liberal philosophy, these ideals are only by-products of the Christian faith. Moreover, Barth, Bonhoeffer and Brunner are emphatic in their denial that any ideals can be

---

2. Matthew 28:18-20.

attained by structural change alone. Structural changes may be helpful in some cases, but they guarantee nothing.

In the plainest terms, the historic view is that *evangelism* means winning converts to the Christian faith. Everything we have said thus far in this book depends upon this one central and fundamental task. The Christian approach to the public philosophy, the effectiveness of vocation, the reality and authenticity of encounter, the presence of the Holy Spirit – all presuppose an ever more widespread conversion of non-Christians to the Christian faith and the revitalization of that faith among nominal Christians. This presupposition was beautifully and powerfully expressed in the Covenant of Lausanne adopted in July 1974 by evangelicals from 150 nations. It is the response to pronouncements from the World and National Councils of Churches and the World Alliance of Reformed Churches.

However far social activists have deviated from the essentials of the Christian faith into a sociopolitical morass, no Christian should draw the conclusion that the Church should have no concern for political, social and economic issues. A narrow individualism is no part of the Christian faith. It is impossible, therefore, to reject social activism *in toto*. There are several reasons why this is so.

The first is that the task of evangelism requires that the Church concern itself with these issues because you cannot reach individuals while ignoring the forces that have so much to do with molding them. There is no doubt that a person's relationships are so important that there is no understanding or reaching him without understanding those relationships. Whether he is married or single, employed or unemployed, employer or employee, educated or uneducated, rich or poor, sick or healthy, satiated or hungry, powerful or weak, socially prestigious or not, all have very much to do with how the Christian faith may be communicated to him. He must be reached through these relationships.

Secondly, service – the ministering to human need – is an essential part of the Christian witness. It was none other than Jesus himself who instructed his disciples to heal the sick, feed the hungry, clothe the naked, and liberate the captives. Now it is indisputable, especially in a complex society like ours, that ministering to human need cannot be done effectively on an individual basis alone. There are things that we can do together that we cannot do separately. This aspect of social activism is non-controversial. There always has been a recognition of the necessity of service in the Church's sponsoring of schools, orphanages, housing for the aged, hospitals and other forms of service. Foreign missions, for instance, always have involved more than the services of preachers and included those of physicians, nurses, dentists, educators and agronomists. Even the most conservative and pietistic Christians have supported these services, and have objected only when they were not accompanied by the Christian message. The preaching of the gospel, of course, is not a condition for responding to human need, but the response is and should be the occasion for presenting the Christian message. It is noteworthy that this aspect of the Church's mission is not divisive and arouses almost no criticism even from agnostics, atheists and secular humanists. It belongs to what the Apostle Paul called things of good report. A concern for human need, therefore, is an intrinsic part of evangelism.

Thirdly, as individual Christians give their witness through the exercise of their vocation, through personal encounter and through the presence of the Holy Spirit, they find themselves in frequent need of guidance. Where can they get it? Theology, historical and systematic, is helpful. So are Christian ethics, Biblical scholarship and Church history. But individual Christians often are very deficient in their knowledge of these aids as they meet the perplexities of day-to-day political, social and economic life. They must turn, therefore, to the one place where these aids are to be found – namely, the Church – to fill this deficiency. They have a right to expect guidance from the Church.

In order to avoid the pitfalls of social activism, the Church must deal with matters of principle only where the principle is very clear. It is at this point that Barth's command of the hour becomes relevant. There are controversial issues in which the principle is unmistakable, and the command of the hour comes through loud and clear. On these issues, the Church must make pronouncements. Few Christians, if any, would find fault with the Declaration of Barmen in which the German Confessing Church condemned Nazism. Again, few Christians, if any, would deny that the Church pronouncement condemning compulsory racial segregation in the United States was right.

But there are other general issues in which facts and motives are mixed, consequences contradict the principles involved, and equally dedicated and knowledgeable Christians disagree. In these cases, the Church should remain silent, letting individual Christians and Christian groups decide for themselves what the Christian witness means. To issue pronouncements on general principles alone in the absence of a particular controversial issue is platitudinous and, therefore, ineffective. One need not go so far as Barth does with his demand that ideas should not be dealt with until they have become "definite and concrete political constellations," since that denies the power of ideas. But there, nonetheless, is something right about Barth's point. Until an idea or principle has become sufficiently crystallized to be an issue on which people divide, pronouncements will pass unnoticed or be dismissed as purely academic and, therefore, will be ineffectual. On the other hand, the Church should not wait until a principle has become crystallized into an issue so urgent that pronouncements are too little and too late. There is a very real problem of timing here.

Another difficulty with Church pronouncements is that, when a principle becomes crystallized into an issue, it gets tied up with many matters whose religious significance is nil, or practically nil, and theologically ambiguous. During the early period of the Watergate crisis, for example, there were journalists and political scientists who argued that the United States should give up the separation of powers and adopt the British parliamentary system because there would have been no delay in getting Nixon out of office. Aside from the political impracticability of this proposal, what could be the prophetic message that the Church could give on the merits of the two systems? The same observation can be made concerning proposals for fighting inflation, lowering interest rates, devaluing the dollar, raising debt ceilings, and federal financing of primary and general elections. For the Church to sponsor a political party, engage in lobbying, form coalitions with secular pressure groups, and become entangled in the decisions of private business corporations would be to take a position in precisely those issues in which the religious significance is unclear, ambiguous or nonexistent.

The secret of the efficacy of the Church can be found in the statement of Jesus when he said that his disciples are the salt of the Earth. The analogy is illuminating and is inherent in the conception of the Church advocated by Bonhoeffer and Brunner. Salt is a preservative, and it also brings out the flavor of those other elements in which it has been dissolved. It does this by losing its own flavor. If it goes beyond bringing out the flavor of other elements, it is briny and will be spewed out of people's mouths. So it is with Bonhoeffer's church, in a world come of age marked by a religion-less Christianity, and with Brunner's *Ekklesia*.

The dissolution of the Church in society gives rise to two misunderstandings. The Church is dissolved by becoming indigenous – i.e., nationalized, naturalized, assimilated. The necessity for this phenomenon is recognized in the foreign mission field. The fruit of missionary work appropriately is described as national churches. As long as Christians are viewed as foreign agents of a foreign culture, they are the object of charges of imperialism and colonialism. A national church develops its own rituals, creeds, hymns and polities. They set up church buildings, schools, seminaries, hospitals and orphanages. Their personnel is completely identified with the nation, and shares the loyalties of other compatriots.

The misunderstanding comes from a curious twist in liberal thinking about assimilation. On the one hand, no one is more insistent than liberals who demand that the Church become completely indigenous – in Korea, India, Zaire, Mexico, etc. On the other hand, they say that the Church in America is too indigenous, too identified with American culture. There is a double standard involved here. It neither is possible nor desirable to separate wholly the Church and the culture in which it exists. When American missionaries bring doctors, dentists, hospitals and agronomists to the peoples of Africa and Asia, they cannot help but bring some parts of Western culture to these countries. These importations inevitably influence the culture of the non-Western countries. But this does not prevent the mission Church from becoming indigenous, since these peoples adapt and assimilate these importations to their own advantage and without losing their identity by so doing. What has taken place is transfiguration, not denaturalization. This important point was made long ago by Augustine when he said:

> "This heavenly city, then, while it sojourns on earth, calls citizens out of all nations, and gathers together a society of pilgrims of all languages, not scrupling about diversities in the manners, laws, and institutions whereby earthly peace is secured and maintained, but recognising that, however various these are, they all tend to one and the same end of earthly peace. It therefore is so far from rescinding and abolishing these diversities, *that it even preserves and adapts them,* so long only as no hindrance to the worship of the one supreme and true God is thus introduced."[3]

The second misunderstanding comes from some of the admirers of Bonhoeffer and Brunner. Unlike Bonhoeffer and Brunner, these admirers downgrade the institutional church and hold the congregation in low esteem. They say that the congregation is a mutual adoration society, self-satisfied and stagnant. They contend that church members spend too much money on buildings – money that should have been spent on service – and do not go out into the world to evangelize it by ministering to human need. What these people forget is that no one can go out who is not already in. The institutional church could be compared to a pulsating heart with venous blood coming in and arterial blood going out. A stream moves into the congregation to be purified, inspired and trained. Another stream moves out to evangelize (convert and serve) those outside the church. To sustain this pulsation, you need a center, an organization, a budget, and a program. To return to Christ's analogy, a salt that has dissolved into other elements, but has no saltiness, has no power – and it is the institutional church whose task

---

3. Augustine; *The City of God* (Random House, Inc.; New York; 1950); p. 696. Italics added.

it is to produce that saltiness.

The institutional church that engenders the Church in the sense specified by Bonhoeffer and Brunner is one that has kept its saltiness by being distinctively Christian. It is a community in which one finds humility and not conceit, serenity of spirit and not existential dread, security and not inferiority complexes, reconciliation and not alienation, acceptance and not rejection, goodwill and not malice, service and not self-aggrandizement, reverence and not irreverence, freedom and not slavery, courage and not fear, kindness and not censoriousness, wisdom and not foolishness.

The effect of such a community is to expose evil by contrast. The mask of evil is torn off and the beguiling disguises of Satan are stripped away. On the other hand, the existence of a Church that has kept its flavor is ineffably and irresistibly attractive. It proves "what is that good, and acceptable, and perfect, will of God."[4] Those who are spiritually weary, morally tormented, intellectually baffled, psychologically insecure and lonely turn to it as an oasis, a fortress, a refuge. In it, they find forgiveness and acceptance. They discover that the life they led is not inevitable. They discover how sweet, good, exhilarating, abundant and ennobling life can be.

What impresses them most is the collective impact of a life that exemplifies the Christian ethic. Secular man, like the citizens of the decadent Roman Empire, always can dismiss an outstanding Christian individual as an exception, the exception that proves the rule, someone whose stature is not attainable by ordinary mortals and does not belong to this world. But when large numbers of quite ordinary people of all races and classes and nations exemplify the Christian ethic, secular man has to take notice.

Among the many people thus attracted will be bureaucrats and politicians. Their incorporation into the Church will bring vocation, encounter, the discerning of spirits, the creativity of the Holy Spirit into being. No one can say in advance what effect these forms of witnessing will have. As Bonhoeffer pointed out, to claim otherwise would be to walk by sight and not by faith. Furthermore, these bureaucrats and politicians will not be alone. They will be associated with similarly attracted business people, farmers, educators, lawyers, workers, ethnic groups, and age groups. The inclusiveness of the Christian community will make Christian statesmanship possible to a degree not attainable in a secular society because there can be no leadership without a following.

This achievement is the aim of evangelism in its political aspect and it is, in essence, the 20th century message that Barth, Bonhoeffer and Brunner send to the troubled 21st century.

---

4. Romans 12:2.

Let the church be the Church

By Parker T. Williamson

It is one of the ironies of our time that in their avowed pursuit of relevance, America's mainline denominations have sidelined themselves into virtual obscurity.

How is it possible that member denominations of the National Council of Churches, once considered a formidable curia in American culture, could have taken such a fall? There was a time when these churches commanded significant moral authority, their spires towering over village greens and cityscapes throughout the nation. Silent sepulchres, those spires still stand as testimony to what was once a vibrant faith.

That faith was, in fact, powerfully relevant, making a foundational impact on America's political philosophy and the institutions that were spawned by its principles. The *Declaration of Independence, The Federalist Papers*, the Constitution of the United States of America, not to mention speeches and writings from the giants of American history, reveal a formative Judeo-Christian influence. America entered the world stage, without equivocation, as "one nation under God."

As Reinhold Niebuhr reminds us in his *Irony of American History*, a distinctly Biblical anthropology underlies the American democratic experiment. Man's capacity for good "makes democracy possible," he said, while man's capacity for evil "makes democracy necessary." Self-transcendence is unique to us humans, who are, as Scripture asserts, made in the image of God. In recognition of this capacity, America's constitutional framers established a system of government that is sufficiently unfettered to allow creativity to flourish. But sin is also a universal human reality. Thus, the framers established a system of government that limits power by providing check-and-balance safeguards.

Given the formative role that the Judeo-Christian faith played in the development of America's political institutions, it is not surprising that, generations later, denominational leaders might be seduced by statecraft. Inspired by the civil rights and anti-war movements of the sixties, and lured by the notion that they might translate ideology into action, they ventured into the world of politics. After all, they asked, of what practical use is a church that remains cloistered in its sanctuary? What good is an irrelevant faith?

Martin Peretz remembers his Harvard days in the sixties when he encountered W. Appleton Lawrence, the distinguished suffragan bishop of Massachusetts. "I asked Lawrence what Anglicans believed," he recalled. "His face took on a deep, pensive look. 'We believe,' he intoned, 'in civil rights for Negroes, the admission of Red China to the United Nations, and friendship with Castro's Cuba.'"

"I did not want at all to belittle the bishop. I like him. He was not pompous. And probably he thought that this clever Jewish boy from New York would not really be asking him a theological question, which is exactly what I was doing."[1]

The fact of the matter is that since the early 1960s, mainline denominational leaders have eschewed theological questions, believing that their ministries would be more relevant if they dealt less with theology and more directly with politics. Tragically, their assumption proved both erroneous and correct. It erred in that, by turning their focus away from the faith, these leaders diminished the church that they purported to serve, thereby rendering it impotent to accomplish in the political realm the very thing that they wanted. Having marginalized matters of faith, they no longer offered to their parishioners the one thing that the church alone can offer. Other institutions can offer them psychology, various forms of lifestyle management and politics, but who else except the church can give them the gospel?

This abandonment of the church's primary mission has resulted in massive membership declines, drastically diminished budgets and the loss of influence at home and abroad. From a purely political perspective, why would a member of Congress heed counsel from leaders of an ecclesiastical institution that has lost more than half its membership in the past 30 years? If the churches' own people do not follow their leaders, why would a politician care what those leaders think? In this sense, the mainline denomination's shift from theology to politics has produced the opposite of its intended effect. From a political perspective, the church has made itself irrelevant.

---

1. *The New Republic*, June 30, 2005.

But there is also a sense – a tragic sense – in which the denominations' abandonment of theology has become powerfully relevant to the American cultural scene. Just as the Judeo-Christian worldview was instrumental in the development of American constitutional government, so the diminishment of that worldview is producing the opposite effect. Deprived of anchoring principles, politics is an exercise in power without purpose, a merely Machiavellian enterprise. The church's failure to challenge postmodern ideologies (and, in some cases, even its endorsement of these ideologies) has resulted in the spread of a pernicious individualism that undermines the rule of law and any sense of communal identity. It has long been an axiom of politics that ideas have consequences. The mainline denominations' acquiescence to an alien faith is undermining foundational principles of constitutional government.

None of this would have come as a surprise to my father, Dr. René de Visme Williamson, a political theorist and constitutional law scholar who tracked and often engaged in vigorous conversations about theology and politics throughout his 50-year academic tenure. Eschewing the behaviorist and deconstructionist trends that infected political science as much as they did denominational life during the latter years of his career, Williamson believed that no secular anthropology could discern the nature of human life or the meaning of human behavior. Concurring with Aristotle, he believed that man is a political animal. But concurring with Scripture, he knew that humans are much more than that. We are, he insisted, made in the image of God.

It was that conviction that led him as a political scientist to converse with theologians, believing that the language of politics can have little meaning unless aided by the language of the spirit. How can one speak of the ordering of human society, he asked, unless one understands what it means to be human? And how can we know what it means to be human unless we know something of the One in whose image humans were made and whose authority humans are inclined to usurp? Anthropology and theology are inextricably entwined.

Tillich, Barth, Bonhoeffer and Brunner, the theologians whose thought Williamson chose to examine in this book, were the giants of his time – and the impact of their thought still is being felt in our time. While they had little to say about politics directly, he found implications in their understandings of the nature of God and the nature and purpose of humanity that apply to the political order.

All four theologians exhibited a profound distrust of ideologies and philosophical systems because they knew that such systems could lead humans into idolatry. That warning has not been heeded by denominational leaders, whose ideological pursuits have led them to accommodate the gods and goddesses of our age. Liberation theology,[2] the doctrinal position utilized by liberals to justify their adventures into the world of revolutionary politics, would have been roundly condemned by the theologians referenced in this book.

There is a particular irony in the fact that liberationists associated with Union Theological Seminary in New York frequently cite Bonhoeffer with adulation, as if he were a symbol of the political ideology that they claim for themselves. In recent years, Union officials have even gone so far as to conduct seminary fund-raising events using themes that celebrate the life and work of Bonhoeffer. In so doing, they conveniently ignore the theologian's description of Union as "notorious" for promoting "the permeation of Christian theology with pragmatic philosophy," and his view of Union's faculty: "They intoxicate themselves with liberal and humanistic expressions, laugh at the fundamentalists, and basically they are not even a match for them."[3]

One might wonder if, in publishing a revised and expanded edition of Williamson's work, some consideration might have been given to theologians worthy of note who have come to the fore since the deaths of Tillich, Barth, Bonhoeffer and Brunner. Such consideration was given, with a telling result: With the possible exceptions of Thomas F. Torrance's recovery of Trinitarian theology and its implications for modern science, and Thomas C. Oden's paleo-orthodoxy that sheds new light particularly on the patristic period, there are none.

This current dearth of excellence in systematic theology in itself testifies to the condition of a church whose passions have been limited to politics. The secularization of mainline denominations has resulted in the transmutation of theology into sociology, a thin-gruel substitute for *theo-logos*, once the primary discipline at the world's great universities that attracted their brightest minds. In the place of theologians, we have welcomed sanctified sociologists who, having ruled out the existence of Truth, promote the foolish notion that all ideas are equal.

Today, evangelical movements are sweeping across the continents of Africa, Asia and Latin America, attracting converts to the Christian faith in

---

2. The use of the word "theology" in this instance is a misnomer, since there is no "theos" in an essentially Marxist ideology that has been employed to justify church support for revolutionary movements in the two-thirds world. The slogan, "God is on the side of the poor," frequently employed by denominational liberationists, hardly qualifies as a theology. Rather, it proves little more than affixing a divine title to a movement whose origin is secular.

3. See Chapter Five, p. 131, for citations.

massive numbers, and powerfully offsetting the decline of mainstream denominations in the United States. But, even here, evangelicalism is making its mark as rapidly growing non-denominational churches and numerous para-church movements appear on the scene. That this evangelical emergence is gaining traction among institutions of American culture cannot be denied, even by the secular media, whose pundits recognize but cannot comprehend such faith-based phenomena.

In their early stage, evangelical movements focus more on Christian experience than on orderly theological inquiry. Thus, the theological vacuum spawned by secularism has not yet been filled by Christian theologians. But that condition will change over time, as people who have experienced a life-changing encounter with Jesus Christ begin to reflect upon their experiences and its implications for the common life. Such periods of reflection will engender the discipline of theology, and once again it will become a credible field of inquiry in the academy. When faith returns, the church will engage theologians whose words prove worthy of reflection.

But first things first: The primary mandate for the mainline denomination is to summon its members to the faith once entrusted to the saints. Either it will return to its first love or it will continue its terminal illness. Despite clear symptoms of its morbidity, the likelihood of an institutional turnaround does not appear encouraging. Denominational leaders appear to prefer a corpse to a cure.

But the Lord will not leave his people without a witness. History reminds us that ecclesiastical institutions are impermanent and imperfect arrangements. But Jesus Christ promised that the Church, the people of God grounded in the Word of God, will not fail. Should current institutional forms die, the Church will appear afresh in some new configuration. The worldwide evangelical revival suggests that this is happening today.

As Christian communities that are self-consciously and unequivocally evangelical reappear in American life and culture, people will be drawn to the gospel that preachers and lay people proclaim. Already, we hear those who have wearied of secularism say, "Lord, to whom shall we go? You have the words of eternal life." These converts will sense their Christian vocation. They will take their places in society, many of them in the fields of politics and law. Christian statesmen will appear on the scene, their worldview influencing the exercise of their craft. Thus, the re-emergence of the Church, a community of faith whose first love is Jesus Christ, will restore a witness that is relevant to the common life, and the salt of the earth will once more flavor the realm.

About The Author

René de Visme Williamson was professor emeritus of political science at Louisiana State University, where he served as chair of the political science department from 1955-63 and again from 1965-68. At the time of his retirement, Cecil Eubanks, then chair of the department, called Dr. Williamson "one of the leading political theorists of his generation, particularly in the field of political theology."

He was a Harvard Ph.D. who held faculty positions at Princeton, Davidson and Beloit colleges and the University of Tennessee before teaching at LSU. Williamson also taught at Vanderbilt, Johns Hopkins and Duke universities and the University of Michigan.

His other books include *Independence and Involvement: A Christian Reorientation in Political Science* and *Culture and Policy: The United States and the Hispanic World,* as well as a number of articles in leading journals.

Williamson served as editor of the *Journal of Politics* from 1949-53 and was a member of the executive council of the American Political Science Association from 1959-61. In 1959, he was elected president of the Southern Political Science Association.

He was a Presbyterian elder, serving on the sessions of First Presbyterian Church in Knoxville, Tenn., and First Presbyterian Church in Baton Rouge, La., and chairing pastoral search committees in both churches. At the national level, he represented the Presbyterian Church U.S. Board of Christian Education as a leader of the Faculty Christian Fellowship, whose ministry was to encourage Christian professors in secular universities to think through the implications of their faith for their professional disciplines.

Williamson traveled extensively throughout South America, where he established Faculty Christian Fellowships at many universities. He served the General Assembly of the PCUS as a commissioner and a member of the denomination's Permanent Theological Committee.

Contributors

Craig M. Kibler, a Pulitzer Prize nominee for criticism, is an award-winning editor, writer, poet and journalist whose work has appeared in numerous magazines, journals and newspapers. His books include *Orthodoxy: The Annotated Edition, Confessing The Faith: Reclaiming Historic Faith and Teaching for the 21st Century* and *Heretics: The Annotated Edition.*

Parker T. Williamson is the chief executive officer of the Presbyterian Lay Committee, editor in chief of its publications, and a longtime leader of the renewal movement within the Presbyterian Church (USA). Prior to his present duties, he served for 30 years as an ordained minister in the Presbyterian Church (USA). A graduate of Rhodes College, Union Theological Seminary (Va.) and Yale Divinity School, his books include *Standing Firm: Reclaiming Christian Faith in Times of Controversy* and *Essays from Zimbabwe.*

A Note on the Text

*P*olitics and Protestant Theology is a timeless book. While its themes do not change, the cultures to which it speaks do. Styles, spellings and word usages change with time. With those and other changes in mind, the approach with this volume was to try to make it more accessible for today's readers.

René de Visme Williamson, to cite one example, included in his text a large and diverse cast of characters – both major and minor. Many readers perhaps can identify Tillich, Barth, Bonhoeffer, Brunner, Calvin and Augustine, for example, but how many have trouble recognizing Thomas Hobbes, Jean Rousseau or Joseph Haroutunian?

And those are just some of the major characters. What about such lesser-known people as George Tavard, Harvey Cox, Carl J. Armbruster or John D. Godsey?

And then there's Williamson's use of political science references, like the Weimar Constitution or the Argentine constitution, forms of government and their application to politics.

Invariably, there will be critics of any attempt to make *Politics and Protestant Theology* more accessible for today's readers by revising it, expanding it and including more modern examples to illustrate its themes. Some will say there are too many notes, for example, just as there will be those who say there are too few. Some will prefer more modern examples included, just as there will be those who prefer it the other way around. Critics will complain about breaking up some of the paragraphs to focus on a single idea or theme, while others will say there wasn't enough of this done. Some will insist that readers should get a history, a biography or some other reference book out and look up arcane or obscure references, just as there will be those who say they want more detail included in the notes.

The only response that can be made to any of these criticisms is to state the simple belief that when today's readers must go in search of outside works to help with difficult passages or references, they are required to leave the book when the goal should be to help keep them in its pages. It is in those pages that the responsive reader will find and understand the timeless themes Williamson addresses.

And that understanding, once achieved, will provide a solid basis for a Christian worldview from which to live in – and actively engage – today's hectic society.

Printed in the United States
35876LVS00005B/1